American Puppetry

American Puppetry

Collections, History and Performance

Edited by PHYLLIS T. DIRCKS

Foreword by STEVE ABRAMS

L.C.C. LIBRARY

McFarland & Company, Inc., Publishers

Jefferson, North Carolina, and London

THIS WORK IS PUBLISHED AS VOLUME 23
OF THE PERFORMING ARTS RESOURCES SERIES
OF THE THEATRE LIBRARY ASSOCIATION

LIBRARY OF CONGRESS CATALOGUING-IN-PUBLICATION DATA

American puppetry : collections, history and performance / edited by
Phyllis T. Dircks ; foreword by Steve Abrams.
    p.   cm.
Includes bibliographical references and index.

ISBN 0-7864-1896-6 (softcover : 50# alkaline paper) ∞

1. Puppet theater — United States — History.   2. Puppets —
United States — History.   I. Dircks, Phyllis T.
PN1978.U6A68   2004
791.5'3'0973 — dc22   2004009586

British Library cataloguing data are available

Cover photograph: A group of Punch and Judy puppets
(Smithsonian Institution)

Manufactured in the United States of America

McFarland & Company, Inc., Publishers
  Box 611, Jefferson, North Carolina 28640
  www.mcfarlandpub.com

Table of Contents

III. Puppetry in Action

Foreword

STEVE ABRAMS

Imagine opening a theatrical trunk and discovering inside all the sets, props and costumes for the original production of *A Midsummer Night's Dream*. We will never know exactly what the original physical appearances of *Oedipus Rex*, *Romeo and Juliet*, or *commedia dell'arte* productions were when they were first presented on stage. But when a work of puppet theater is preserved, we can look at not only the sets, props, and costumes of an original production but we can also look at the faces of the actors!

All objects have a story to tell, but puppets are objects with rare power. They are objects made purposely for theatrical expression. Masks have similar power and intent. Masks and puppets were not made to be seen as silent, still artifacts in a museum case, but viewing them generates interesting questions beyond identifying the origin and age of such objects. How did they move? What did they say? Why was this kind of puppet crafted and what role did it play?

Viewing puppets is a unique experience. Even if a puppet is well known from photographs, seeing the actual figure often surprises us. Some puppets charm us because they are crude and rough, while others enchant us with tender, delicate beauty; still others startle us with their power and intensity. Walking under the outstretched wings of a huge Bread & Puppet Theater bird, for instance, is not easily forgotten.

During the 1950s, Lettie Connell Schubert, a beloved and respected West Coast puppeteer, worked with puppet legend Ralph Chessé, doing television puppetry in San Francisco. I asked this seasoned professional if a puppet ever inspired her, standing still, in a collection. "One year I went to a puppet festival in Buxton, England," she answered. "The exhibit was full of small and mostly crudely made old puppets (which I am sure delighted and interested many audiences), but then I came across a beautifully designed display with the magnificently designed puppets of John Blundall from Cannon Hill Theatre at Birmingham. I knew I had to go to meet the artist, so just as soon as the festival was over, I took a train to Birmingham, a taxi to Cannon Hill and asked to buy a ticket to that afternoon's performance. I mentioned I was a puppeteer from the United States. John appeared and took me to tea and showed me his studio, his fabulous book collection and his puppet collection. ... I was inspired, awed and impressed."

After reviewing the collections profiled in this book, I find it gratifying that puppets of every type — shadow, hand, rod and string — have found homes in museums and libraries. And the retrospective collections devoted to one artist, such as Dwiggins, Baird, Ballard, or Henson, provide the rare opportunity to understand the full scope of a career.

This book is especially helpful, too, because some of the collections described herein are safely packed away in storage. One of the largest and best storage facilities is at the Detroit Institute of Arts. One day, I watched museum technicians dressed in white lab coats lean over a workbench that looked more like an operating table; they were restoring, with careful, delicate movements, a huge puppet figure made by Remo Bufano. The puppet looked a bit like Frankenstein's monster. It was very touching to see a "puppet sculpture" given the same respect that a seventeenth-century Flemish tapestry would command. For a museum to preserve and exhibit puppets confers dignity and respect on the art of puppetry. Those who work at making puppet theater are truly grateful to the museums and libraries that preserve our ephemeral art form and to this book for communicating its knowledge to all lovers of puppetry.

Introduction

PHYLLIS T. DIRCKS

Critics and playgoers alike have noted the significant impact of puppetry on performance art during the last decade. That this most ancient and most widespread form of performance, in which dramatic energy is generated by a material object, could influence the course of sophisticated modern and postmodern theatrical productions is, in itself, remarkable. Moreover, the outstanding success of *The Lion King* on Broadway in 1997 focused popular attention on puppetry as a significant element in mainstream theater. Though years have passed, theater audiences still burst into applause at least five or six times each night when they catch sight of *The Lion King's* oversized puppets and puppet masks.

Further testimony to the significance of puppetry in contemporary theater abounds. The recent successful New York production of *Peter and Wendy,* featuring an all-marionette cast, and *Carnival,* in which Lili believes puppets are people, as well as Basil Twists's imaginative all-marionette staging of Stravinsky's poignant ballet, *Petrouchka,* and Ariane Mnouchkine's recent *Drums on the Dike,* in which actors simulate the movements of puppets, all attest to the continuing influence of this ancient dramatic mode on cutting-edge performance art. Recent productions such as *Avenue Q* and works of Eugene Ionesco and Paula Vogel that feature puppets interacting with live performers offer a promise of future possibilities for puppetry on the American stage.

Despite the surge of puppet popularity, however, little attention has been paid to puppets as art objects or as cultural indices. Fortunately, thousands of puppets from various cultures and many time periods have been collected by scholars, enthusiasts and curators, who wisely realized that these material images can teach us much about the society for which they were crafted. Magnificent puppet collections are housed in some of our most renowned American institutions and in outstanding university collections. This book includes twenty-one essays written by curators of puppetry collections, anthropologists, puppet conservators, and distinguished scholars who, through their collaborative efforts, provide a valuable guide to American puppetry and puppet collections.

Vincent Anthony, founder and executive director of the Center for Puppetry Arts in Atlanta, introduces the subject in his chapter in which he discusses the many modern American and Canadian puppet artists who have contributed significantly to "the long tradition of disseminating folklore, fairy tales and myths of diverse cultures." And Lowell Swortzell's chapter deftly explores the link between today's artists and their American predecessors, tracing them back to 1776.

Other contributors provide analytical descriptions of fascinating puppet collections at major American cultural institutions. The puppet collection at the National Museum of American History of the Smithsonian Institution contains marionettes, rod puppets, hand puppets and ventriloquist figures spanning 150 years of our national history. In their chapter on this collection, Ellen Roney Hughes and Dwight Blocker Bowers describe how these artifacts "uniquely represent how Americans have experienced puppetry." Nancy Staub's chapter takes us into the making of a collection, as she details the growth of the Center for Puppetry Arts' holdings from its first donation of approximately 150 puppets to its current total of nine hundred, supplemented by an impressive collection of posters and other graphics — all collected within a quarter of a century. In discussing the collection at the American Museum of Natural History, Kathy Foley and Ann Wright-Parsons provide full descriptions of the puppets and consider the forces that shaped the collection, acknowledging the museum's debt to the work of Margaret Mead and others.

John Bell's description of puppetry at the Detroit Institute of Arts lends historical perspective to its collection, with a focus on puppet modernism in the Midwest, especially in the work of renowned puppeteer Paul McPharlin. Roberta Zonghi's chapter provides a personal glimpse of William Addison Dwiggins, the renowned illustrator and type designer who created the distinctive Dwiggins marionettes, which Zonghi describes as "lighthearted and amusing," as well as "marvelous examples of engineering and design."

University collections of puppetry are also rich and varied in their holdings. Fredric Woodbridge Wilson carefully details items in the Harvard Theatre Collection, assuring us that "puppetry has ... been present in the general holdings of the Harvard Theatre Collection from its earliest years." Annette Fern lends rare insight into the soul of a puppeteer in writing about the Marionette Theatre of Peter Arnott, a special collection at Harvard. She describes in detail how puppetry enabled Arnott to present ancient plays to modern audiences. In his chapter, John Bell notes that Brander Matthews, the first professor of dramatic literature in the country, embraced puppetry fully in his quest to capture the whole range of theater experience. Bell celebrates Matthews's "unabashed inclusion of puppets into his sense of essential theater," which led him to collect puppets himself and include them in the Brander Matthews Dramatic Museum.

The impact of the personalities of legendary puppeteers is felt throughout this volume. Frank Ballard's enlightened view of the importance of puppetry studies and his establishment of the first degree program in puppetry at the University of Connecticut is detailed in "The Ballard Institute and Museum of Puppetry Collection," which includes precise descriptions of numerous Ballard puppets. Similarly, the personal imprint of Lou Harrison is seen in Kathy Foley's chapter which details puppet-music performances inspired by Asian models. Roy W. Hamilton's scholarly treatment of Asian puppets describes the UCLA Fowler Museum's collection of over thirteen hundred puppets, a testament to the significance of puppetry in our growing embrace of non–Western arts.

The current popularity of puppetry with the general public seems to be on a dizzying upward spiral. Two puppeteers whose work has been seminal in this movement are studied in abundant detail. Elka Schumann combines narrative and history in describing the making of The Bread & Puppet Theater's collection; her chapter offers unique insight into the fierce energy of that company, whose founder, Peter Schumann, stoutly maintains that "puppet theater is the theater of all means. Puppets and masks should be played in the street." Alan Woods traces the career of Julie Taymor, the most visible, albeit reluctant, puppeteer of this moment.

The contributions of puppeteers who performed in venues other than onstage are also celebrated. Richard Leet tells the story of the development of the Bil Baird puppet collection at the Charles H. MacNider Museum. My chapter, "Howdy Doody in the Courtroom: A Puppet Custody Case," details the iconization of a puppet hero and his later significance in juridical history. Bernard F. Reilly inventories the Kukla, Fran and Ollie holdings in the Chicago Historical Society. And Leslee Asch describes a series of successful exhibitions of the Jim Henson puppets. Puppet conservators Mina Gregory, Maureen Russell and Cara Varnell consider the necessity of observing strict standards for the preservation of puppets so that these art objects may be enjoyed for years to come. And Mary Flanagan speculates on the future of puppetry and the means of using them in cyberspace.

All puppet lovers are invited to further enjoyment of the limitless world of puppetry by savoring the appendices. The first appendix is a listing of selected puppetry collections that have not been described in the preceding chapters. Meticulously compiled by puppeteer Steve Abrams, the list is a treasury of useful, little-known information. The second appendix, Joseph Yranski's listing of puppetry films at the Donnell Media Center of the New York Public Library, invites readers to experience the joys of both puppetry and film in one sitting.

In tracing the history and illuminating the current state of puppetry in the United States today, in describing leading American puppet collections, in citing the work of renowned puppeteers, and in detailing the required professional care of puppets as art objects, this book seeks to whet the interest of novices, to enhance the knowledge of advanced students of puppetry, and to heighten the pleasure of all readers in this most ancient and popular dramatic art form.

I am personally grateful to so many who have actively participated in the making of this book. I wish to thank my colleagues in the Theatre Library Association and Larry Baranski, Rita Bottoms, Gary Chelius, Daniel deBruin, James Fisher, Stephen Johnson, Susan Kinney, Paul Newman, Madeline Nichols, Kenneth Schlesinger, Daniel Watermeier, and Don Wilmeth for their most generous assistance. The Research Committee of Long Island University has kindly awarded me time to complete this project.

I

American Puppetry Today and Yesterday

A Snapshot of Puppeteers of the United States and Canada

Vincent Anthony

Puppetry today mirrors America today: it is a rich blend of cultures and traditions; it is rooted in familiarity, yet constantly reaches toward the cutting edge; it is ethnically diverse, politically driven and alive with exciting and challenging concepts. This is contemporary puppetry: an old friend, vibrant with new ideas, reaching out to audiences of adults as well as children.

Performances that are culturally and ethnically diverse are the cornerstones of American puppetry. This is amply demonstrated by reviewing the UNIMA-USA *Directory of Touring Companies and Professional Puppetry Services*. Over one hundred companies are listed in the 2002 edition; they perform in English and ten other languages: Balinese, Cantonese, Dutch, French, German, Indonesian, Japanese, Mandarin Chinese, Romanian and Spanish. The field is rich with performances by artists who are sometimes several generations removed from their cultural roots, but who draw on the past while incorporating contemporary concepts in their work. An excellent example of this is *Between Two Worlds* by Mark Levenson of New York City. Mark has drawn on his Jewish heritage to tell the classic story of the Dybbuk. Vermont puppeteer Eric Bass's production of *Invitations to Heaven* is a masterful telling of the story of his Jewish grandparents. The Mermaid Theatre of Nova Scotia explores Canada's French and English roots. Cultural influence is evident in the

9

incredible performance of *Fiesta* by René of Los Angeles, who is a second-generation Mexican-American. This fast-paced variety marionette act is highly entertaining and celebrates René's Hispanic roots. There are also puppeteers newly immigrated to America who have brought with them their family traditions in theater, such as Yang Feng, formerly of China, who is now a resident of Seattle. In his performance of *The Hungry Tiger*, he shares with his new homeland the culture of his native one. Mark, Eric, René, Feng and many other talented artists enrich the cultural brew of contemporary American puppet theater. There is even a revival of puppetry among some of America's first puppeteers: the Native Americans of the Northwest coast. Puppetry is included in some ceremonies, including those of the Lelooska family of Ariel, Washington, who give performances to educate the public.

Carrying the long tradition of disseminating folklore, fairy tales and myths of diverse cultures, puppeteers are still challenging themselves to be great storytellers and keep these timeless traditions alive; the results can be stunning. Akbar Imhotep, an Atlantan and African-American, could make the simplest tale riveting, but when he presents stories rooted in African myth, the result is mesmerizing. His *Anansi the Spider and Other Tales* relays ancient tales to young and eager audiences. Akbar also transforms the material of Georgia's Joel Chandler Harris and his Uncle Remus and the Briarpatch "critters" into modern tales for young and old. Although this material was considered taboo for decades, Akbar has modernized it and opened it to new audiences. Chris and Stephen Carter of the Carter Family Marionettes in Seattle are well known for their research and reputation for authenticity. They have worked with Northwest Native American tribes to bring to life some of their rich folkloric traditions. They have twice presented works based on these traditions, and both times they incorporated Native Americans, from whose culture the legends came, not only as consultants, but also as performers. Carol and John Farrell's Figures of Speech Theatre of Maine explores Eskimo culture in the Japanese *bunraku*-inspired *Anerca*. Paul Mesner of Kansas City, Missouri, adds the sheer fun of multiple voices and humor to his versions of European fairy tales, like *Sleeping Beauty*, and folktales, including the Appalachian *Wiley and the Hairy Man*. Kathy Foley, of Porter College of the University of California at Santa Cruz, specializes in the myths and culture of Asia in her teaching, and her extensive travels have included formal study of puppetry in Indonesia. During this time, she became so

Atlanta puppeteer Akbar Imhotep brings to life tales of African folklore. (Photograph by Joe Boris, courtesy the Center for Puppetry Arts.)

entranced by this art form that she became a *dalang* (puppeteer) of *wayang golek* (rod puppetry). She is one of the few females performing *wayang golek* in Indonesia, as well as in America. Her retelling of stories from the *Mahābhārata* and *Rāmāyana* epics is both refreshing and in keeping with tradition. San Franciscan Larry Reed became a Balinese *dalang* and performs traditional *wayang kulit* (shadow puppetry) and a version of Shakespeare's *Tempest* with traditional shadow puppets. Both Kathy and Larry apply the principles of Indonesian *wayang* to modern theatrical productions.

American puppeteers are often politically driven. There are few other cultures wherein artists can skewer political foibles. Quite recently puppeteers were involved in a test of First Amendment rights during the 2000 Republican Convention in Philadelphia. During this time, numerous members of the artistic company Spiral Q. and their leader, Mathew Hart (a.k.a. "Matty Boy"), were embroiled in political controversy; while planning street protests during the convention, they were, in fact, arrested and detained. Although the charges were subsequently dropped, the incident sent shock waves through the entire puppetry world. Just how important does the FBI think we puppeteers are, anyway? Best known for their work in the political arena are the Bread & Puppet Theater and its fiery founder, Peter Schumann. Bread & Puppet has tackled subject matter ranging from the deforestation of South American rain forests to the unethical business practices of a power company in their home state of Vermont. Thousands flock to their farm each year to visit the Bread & Puppet Museum, which fills a large barn. According to Schumann in an article titled "The Radicality of the Puppet Theatre," published in 1990, "[Puppetry] is also, by definition of its most persuasive characteristics, an anarchic art, subversive and untamable by nature, an art which is easier reached in police records than in theatre chronicles, an art which by fate and spirit does not aspire to represent governments or civilizations, but prefers its own secret and demeaning stature in society, representing, more or less, the demons of that society and definitely not its institutions." Through his enlightening performances and extravagant parades, including giant puppets that require several puppeteers, Schumann has been a beacon for those who believe that puppeteers have not only the right, but also the obligation, to speak out emphatically. There are many groups founded by those who have apprenticed and worked with Bread & Puppet Theater. One of the most successful is In the Heart of the Beast Puppet and Mask Theatre in Minneapolis. Performing both in their own space and in annual outdoor events, the artists, under the direction of Sandy Spieler, tell their own political stories and assist others in their community who have a need to be heard. I was present at a poignant event for La Peña, a monthly Hispanic community arts and culture gathering, where they performed *Circle of Love Over Death*, about missing men and women in Argentina. The performance was preceded by singing and celebration and, to my shock, was followed by weeping and cheering from the audience; thus the performance was a celebration of cause and a sharing of common sorrow.

History has long fascinated and frustrated many puppeteers who have chronicled the past; they have even shed new light on significant historical moments. Theodora Skipitares of New York is undoubtedly the master of recounting the past and holding accountable those responsible for some of its greatest blunders. In her *Defenders of the Code*, she shines new light on the discovery of DNA, as well as famous, yet incorrect, assumptions as to race and character that preceded it. In her detailed and accurate drama *Age of Invention*, she focuses on the fame and foibles of Thomas Edison and Benjamin Franklin. Schroeder Cherry of New York City, an African-American puppeteer, has chronicled the compelling story of Harriet Tubman, who led many slaves to freedom on the Underground Railroad. On that same subject, The Underground Railway Theatre of Cambridge, Massachusetts, compares the current movement to aid Latin American refugees to that effort during the Civil War to assist escaped slaves in one of their productions. A giant African puppet face hovering over the stage is transformed into a Mayan Indian to visualize the comparison.

The politics of sexual orientation is also a very heated topic focused upon by noted puppeteers. Bobby Box, producer and writer at the Center for Puppetry Arts in Atlanta, recently performed his moving *Towing the Line* for the national Puppeteers of America conference. With a complex plot, Bobby managed to make a strong case for being true to yourself, no matter who you are, even if that means acknowledging a gay identity. Ronnie Burkett of Canada also deals with gay issues in his recent *Street of Blood* production by detailing the persecution of gay people. Ronnie has made his reputation on his singularly magnificent manipulation of his exquisitely crafted marionettes. Many Americans, including many puppeteers, consider gay and lesbian rights as the final chapter in the battle for equal rights.

Puppetry is a vital part of the modern performing arts movement. Today's demand for the creativity of puppetry artists is unparalleled. This is due largely to the success of such artists as Jim Henson and Julie Taymor, who proved that adults, as well as children, would respond to puppet performances.

Jim Henson was the visionary who dreamed of puppet images created solely for television and film. "The Muppet Show" reached millions of adults around the world each week in prime time. His film *Labyrinth* still stands as a work of creative genius. He led the way with this vision and a plethora of artists have rushed to fill the need he created. These artists work on such projects as "Sabrina, the Teenage Witch," a popular television series with a "cat" named Salem; the eight puppeteers who manipulate this puppet are led by Thom Fountain of Los Angeles. He is but one of hundreds of professional puppeteers who are gainfully employed in projects ranging from movies, such as *Men in Black,* to the "Between the Lions" TV series. The central character in the recent hit film *Being John Malkovich* was a puppeteer.

Julie Taymor has created many incredible productions, the most notable of which is, without question, *The Lion King.* It is a huge success on Broadway and is now also playing to packed houses of adults, with or without their children, in Los Angeles, Toronto, London, and Tokyo. A touring company is also playing in several cities across the country. Julie, based in New York City, has had numerous prior successes, but this single work exemplifies the blending of puppet and mask artistry and popular musical theater to create a masterpiece. A close collaborator of Julie Taymor on *The Lion King* and other productions is Michael Curry of Mount St. Helena, Oregon. He has emerged as a major force in the world of puppetry and has created puppets for some ambitious and high-profile projects. His credits include a half-time extravaganza for the ever-popular Super Bowl football game and the Year 2000 New Year's Eve celebration in New York's Times Square, which was broadcast to millions of people around the world. Barbara Pollitt, who has also worked with Julie Taymor over the years, has collaborated with other New York theater directors as puppeteer and designer. She cooperated with Lee Breuer of Mabou Mines on several productions, including *MahabarANTA* and *Peter and Wendy,* and with George C. Wolfe in his Public Theater production of *The Caucasian Chalk Circle,* in which she created puppets and masks that acted as a focal point to merge Wolfe's vision with the intent of the author, Bertolt Brecht. This allowed for a startling new interpretation by the audience. She also worked on Wolfe's *Spunk,* as well as his Broadway success, *Jelly's Last Jam.*

Numerous other puppet artists are making their marks with compelling innovative works. Mark Fox and his Saw Theater of Cincinnati, Ohio, has recently dazzled audiences with *Account Me Puppet,* a fanciful retelling of Milton's *Paradise Lost.* Some of its very modern music is actually played on an amplified saw; the puppets are of a highly stylized modern style. New York City's Hanne Tierney also lights up the sky with her abstract sculpture in motion. Her *Salome* was probably the most "out there" retelling of the Oscar Wilde work ever done. Salome was merely shimmering fabric manipulated by Hanne with an elaborate system of strings connected through a grid to weights attached to a precisely mapped control wall. Paul Zaloom of Los Angeles has captured the hearts of American children as the Mad Scientist in "Beakman's World," a TV favorite that uses puppets. Zaloom, however, is also the undisputed king of trash (literally): false eyeballs in a jar become tourists in a sightseeing bus; a stack of egg cartons becomes an apartment building; a scrap of cloth is a road on which to play with toy cars. His hip, all-junk shows of social satire for adults really rock, including his recently performed gay-themed *Punch and Jimmy,* which brings the traditional *Punch and Judy* kicking and screaming into the twenty-first century.

Speaking of twenty-first-century artistry, that is just what Jon Ludwig does in a series of science-based shows for children, such as *Weather Rocks* and *The Body Detective.* He uses overhead and slide projectors, video cameras, and multiple movable light sources. The shadow figures are three-dimensional, as well as traditional flat cutouts. He has masked actors appear in front of and behind the screen for dynamic images. His adult works are as compelling, such as his recent *Wrestling Macbeth,* which combined the popular fad with Shakespeare. With a ring for a stage and pumped-up puppets manipulated by puppeteers dressed like wrestlers, with lights flashing, pop music blasting away and video cameras offering simultaneous projections, this production was as big as it was bold. According to an article in *Puppetry International* by Andrew Periale, "Shakespeare's Macbeth and pro wrestling: clearly a match made in heaven or in hell! ... Ludwig ... brings about this unholy union in a wild head-banging extravaganza that is so far over the top it fairly escapes the pull of gravity."

Detective Sam Flat Foot from Jon Ludwig's award-winning *The Body Detective.* (Photograph by David Zeiger, courtesy the Center for Puppetry Arts.)

Wrestling MacBeth by Jon Ludwig. (Photograph by Joe Boris, courtesy the Center for Puppetry Arts.)

We are constantly experimenting and learning. There are many organizations offering support so that puppeteers may take risks without fear, and there are many puppeteers willing to take those risks. The O'Neill Puppetry Conference, held annually at the Eugene O'Neill Theatre Center in Waterford, Connecticut, has become the premier learning arena for hundreds of puppeteers of diverse ages and backgrounds. Founded by Jane Henson and led by artistic directors Richard Termine and George Latshaw, the conference has managed to draw top puppetry artists each summer to lead interactive workshops. All participants work with one of these artists and develop their own projects as well. A list of the artists who have led these workshops reads like a Who's Who of puppetry: Phillip Huber, Janie Geiser, Eric Bass, Jon Ludwig, and many more gifted and distinguished artists. Puppet Parlour at the hip New York City arts space, Here, showcases the best of the Puppetry Conference pieces and offers unique performance opportunities for other new work. Interesting opportunities for works-in-progress and new short works have emerged. Three Legged Race of Minneapolis offers object theater artists an opportunity to be seen in their *Hand Driven III* project; new artists, such as Erik Blanc of North Carolina, Heather Henson of Florida, and Soozin Hirshmugl of Vermont, have all premiered work there. Puppet slams at the Puppet Showplace in Brookline, Massachusetts, are also popular with the younger artists as spaces where they can try new ideas and new works.

Education opportunities are essential to the progress of any field, and puppetry is no exception. The University of Connecticut has one of the few bachelor's and master's degree programs in puppetry in the United States. Founded by Professor Frank Ballard and now run by Professor Bart Roccoberton, this renowned program has been fueling the puppet machine with new, energetic students brimming with talent, who have gone on to the Muppets, Hollywood and beyond. In Los Angeles, Janie Geiser, famous for her striking new innovative work with puppetry and with film, has taken on a new task at the California Arts School of Theatre by directing a new division devoted to puppetry. The Cotsen Center for Puppetry and the Arts offers a laboratory for training and experimentation in the art of puppet theater. Janie's influence and the influence of the artists she draws to this center will add significantly to the training and growth of students. Several Americans have attended puppet workshops and academies in Europe. New York puppeteer Basil Twist graduated from ESNAM, *École Supérieure Nationale des Arts de la Marionnette*, a three-year puppet academy in France. After many years of international performances, guest directing, and teaching, New York puppeteer Roman Paska became the director of ESNAM. UNIMA-USA, a branch of *Union Internationale de la Marionnette* (UNIMA), when under the guidance of General Secretary Allelu Kurten, established a scholarship program for Americans to study abroad, which still exists today. Lest we forget, the training I found available when I joined the field is still in place, that is, OTJ or "on the job." My former boss, Nick Coppola, now of Puppetworks in New York, is one of those guys who will still hire and train. There are many out there willing to make this investment of time and energy, and they have helped launch many careers.

We as puppeteers have organized ourselves in order to accomplish Herculean tasks. The patriarch of puppetry in North America is the organization Puppeteers of America. Founded in 1937 and now over two thousand puppeteers strong, it still accomplishes its original goal of being the foundation of the field by encouraging and nurturing grassroots puppeteers. Whether they are public schoolteachers, hobbyists, amateurs or professionals, they all are welcome here. P of A's festivals have become the bedrock of the American puppeteer. They include invaluable workshops and seminars, as well as performances. Its publication, *The Puppetry Journal*, is sent to members four times a year. UNIMA-USA, the other important American organization that represents the global perspective, with a membership of over five hundred, publishes the previously mentioned *Directory of Touring Companies and Professional Puppetry Services*. Its magazine, *Puppetry International*, established in 1994, is ably edited and designed by Bonnie and Andrew Periale of New Hampshire. It underscores the uses of puppetry in contemporary theater, film and media. This publication is a shining example of the public's current interest in information on puppetry. Articles have ranged from "Puppetry into the Next Millennium," by noted puppeteer Stephen Kaplin of New York City, which was in the 1994 premier issue, to a recent article, "Puppetry in the Media," by Leslee Asch, formerly of Jim Henson Productions in New York City. Dedicated to promoting peace through the art of puppetry, UNIMA, a member organization of UNESCO, encourages international pluralism. UNIMA-USA, in cooperation with Puppeteers of America, hosted the thirteenth Congress of UNIMA and the World Puppetry Festival in 1980, which was attended by over two thousand puppeteers. The John F. Kennedy Center for the Performing Arts and Georgetown University were the primary sites; also included were the Smithsonian Institution and The Corcoran Gallery. This brought puppetry to the attention of the National Endowment for the Arts and major performing arts presenters.

The Jim Henson Foundation was created by Jim Henson at the urging of Nancy L. Staub, director of the 1980 World Puppetry Festival, in order to help fund new and exciting work by the burgeoning core of new artists. The foundation has continued to fulfill Jim's mission by providing grants to produce "cutting-edge" new works. Just before his death in 1990, Jim had hired Nancy to direct an international festival of puppet theater in New York City. After the initial planning stage, Leslee Asch, executive director of the Henson Foundation, and Cheryl Henson, one of Jim's daughters, who became president of the foundation, nurtured the first festival to maturity in 1992. Since then it has been held there every two years and makes use of a dozen or more prestigious Manhattan venues. During that time, New York becomes the Mecca for works of puppetry artists of global significance. The event was designed to showcase the art of puppetry to the New York theater audience and critics, but it is attended as well by people who travel from all parts of the world to avail themselves of this singular event.

Several puppetry centers have emerged that are responsible for propelling the field forward at a breathtaking pace. The largest is the Center for Puppetry Arts in Atlanta; since I am its founder and executive director, I can boast a little of its accomplishments. We have several performance series of note. The New Directions Series offers adult audiences a chance to experience innovative works from America and around the world. The Xperimental Puppetry Theater allows new and emerging artists a chance to be seen. The Family Series offers our resident company, as well as guest artists globally, to find enthusiastic audiences. Our education program not only offers traditional puppet-making workshops for children and adults, but it also partners with community agencies; we also now offer distance-learning opportunities nationwide via sophisticated interactive television. Our museum offers our permanent collection and special exhibits focused on specific areas of the field. Other very important puppetry centers exist around the country. The Northwest Puppet Center in Seattle, established by Chris and Stephen Carter, offers a diverse program of top quality family shows by the Carters themselves, in addition to regional, national, and international performers; they also have educational workshops and courses and a museum. The Greater Arizona Puppet Theater in Phoenix, run by Nancy Smith, offers performances by in-house puppeteers and by guest artists. The Puppet Showplace in Brookline, Massachusetts, was founded by Mary Churchill and is now administered by Paul Vincent Davis; it features his excellent productions and hosts guest performers from New England and beyond.

For eons we have been vagabonds. As such, we have always traveled to find audiences of all ages. As the previously mentioned *Touring Directory* points out, that tradition is still intact. Whether it be the Icarus Puppet Company of San Diego enchanting young audiences with their Japanese stories, or Cherokee legends enacted by Hobey Ford's Golden Rod Puppets of Weaverville, North Carolina, or the elaborate Huber Marionettes dazzling crowds in Las Vegas, puppeteers are still on the move. The brother/sister puppetry team from Toronto, Ann and David Powell, take their award-winning Puppetmongers performances worldwide. Former airline pilot and now full-time puppet entrepreneur, Jim Gamble, travels the globe to entertain with his children's and adult shows. Drew Allison of Grey Seal Puppets in Charlotte, North Carolina, straps on his plumber's belt and incorporates it into his delightful show, *Bathtub Pirates*, presented for children near and far. Patti Smithsonian of Manitou Springs, Colorado, puts her puppets, newly made from cast-off junk, into her car and is on the road to dazzle hip young adults. Those same hip audiences might be perched on street lights in New York's Greenwich Village in order to see one of the dazzling creations in Ralph Lee's perennial Halloween parade. Husband-and-wife team Tom and Marianne Tucker travel with their Tucker's Tales Puppet Theatre, performing with hand puppets in their home territory of Abington, Pennsylvania, and down the I-95 corridor to Florida. Preston Foerder of Jersey City, New Jersey, collects his trash pail, brooms and brushes to tell the classic tales of the Brothers Grimm in a new way to new audiences. Professor John Bell of Emory College in Boston readies his miniature toy theater of Great Small Works in New York City to tell the grand story of Bertolt Brecht's life to puppet aficionados somewhere, someplace.

And on and on we go. We have followed the tribes of the past, and we will follow the tribes of the future because we are the past and the future. We will always be the chroniclers of our time. Whenever that time may be, we as puppeteers are its reflection: the mirror image of the creativity, crises, passions, politics, foibles, foolishness, and fun that make up contemporary American life.

The author wishes to thank Nancy L. Staub and Dave Martin for their assistance in writing this essay.

A Short View of
American Puppetry

LOWELL SWORTZELL

Perhaps no single celebration better exemplifies the popular advancement of puppetry in America at the beginning of the twenty-first century than the Jim Henson Foundation's International Festival of Puppet Theater, held biannually in New York City. Starting in 1992 with seventeen puppeteers representing eight countries, who performed in one theater over a two-week period, the 2000 festival expanded to include twenty-six companies from fourteen countries, appearing at fourteen venues over three weeks, offering a total of one hundred forty-six artists and their estimated six hundred puppets, who gave two hundred performances. Almost every type of puppet appeared, from traditional forms of glove, rod, string, paper, doll and shadow to abstract experiments with found objects, film, machines, electronics, video and computer-digital collage. Executive producer Cheryl Henson has defined puppetry as "the magical art of bringing inanimate objects to life," but, as festival participants continue to demonstrate, the magic extends equally to animate objects, particularly to the human body, which can transform its face, fist or foot (yes, even its belly button!) into new and imaginative articulations. At the Henson Festival actors and dancers become puppets and puppets become actors and dancers; masks move and sing; lights and sounds discover identities of their own, and, in doing so, create constantly broadening definitions of their own.

The festival has grown over the years, not only in attendance and in the participation of additional companies, but also in its critical coverage and recognition by the press and media. This enthusiasm has helped to reverse the traditional American attitude that puppetry is largely child's play, an entertainment emanating from the nursery love of dolls and only extending through the elementary grades. But now, with major New York reviewers giving their full attention, as much as they would to a Broadway opening, theatergoers are realizing that puppetry is an art form worthy of their appreciation and patronage. Not that children are overlooked, for the festival schedules weekend morning and afternoon performances for them, as well as designating certain other productions as suitable for all ages. This achievement comes after more than two hundred years of pioneers, whose artistry served their own time and contributed to puppetry's flowering today.

Native American Examples

The theatricality of Native American communities is nowhere better observed than in the Kwakiutl art of British Columbia, particularly in the region of northern Vancouver Island. At potlatch ceremonies, dancers wore masks and headdresses to celebrate traditions and to illuminate their carefully preserved legends. Transformation masks operated with hidden manipulating strings to reveal faces within faces; animals and birds, such as the beloved raven, spoke with mouths opening and shutting and beaks snapping and biting. An octopus spread its tentacles and moved its hinged jaw as it glided in underwater rhythms. And along with these animated faces, full-fledged puppets appeared. A bright blue frog mounted on a wooden roller could crawl with its legs moving in tandem, even its cloth throat and underbelly bloating to add to its life-like image. A wooden crab puppet with movable legs and huge bulging eyes suggests it was employed for comic effect. Such masks and puppets reveal a technical command of strings and rigging that is as intricate as it is theatrical. While no claim is made here that they either were influenced by other cultures or that they, in turn, inspired puppeteers elsewhere, their indigenous presence establishes their place in the pageantry of American puppetry.

Wandering Showmen

As Paul McPharlin delineates in *The Puppet Theatre in America: A History 1524–1948*, the eighteenth and nineteenth centuries witnessed a series of itinerant performers from whom we can glean scattered glimpses of their hardy figures roaming muddy roads in the wilderness. These adventurers eventually were mentioned in print in such places as Charleston, Williamsburg, and New York. George Washington entered the price of a "Puppet Shew" in his expense account for November 16, 1776, for a performance that took place in Williamsburg at 6:00 P.M., when Peter Gardiner and his four-foot figures appeared in a variety of scenes and characters, including "all manner of sea monsters sporting on the waves" (50–51).

John Durang, a self-taught actor and entrepreneur, brought before the public such attractions as equestrian and pantomime performances, the first theater for and run by children, and, to be sure, his own puppet company. He recorded these accomplishments in his colorful travel account, *The Memoirs of John Durang*. In summer 1786 while vacationing in Philadelphia, he made a "company of wooden actors to entertain and amuse my friends as well as myself" (25). Using figures about two feet high, he performed *The Poor Soldier* on a stage with a curtain, scenery, lamps and chandeliers with his sister and "several young men of some talent and accompanied by six musicians." At "fifty cents a ticket," he claims to have attracted "crowded houses every night" (26). Whether or not, as Durang insisted, every performance was of the highest professional quality, an entirely American company had been created and welcomed by the public.

It would appear that the two-foot "Punch and his wife Joan" performing in Philadelphia on December 30, 1742, was indeed a version of puppetry's most dysfunctional, yet best-loved, couple, the irrepressible Punch and the long-suffering Joan (later to be known as Judy). McPharlin believed that the advertisement boasting their ability to move and to change meant they were string puppets rather than the customary glove formations. The first traditional Punch and Judy show came from London in 1828 in the person of a Mr. Mathews, whose "tragical Comedy or Comical Tragedy" played at the Park, New York City's most prestigious theater (118). Punch and Judy shows remained a staple of American puppetry, with numerous exponents throughout the nineteenth to the mid-twentieth centuries.

Trouping Professionals

One example of the Americanization of the marionette show may be charted through the popular success of *Little Red Riding Hood,* an extravaganza that began in 1873 and continued well into the next decade, with rival companies appearing in major cities throughout the nation. Billed as the Royal Marionettes, the original company consisted of a group of manipulators, readers, and singers, perhaps as many as twenty, contracted in London to give nine weekly performances and various added matinees. With no connections to actual royalty, their program opened with a variety act composed of traditional comic antics: tightrope walkers, contortionists, Irish dancers, and a chorus of Chinese bell ringers. A minstrel show followed that replicated in miniature live shows then widely patronized (even at nearby theaters), complete with their "Gentlemen, be seated" half circle of burnt-cork comedians and tellers of intentionally terrible jokes. The major section of the evening offered a marionette version of the great musical hit of the 1860s, *The Black Crook,* a blend of British fairy-tale pantomime and Faustian spectacle of nineteenth-century melodrama. Largely an excuse for transformations of scenery from fairy grotto to enchanted island, the live musical was most famous for its girls in pink tights, and even they seem to have had their stringed counterparts. As *Little Red Riding Hood* made its way in one version or another to Chicago and eventually throughout the West Coast, with imitators venturing into Canada and on to Hawaii, the company's name changed to the Anglo-American Marionette Combination. By the 1880s professional puppetry had proved its viability among American audiences, and had incorporated materials and characters of the American experience. Marionettes still remained a novelty, but by then were an established novelty (180–182, 191–193).

Vaudeville grew out of the tradition of the variety show in the 1880s and lasted through the coming of radio and talking movies, giving puppetry a home on the bill among the acrobats, singers, comedians and even as the major-name attraction. Full-season engagements made vaudeville a far more professionally secure avenue than city-to-city freelance touring. Following the pattern of the Royal Marionettes, manipulators often demonstrated a range of comic and trick turns in the brief time allotted to each act; short versions of plays such as *Humpty-Dumpty* also might be included. In such a restricted lineup of offerings, performers were not likely to break new creative ground, but, and this was no small accomplishment, they did keep puppetry before the public.

Twentieth-Century Expansion

The contributions of countless amateurs — those who fostered the legacy of Punch and Judy, and string performers in their homes, communities, and workshops — should be celebrated. In the first three decades of the twentieth century, puppetry came to be recognized for its educational values in teaching a variety of subjects, as well as in the production of plays that students wrote, designed, constructed, and performed. Playgrounds began to sponsor puppet activities and performances; performers sometimes traveled from park to park throughout summer seasons. Extending beyond education and recreation, puppetry also made advances in its therapeutic applications in hospitals and private practices.

In what Bil Baird has called "the surge," that swelling of puppetry popularity among Americans in the 1920s and 30s, the single most central force was Tony Sarg (1880–1942). Born in Guatemala to German parents and educated in German military training, as well as in music and drawing, Sarg established himself as an illustrator and collector of antique toys in London, where he also developed his interest in marionettes. Arriving in New York City in 1915, he rented a studio in the Flatiron Building and performed a 1916 revue, *A Night in Delhi*, complete with a snake charmer and a loosely jointed dancing cobra. His trick marionettes, such as a come-apart skeleton, so impressed producer Winthrop Ames that he invited Sarg to appear on Broadway. Later, his company, advertised as "Tony Sarg's Marionettes," presented *Rip Van Winkle* to national audiences, who became enthralled by its fourteen scenes of spectacle and fantasy created by five operators, a floorman, and a pianist. The young Bil Baird, upon seeing this production in 1921, determined to become a puppeteer. In this and other successful tours of *Ali Baba, Treasure Island* and *Alice in Wonderland*, Sarg insisted on strong scripts and able speakers in order to give full dramatic effect to performances lasting from two to three hours. After his early success, he left the execution of his designs to associates, but always under his supervision, as he did with other shows that played to crowds at fairs, expositions and amusement parks. His concepts for giant animated helium-filled balloons, some one hundred twenty-five feet long and requiring fifty handlers, began the tradition still seen in the Macy's Thanksgiving Day parade. Sarg also operated a school in Manhattan that trained a generation of professional puppeteers. While he aimed his work largely at young audiences, untold thousands of all ages experienced the pleasures of puppetry for the first time, and his name became synonymous with modern marionettes in America.

The Provincetown Playhouse, a converted Greenwich Village stable dedicated to producing new American plays, became home in the 1920s to the early works of Eugene O'Neill and Susan Glaspell, as well as becoming a center of puppet activity. Here Remo Bufano (1894–1948), drawing on his Italian heritage, which had prompted him to perform his own satiric version of *Orlando Furioso* (1914), produced puppet plays by noted contemporary poets, such as Alfred Kreymborg (*Lima Beans*, 1920) and Edna St. Vincent Millay (*Two Slatterns and a King*, 1923). Moving uptown, Bufano created the Walrus and the Carpenter for Eva Le Gallienne's acclaimed *Alice in Wonderland* (1933, repeated in 1946) and a clown thirty-five feet tall in the Rodgers and Hart Broadway musical *Jumbo* (1935). Far shorter, at only ten feet in length, but no less imaginative, were the figures he constructed from designs by Robert Edmond Jones for Stravinsky's *Oedipus Rex* (1931). Operated by cords from above and supported by rods from below, these übermarionettes dominated the stage of the Metropolitan and other opera houses where the oratorio was enacted above the heads of the chorus. After leading the New York Marionette unit of the Federal Theatre Project, Bufano built masks and played the role of the Dinosaur in the prize-winning Broadway comedy, *The Skin of Our Teeth*, by Thornton Wilder. Upon moving to Hollywood in the 1940s, he experimented with puppets and stop-action techniques until his career ended tragically when he was killed in an airplane crash.

Beyond the contributions of individuals such as Sarg and Bufano, growing puppet popularity in the first half of the twentieth century prospered most from the formation of a Marionette Unit within the Federal Theatre Project (FTP). Operating from 1936 through June 1939, under the aegis of the Welfare Progress Act (WPA) as a relief measure of the Great Depression, FTP employed out-of-work actors, musicians, vaudevillians, circus performers and puppeteers. In order to qualify, performers had to have held one previous professional engagement, so soon old-timers and young apprentices were working side by side in twenty-two marionette companies presenting a weekly average of one hundred shows across the country. Headed by theater educator Hallie Flanagan, who believed that marionettes should be integral to a national theater movement, FTP had more puppeteers working in New York City alone than had been employed previously throughout the country (Brown and O'Connor 24). Bufano, director of the New York unit, focused mainly on dramatizations of childhood classics, such as *Treasure Island* and *Oliver Twist,* while Ralph Chessé, head of the California unit, concentrated on what he termed "high-class adult entertainment," which included Eugene O'Neill's *The Emperor Jones* and variety shows. The Marionette Unit also offered patterns, instructions and materials for children to make puppets for their own classroom shows.

The Yale Puppeteers, who began performing in 1923 at the University of Michigan before reassembling in New Haven, where they took theater courses, are best remembered for their quarter-century tenure at Hollywood's Turnabout Theatre. Creating their own satirical material in songs and sketches, they directed their wit at sophisticated adult audiences.

Bil Baird

Bil Baird (1904–1987), arguably the twentieth century's seminal puppeteer as a performer on Broadway, in film and on television, as a teacher (of Jim Henson, among many other artists), and as author of the classic and lavishly color-illustrated *The Art of the Puppet* (1965), defined a puppet as "an inanimate figure that is made to move by human effort before an audience" (13). Along with movement, he believed the figure must possess form and sound that communicates its creator's intentions because a puppet is an extension of the puppeteer (20). If so, Baird, in his more than half-century career, had an estimated three thousand extensions as diverse as Slugger Ryan, who actually smoked as he played a honky-tonk piano, Mme. Swanova, the long-legged dancing swan, and the yarn-fringed cowardly lion from his version of *The Wizard of Oz.*

Given a puppet as a child of eight, he performed with one of his own construction at fourteen, a love he continued to develop as he also studied stage design. But it was his five-year association with Tony Sarg that turned him into a professional puppeteer as he toured *Ali Baba and the Forty Thieves* in a forty-week season of one-night stands across the country. While working as an acrobat in the Federal Theatre Project's farce *Horse Eats Hat,* Orson Welles's energetic version of Labiche's *The Italian Straw Hat,* Baird agreed to construct Welles's design for the two-person costume of the horse. "Everybody tried him out and liked him," Baird recalled, and next Welles had him creating puppets representing the Seven Deadly Sins for his WPA 1936 production of Marlowe's *Doctor Faustus* (Brown and O'Connor 46). The voices were supplied by a young actress whom Baird later married and who remained his artistic collaborator until her death in 1967.

The Bairds operated their own Greenwich Village Theatre on Barrow Street where, in addition to original full-length works, such as *Davy Jones' Locker,* they also maintained a workshop and museum filled with their own puppets, as well as those they had collected from around the world. While the Bairds extended puppetry into mainstream entertainment with their television show, as well as guest appearances on the Ed Sullivan, Jack Paar and Sid Caesar variety shows, they also, through such productions as Stravinsky's *L'Histoire du Soldat* (1982), pursued new applications of the puppet's mission. Baird declared, "A puppet must always be more than his live counterpart — simpler, sadder, more wicked, more supple. The puppet is an essence and an emphasis. For only in this way does a puppet begin to reflect the truth" (15). At the time of Baird's death, Jim Henson said he had learned most of what he knew from Baird and that at least thirty of his Muppeteers had trained at the Bairds' Greenwich Village theater.

Variety Acts

Big city nightclubs and supper clubs in the mid–twentieth century spawned circuit careers for individual puppeteers who aimed their variety acts at adults. Typical among them was Frank Paris's *Stars on Strings,* which mimicked song stylists such as "Latin bombshell" Carmen Miranda. Such solo performers abolished the anonymity operators once had sought behind the scenes; now in full view, they became equal partners with their wooden figures. Ventriloquists also flourished in the spotlights by playing straight men to their so-called dummies, who often could outsmart them on every subject. Dressed in a tuxedo to match that of his creator

Edgar Bergen, Charlie McCarthy, the monocled top-hatted sophisticate, became such a full-fledged favorite personality that, by the 1930s, he had his own radio show in which his repartee parried masterfully with that of W. C. Fields and Bergen himself. Although never Charlie's true rival, Mortimer Snerd, the hayseed country cousin, was his total opposite, as dense as Charlie was alert, and further demonstrated Bergen's remarkable vocal versatility and sense of comic timing.

Political Agendas

The potential of puppetry as a political consciousness tool has long been sustained by the Bread & Puppet Theater, first established by Peter Schumann as the New Dance Group in Munich in 1961, then transferring to New York City and, finally, in 1974 headquartered on a farm in Vermont. They protested issues such as governmental bureaucracy and American involvement in the Vietnam War, and they supported such causes as peace and voter registration. Although he denies the agit-prop label often associated with his largely amateur company (of one production he said, "It glorifies the hero who opposes taxes, and people can take from that what they want to take"), Schumann calls his once annual August collective event *The Domestic Resurrection Circus*. Employing puppets and masks of varying dimensions (from a few inches to eighteen feet high), the productions emphasize theatrical mime and movement, rather than dramatic narrative. Depending on financial contributions rather than on grants or subsidies that might influence his critical views, Schumann has traveled widely abroad to conduct workshops and performance residencies. His provocative productions and parades include *Masaniello* (1977), based on a seventeenth-century Italian uprising against Spanish captors, and *Columbus: The New World Order* (1992), which indicted Columbus as the perpetrator of crimes that continue to resonate today.

Television

Numerous American puppeteers found employment at their local television stations in the early years of programming. But once Burr Tillstrom's Chicago-produced "Kukla, Fran and Ollie" appeared on ABC in

1947, national audiences began to welcome puppets into their living rooms for fifteen minutes of live broadcasts five days a week. With Fran Allison poised in front of their curtained booth, the hand-manipulated Kuklapolitan Players (all played by Tillstrom) ad-libbed, sang (even opera) and commented on their distinctly varied lives. Through their affection for each other, they became television legends, still to be appreciated today in video archives. After the series ended in 1957, Tillstrom won new recognition for his bare-hand pantomimes of choreographed gestures on subjects as serious as the Berlin Wall.

Millions of children further explored puppets as they watched two long-running programs: "Howdy Doody," which began on NBC in 1947 and played until 1960, and "Mister Rogers' Neighborhood," presided over by the gentle conversationalist Fred Rogers, who welcomed viewers to his neighborhood for over two generations. Other puppeteers who found television responsive to their appearances on variety shows and in commercials included Bil Baird, Shari Lewis, Señor Wences, George Latshaw, Ralph Chessé, and Rufus and Margo Rose. It would be Jim Henson (1937–1990), however, experimenting first in Washington, DC, and later in New York with studio production and camera techniques, who eventually dominated the nation's TV screens. His Muppets, as the name implies, combined marionettes and puppets, but no longer confined them to traditional stages or to conventional sizes. Kermit the Frog and Miss Piggy, one of puppetry's most memorable couples, performed by Henson and Frank Oz, respectively, first appeared on "Sesame Street" and then became the superstars of "The Muppet Show," which ran five seasons from 1976 through 1980. American puppetry had become an entertainment attracting audiences of all ages and levels of sophistication (at one point the show was said to have aired in one hundred countries). Respected artists, such as Beverly Sills and Rudolf Nureyev, willingly satirized themselves by joining the Muppets in their comic versions of the worlds of opera and ballet.

Films

Hollywood's incidental interest in puppetry was strengthened notably in 1943 when it bestowed a special Academy Award on George Pal (1908–1980) for his novel techniques of stop-motion filming of carved figures. Known for his series of short Puppetoons, Pal later expanded his methods into the full-length films, *Tom Thumb* (1958) and *The Wonderful World of the Brothers Grimm* (1963). The MGM musical *Lili* (1953), featuring the hand puppets of Paul Walton and Mickey O'Rourke, and Twentieth Century–Fox's *The Sound of Music* (1965), with dancing marionettes by Bil Baird, further charmed audiences worldwide. But it was not until Jim Henson brought his Muppets to the big screen that puppets became true Hollywood stars: Kermit the Frog, Miss Piggie, Fozzie Bear, Bert and Ernie and many of the TV company reigned as both box-office and household names in *The Muppets Take Manhattan* (1984). Henson branched into experimental fantasy with *The Dark Crystal* (1982), based on drawings by British illustrator Brian Froud. Believing that music and movement mattered more than dialogue in bringing Mystic Valley and the Pod People to life, Henson developed this film from visions of imaginary landscapes, rather than from an established script. In *Labyrinth* (1986), he mixed remote-controlled animatronic figures from his Creature Shop with on-screen live actors who together become lost in a topiary Escher-esque maze symbolizing the heroine's entrance into adolescence. In his final film he experimented with *Muppet-Vision 3D* (1991), often successfully giving the illusion of motion through real space as the digitally created Waldo (Henson had been working with computer-generated characters and settings since 1983) became his ultimate technological expression.

The Philadelphia-born identical twins, Stephen and Timothy Quay, have pursued their puppet animation abroad in films such as *Street of Crocodiles* (1986) and *Can't Go Without You* (1993). Described as a macabre theater of anxiety, these films created a world as dark and mysterious as it is foreboding and fascinating in imaginative despair.

Hollywood has continued to develop Henson's animatronic legacy in a series of popular films such as *Toy Story* (1995), and *Chicken Run* (2000), aimed at young audiences, and in *Being John Malkovich* (2000) for adults. Perhaps the most original work is that of Tim Burton, a former Disney animator, and director of such films as *Beetlejuice* (1988), *Batman* (1989), and *Edward Scissorhands* (1990), whose *The Nightmare Before Christmas* (1993) combined both stop-motion filming of 227 molded movable figures with computer synchronization of voices and sound effects. His decade-long effort to bring Jack Skellington's story to the screen was realized with the help of director Henry Selick and one hundred forty artists and technicians in production for two years.

The Philadelphia-born identical twins, Stephen and Timothy Quay, have pursued their puppet animation abroad in films such as *Street of Crocodiles* (1986) and *Can't Go Without You* (1993). Described as a macabre theater of anxiety, these films created a world as dark and mysterious as it is foreboding and fascinating in imaginative despair.

Julie Taymor, Ralph Lee and Other Contemporary Artists

Julie Taymor, long familiar to audiences of experimental theaters in Boston and New York, became America's best-known designer of puppet-mask-costume and makeup concepts almost overnight when *The Lion King* opened on Broadway in 1997. Showcasing her distinctive union of animal constructions and human forms, Taymor won for the Walt Disney musical critical approval and box office triumphs in New York, London and on tour.

Taymor, at the age of ten, participated in activities of the Boston Children's Theatre, which nurtured her theatrical and multicultural interests that, as a teenager, led her to visit India, Sri Lanka and Paris, where she studied at Jacques Lecoq's *L'Ecole de Mime*. Later travel took her to Indonesia and Japan to study traditions of puppetry and masked-theater dance, which, along with Balinese ritual and *wayang* silhouettes, would shape much of her creativity in later works: *The Haggadah* (New York Shakespeare Festival, 1980), Carlo Gozzi's fairy-tale *commedia dell'arte* fantasia, *The King Stag* (1984), *The Tempest* (1986) and *Juan Darien: A Carnival Mass* (1988, 1990). She also has brought theatricality to her films, *Fool's Fire* (1992), *Oedipus Rex* (1993) and *Titus* (1999), an adaptation of Shakespeare's *Titus Andronicus*. Her version of Gozzi's *The Green Bird*, previously well received off–Broadway failed to win Broadway audiences in 2000, despite its Tony nominations. But as companies of *The Lion King* continue to multiply, Taymor's puppets, masks and makeup designs remind audiences of past puppet techniques put to imaginative new directions of musical staging.

Ralph Lee, whose Metawee River Theatre Company specializes in plays largely developed from mythology and legends, has received two Obie and other major awards and has been the subject of a retrospective exhibition of his masks and puppets, large and small, at Lincoln Center. Touring each summer through New England, he also schedules frequent performances in New York at La MaMa, the Cathedral of St. John the Divine and the Henson International Festival of Puppet Theatre. The *New York Times* called his 1999 production of *Psyche* "a performance of high style, sophistication and good humor." Lee, the founder of the Greenwich Village Halloween parade, also teaches at New York University and conducts annual workshops in Mexico.

Gulliver's Travels by Lowell Swortzell. Puppets designed by Ralph Lee. (Courtesy NYU/L. Pellettieri photograph.)

The 1980s and '90s witnessed increases in the interaction between puppets and actors, the incorporation of dance and mime and the integration of live musicians and original scores in such productions as *Underground* and *Harlot's Progress* by Theodora Skipitares, *The Village Child* and *Never Been Anywhere* by Eric Bass, *Peter and Wendy* by Lee Breuer and the Mabou Mines, *Kwaidan* by Ping Chong and in Paul Zaloom's performance art. Yet solo puppeteers such as Bruce Schwartz, Roman Paska, and Canada's Ronnie Burkett also continued to enlarge adult audiences with their charm, wit and innovations in rod, string and glove puppets, sometimes masterminding as many as thirty-seven marionettes in a single performance.

The numerous American companies selected to appear at the Henson Foundation's International Festival of Puppet Theatre represented much of today's best work that incorporates new concepts in texts, technology

Opposite, top: The Woman Who Fell from the Sky, designed and directed by Ralph Lee. *Bottom:* Parade figure, designed by Ralph Lee. (Mettawee River Company.)

and manipulation. Notable among these explorations are the film artistry of Janie Geiser, the sensory interplay of Heather Henson, the epic spectacle of Redmoon Theater, the blending of traditional and contemporary visions of Michael Sommers, the light environments and projections of Rudi Stern, the abstract imagery of Hanne Tierney and the radiophonic plays performed by the electronic puppets of Valere Novarina, Allen S. Weiss and Zaven Pare. This last-named company is only one of several collaborations between Americans and members of foreign companies.

What with ever-widening audiences, young and old, to be found at live performances, at critically praised films, and watching television programming, historians may conclude that puppetry is now recognized as an art form firmly, if still not yet fully, established in American cultural life. As long as it continues to redefine itself through experimentation with new subjects and concepts and through explorations of new forms and styles, it will continue both to honor its past and to extend its magic.

Works Cited

Baird, Bil. *The Art of the Puppet*. New York: Macmillan, 1965.

Brown, Lorraine, and John O'Connor, eds. *Free, Adult, and Uncensored: The History of the Federal Theatre Project*. Washington, DC: New Republic Books, 1978.

Durang, John. *The Memoirs of John Durang*. Pittsburgh: University of Pittsburgh Press, 1966.

McPharlin, Paul. *The Puppet Theatre in America: A History 1524 to 1948*. With a supplement: *Puppets in America Since 1948*, by Marjorie Batchelder McPharlin. Boston: Plays, Inc., 1969.

II

Significant Collections

Puppetry and Related Materials in the Harvard Theatre Collection

FREDRIC WOODBRIDGE WILSON

The Harvard Theatre Collection was established in a modest way in 1901, through a gift to the College Library of a significant collection of engravings related to the actor David Garrick.[1] Almost immediately thereafter, largely through the advocacy of Professor George Pierce Baker, the collection grew through further significant gifts; and by 1918, augmented by the combined collections of Robert W. Lowe, Robert Gould Shaw (Harvard class of 1869), and Evert Jansen Wendell (class of 1882), it had achieved the distinction of being the largest and certainly the richest theater collection in existence.[2]

From its earliest years, the scope of the collection included areas outside of the realm of the legitimate stage. Many forms of popular entertainment — fairground entertainments and pleasure gardens, minstrel shows, circuses and acrobatics, conjurors and spiritualists, festivals and masques, menageries and zoological gardens, trained animals, sideshows and anomalies, music hall, vaudeville, and variety shows — were represented on almost an equal footing with literary drama that ranged from Shakespearean tragedy to modern farce. Among these so-called irregular forms, puppetry has also been present in the general holdings of the Harvard Theatre Collection from its earliest years.

In the decades following, however, some named or archival collections (nowadays more often referred to, in librarians' language, as "special"

Le Malade Imaginaire. Scène imaginaire by Etienne Bertrand Weill. Gift of Lily and Baird Hastings. (Harvard Theatre Collection.)

collections) and other acquisitions have further strengthened Harvard's holdings in this interesting area. In the following outline, some of these resources are enumerated.[3]

Collections of Puppets

The Ralph C. McGoun Collection of Puppets and Masks

A large collection of contemporary puppets, folk masks, and theatrical and dance figures from many traditions, gathered from all over the world between about 1955 and 1985. The collection includes Italian hand puppets, miniature Sicilian rod puppets, Greek Karaghöz shadow puppet figures, a Polish folk art figure, Indian string puppets, Indian Kathakali figures, Pakistani hand puppets, Turkish shadow puppets, a Tunisian rod puppet, Japanese Noh figures and Kabuki dolls, Chinese opera make-up characters, Kabuki and Noh prints, Balinese puppets, Balinese masks, Cambodian temple dancers, Ceylonese devil masks, Thai classical dance figures, Thai shadow puppets, Argentinian Indian masks, Brazilian Carnival puppets, Colombian Indian masks, an Ecuadorian cowboy folk dancer, Guatemalan masks, Mexican puppets, Panamanian dancers, Peruvian hand puppets, *commedia dell'arte* devil figures (all reproductions), Danish toy theaters (including the Tivoli Chinese Theatre), and English Regency toy theater (all reproductions). In all, the collection contains approximately one hundred forty puppet figures and masks. It also includes related prints, programs, and posters. The gift of Ralph Cleland McGoun, 1986.

Punch and Judy Hand Puppets

A set of Punch and Judy hand puppets, presumably English, nineteenth century, made of carved wood and cloth. These puppets do not appear to constitute a uniform set. There are four puppets complete with dresses: Punch, approx. eighteen in., Judy, approx. fourteen in., a uniformed officer (possibly a postman), approx. seventeen in., and another Punch, of different construction, approx. nineteen in. Six other puppets, consisting of heads with an assortment of loose arms, legs, and dresses, include an alligator, a horned demon, and several other monsters.

The Polichinel Vampire Puppet

A puppet made to represent the dancer Charles Mazurier as the Polichinel Vampire (i.e., the Punchinello Vampire, dressed as Punch), made about 1823, approx. nine in. The gift of Marian Hannah Winter, 1980.[4]

Harlequin Puppet

A miniature Harlequin puppet made by the artist Fritz Kredel (1900–1973) for his daughter, Judy Kredel Brown. A toy, made of wood and paper with wire joints, approx. 2½ in. The gift of Mr. and Mrs. Paul Gourary, 1981.

The Doug Fitch Puppet Collection

Hand puppets and properties for James Thurber's children's book, *The Thirteen Clocks*. Nineteen pieces, each approx. eighteen to thirty-six inches, together with a typescript and stage directions. The gift of Doug Fitch.

Greek Shadow Puppets

Manufactured shadow puppets, made of heavy uncolored brown pressboard, with perforations, fastened with metal grommets, eight pieces, approx. thirty in. each, with long-playing recordings. The gift of Robert B. Shaffer, 1976.

Vietnamese Hand Puppets

Puppets from Hanoi, then the French colony of Cochin-Chine, made of papier-mâché, elaborately painted and decorated, ten pieces, each four to nine inches. The gift of Langdon Warner, 1945.

The LaMont Medieval Marionettes

A set of marionettes representing characters of the medieval court, ceramic and cloth, nine figures, approx. twelve in. each, with a throne, made by Mrs. Katharine R. LaMont of Philadelphia. The gift of Robert E. LaMont, 1946.

The Peter Arnott Marionette Collection

A large collection of marionettes, relating to puppet adaptations of Greek tragedies. Peter Arnott was the chairman of the theater department at Tufts University and author of *Greek Scenic Conventions of the Fifth Century B.C.* (Oxford University Press, 1962), among other works. The Theatre Collection received Professor Arnott's papers, which contain his research files and the artifacts of his own performance work in puppetry.[5]

Marionettes by W. A. Dwiggins

Two marionettes made by W. A. Dwiggins, representing Noël Coward and George Bernard Shaw. It is well known that the graphic designer W. A. Dwiggins made marionette puppets and presented entertainments at his home, using the stage name "Dr. Hermann Puterschein." Most of his puppet collection is located at the Boston Public Library, but these two figures were given to the Harvard Theatre Collection.[6]

Asian Puppets

Japanese Hand Puppets

A hand puppet made in 1882 by Kusaka Kaizan, Wadamura, Japan. Richard Fyfe Boyce, American consul to Japan, used this puppet in public presentations. It is accompanied by scripts of Japanese-English routines. Bunraku-style male puppet, called by the name of "Hajime Hayashi," beautifully constructed of wood and cloth, with movable eyes and mouth, approx. twenty-seven in., accompanied by two fans and an extra pair of cloth arms. The gift of Richard Fyfe Boyce, 1966.

A pair of Japanese bunraku hand puppet heads, male and female, made of porcelain and cloth, approx. eleven in. each. The gift of Mrs. Pease, 1944.

A pair of beautifully constructed male and female hand puppets from Osaka, Japan, with movable mouths, heads only, with hair, approx. 12 in. each.

Formosan Hand Puppet

A hand puppet made in Formosa (Taiwan), painted wood and cloth, approx. eleven in. The gift of Richard Fyfe Boyce, 1966.

Harvard Theatre Collection assistant Mary Reardon with the W. A. Dwiggins
marionettes of Noël Coward and George Bernard Shaw, in the Theatre Collection stacks, 1953. (Photograph by Gordon N. Converse, *Christian Science Monitor*. Harvard Theatre Collection.)

The Alice Stern Hart Collection
of Chinese Shadow Puppets

A large and attractive set of Chinese shadow figures, made of thin
vellum painted in watercolor, more than three hundred pieces, approx.
twelve in. each, excluding sticks. The gift of Alice Stern Hart.

The Anne and Roy Freed Collection
of Indonesian Shadow Puppets

A superb old set of Balinese shadow puppets in the *wayang kulit* tradition, made of painted leather, with wooden reinforcements and sticks, with signs of heavy use. The large collection contains 147 figures from at least four distinct sets, various sizes up to approx. 20 in., including named characters and unnamed figures, weapons, animals, etc. The gift of Anne and Roy Freed, 1991.

The John Ward Collection
of Indonesian Shadow Puppets

A large set of Javanese shadow puppets in the *wayang kulit* tradition, painted leather, with bamboo reinforcements and sticks, about twenty pieces, approx. twenty-six in. to thirty-three in. each, together with animal figures, weapons, scenes, etc. There is also a smaller set made of lighter weight vellum, lightly tinted. The gift of John M. Ward, 1994.

The Fredric Wertham Collection
of Indonesian Shadow Puppets

A fine set of Javanese shadow puppets in the *wayang kulit* tradition, twentieth century, twenty-six pieces, approx. fourteen in. to twenty in. each, with screen and batik cloth. From the Wertham bequest, on extended loan from the Busch-Reisinger Museum, 1989.[7]

Indonesian Shadow Puppets

Shadow puppets made of tooled and printed leather, some without sticks, from several sets, about twenty-five pieces, in various sizes. Some pieces may have originated from China and Malaya.

The Kraton Silver Wayang Kulit Set

The Theatre Collection recently acquired a large souvenir set of 124 miniature *wayang kulit* shadow figures, two in. to five in. high, complete with set pieces and orchestral instruments, 160 pieces in all, executed in silver, including sticks. This unique set, made by the smithery in the Kraton of Djogla, Indonesia, was exhibited in 1914 at the Colonial Exhibition at Samarang, where it won a first prize for "perfect artistic work."

The Ralph McGoun Collection, described earlier, also contains a significant number of Asian puppets.

Other holdings at Harvard University include shadow puppets and masks in several ethnographic and anthropological collections, most notably in the Peabody Museum of Archaeology and Ethnology. A few of these are on permanent exhibition.

Collections of Material on the Subject of Puppetry

Czech Puppet Play Collection

An acquisition of more than four hundred printed puppet play scripts, in the Czech language, made in 1996. These fragile and ephemeral pamphlets, mostly published in Czechoslovakia in the early twentieth century, are fully catalogued and maintained as a discrete collection.

The Marian Hannah Winter Collection

The Winter Collection is the Theatre Collection's richest trove of material relating to popular entertainments of all kinds, including puppetry. It includes posters, bills, programs, prints, objects, and other material, collected by the noted authority and author of *The Theatre of Marvels*.[8]

Bread & Puppet Theater Papers

The Bread & Puppet Theater, in Glover, Vermont, has made periodical deposits of programs, posters, advertising material, and other documentation of its activities. The records of the Bread & Puppet Theater range from 1962 to 1984, with some later additions.[9]

Essays and Articles on Puppetry

Robert Edmond Jones (Harvard class of 1910), the principal advocate of the New Stagecraft, used puppets in several of his productions, including Eugene O'Neill's *The Great God Brown*, and wrote an essay, "The Italian Marionettes." The archive of his papers includes those puppets and the annotated typescript of the essay.[10]

Edward Gordon Craig was certainly Jones's spiritual mentor, and among Craig's influential publications was the short-lived journal called *The Marionette*. Its twelve issues, published over slightly longer than a year (1918–1919) during Craig's residence in Florence, contain essays on puppetry, as well as the texts of puppet plays. The Theatre Collection includes several runs of this journal as well as the entire archive of Craig's working papers and correspondence concerning both *The Marionette* and *The Mask*.

The American Repertory Theater Archive

Among the most popular productions by the American Repertory Theater, which is resident at the Loeb Drama Center in Harvard University, was an adaptation of Carlo Goldoni's play *The King Stag*, designed by Julie Taymor and directed by Andrei Serban. This production, which includes larger-than-life-size puppets, has become the A.R.T.'s signature production, revived in many seasons, given an extended tour in 2000–2001, and often presented during the holiday season, à la *The Nutcracker*. The A.R.T. archive contains production texts, videotapes, and other documentation.

Harvardiana

Among the countless stage performances at Harvard that have taken place over at least a century and a half, nearly all of which were produced and directed by students, there have been occasional productions in which puppets were used. Typically, these productions are represented in the Theatre Collection by programs, flyers or posters, photographs, and (for a few recent productions) videotapes.

Among the more recent of these productions was a presentation of Mozart's *The Magic Flute* at Dunster House in 1996, using large hand puppets, and a production of Purcell's *Acis and Galatea,* presented by the Harvard Early Music Society in Lowell Hall in 1999, using shadow puppets with full orchestra and live singers.

The Onion Weavers Puppet Company, founded by Tanya Bezreh and other Harvard students, produced several puppet entertainments during the 1990s, including *The Frogs of Aristophanes* (Fall 1993), *The Star Wars Trilogy* (Spring 1994), *Elvis: A Rockumentary in Puppets* (Spring 1995), and *West Puppet Side Story* (Spring 1999).

During his undergraduate years, the director Peter Sellars, Harvard class of 1980, produced the Edith Sitwell–William Walton performance piece *Façade* at the Loeb Drama Center, using puppets and student actors. Still legendary at Harvard is his two-hour-long condensed version of Wagner's Ring Cycle, performed to recorded music, that included a puppet cast ranging from finger puppets to twenty-foot-tall giants fabricated from burlap bags and wooden crates. (The dragon Fafner was created out of inflated plastic garbage bags and bamboo sticks.)

Books on Puppetry

Nearly all of the numerous books on puppetry in the Harvard Theatre Collection can be identified using the Harvard on-line catalogue, which is known as Hollis.[11] Several search strategies may be suggested to locate these holdings, in addition to the usual searches using the author's name or the title.[12]

The Theatre Collection includes books on puppetry in at least three areas of its collections of books and monographs. The "TS" classes, consisting mostly of early and rare books, classifies puppetry as TS 561, with some related material under TS 560 and 562.[13] There are about three hundred fifty books on puppetry in this class. The "Thr" classes, consisting of books formerly in the Widener Library collection, but since transferred to the Theatre Collection on account of their rarity or age, classify puppetry as Thr 150, with some related material under Thr 151 and 154.[14] There are about two hundred books in this class. In the "HTC-LC" classes, consisting mostly of books published since about 1970, puppetry is classified as PN 1970 through PN 1979. There are more than one hundred fifty books on puppetry in this class.[15]

The Harvard University Library is the largest university library system in the world, and there are many other books on puppetry in Harvard library collections other than the Theatre Collection. These can also be identified in Hollis, using subject headings such as Puppetry and Puppet Theatre.[16] Many rare books, notable among these being a large number of festival books and printed play texts, are found in other Harvard library collections in the Houghton Library, especially the Printing and Graphic Arts Department and the Fine Arts Library. However, although the holdings of the Harvard Theatre Collection and the Houghton Library, together with some other special collections, are available to all researchers regardless of university affiliation, the holdings of most Harvard libraries are available only to holders of Harvard identification cards.

Material Related to Puppetry

In the realm of entertainment, genres are difficult to establish rigidly. Hand puppets and marionettes may sometimes be treated as aspects of the same subject; it is no large distance from hand puppets to ventriloquists' dummies, and then perhaps to dolls and figurines. The hand-puppet Punch and Judy shows are certainly related, at least by heritage, to the Harlequinade of the Victorian pantomime, the Punchinello street performers, and back to the *commedia dell'arte*. Puppets representing

Cinderella. Marionettes by George and Mabel Kegg. Photographed by Gabriel Moulin, San Francisco, inscribed to Lotta Crabtree. Gift of Julian Hawthorne Hatch. (Harvard Theatre Collection.)

"alter egos" are certainly related to mask disguises, which figure in many kinds of theater from the ancient to the modern; their lineage to masques, masked balls, and courtly entertainments is also easily traced. Puppets and toy theaters have had a historical affinity.[17] And, of course, all of these genres may have dance components, and indeed not a few ballets have been fashioned on the ideas of puppets, dolls, toy theaters, masked balls, and the *commedia dell'arte* conventions.

In the Harvard Theatre Collection, then, will be found material that falls outside the strict boundaries of puppetry; yet it may appeal to those who are attracted to the various manifestations of this form of entertainment. Some of that material is outlined below.

Ephemera for Puppetry and Related Subjects

The Harvard Theatre Collection contains extensive collections of theatrical ephemera, including playbills and programs, handbills and advertisements, engravings and lithographs, photographs, sheet music, and posters, related to many forms of popular entertainment. Among these collections will be found material concerning puppetry in many forms and of many periods, but also to related types of performance such as Punch and Judy shows, marionette theaters, fairground and street performances, ventriloquism, toy theater, and shows with automata and mechanical puppets. Although the largest portion of such collections originates in the nineteenth century, there are examples in the Theatre Collection that

Teatro dei Piccoli. Marionette of Josephine Baker. Gift of Charles H. Taylor. (*Boston Globe* Entertainment Desk Archive. Harvard Theatre Collection.)

date from the seventeenth through the twentieth centuries. It should be noted that puppeteers and other related forms often shared bills with other kinds of entertainment, particularly in music hall or variety programs. Automata — mechanical figures supposedly capable (and some actually capable) of performing technical feats such as playing musical instruments or games of strategy such as chess, or telling fortunes — were often demonstrated in the context of a magic performance. Ventriloquism — most often involving the use of a puppet or dummy — was often a feature of acts of trained animals, minstrel shows, spiritualists, or comedy turns; portable theaters were often present in fairground or circus shows; and so on. It is frequently worthwhile looking through more general collections of variety and popular entertainment where material of interest may appear.

Shadow Theater

The many collections of Asian shadow puppets have been enumerated previously. In this category may also be included *Ombres Chinoises,* toy cut-outs, to be shown and manipulated within a shadow-box theater, according to a script or following a well-known story. Among the Theatre Collection's holdings are a cardboard box theater, with its continuous scenic roll; intact cut-out sheets; and several books of plays and instructions. The Theatre Collection has several theaters of this kind.

Toy Theater

Toy theaters, consisting of cardboard or paper figures ("penny plain, tuppence coloured," as the old expression goes) together with stage, scene, costume pieces, and properties, and often accompanied by playscripts, represented a very popular form of children's entertainment, especially in the eighteenth and nineteenth centuries. The Harvard Theatre Collection has a choice collection of these, mostly of English and German manufacture. A few toy theaters are kept assembled and set up; some other sets have been cut out, colored, and mounted; most, however, remain in their original flat, uncut state.

More than two thousand toy theater sheets are preserved in a beautifully assembled set of ten large albums, whose gold-tooled leather covers are titled "Penny Plain and Tuppence Coloured."[18]

The extensive E. Raymond Ellis Collection of toy theater materials includes a large number of uncut sheets, as well as sets of figures that have been mounted on cardboard and cut out. Many of the sets of sheets are accompanied by their original play texts.

A collection of toy theater booklets and play texts was given by Beverly Anderson in 1994.

The toy theater sheets in the Theatre Collection represent British publishers West, Skelt, Redington, Pollock, Hodgson, Lloyd, and Webb; Austrian publisher Trentsensky; German publishers Schreiber and Kuhn; French publisher Pellerin; and Danish publisher Jacobsen, among others. The series of Webb, Pollock, Schreiber, and Trentsensky are particularly well represented. There are also examples originating in Czechoslovakia, Spain, and other regions.

Among the assembled toy theaters are several made by Pollock's; a toy theater representing the famous Chinese Pantomime Theatre in Tivoli Gardens, Copenhagen; and another Danish toy theater, *Ei Blot Til Lyst*, all given by Ralph C. McGoun. There are other assembled examples from Germany, Spain, England, and the United States.

Some of the publishers of toy theaters also produced penny prints of popular actors, and the Theatre Collection has a large number of these.

Masks

Depictions of theatrical scenes or characters wearing masks are plentiful in the Theatre Collection's series of prints, engravings, and photographs. Among the earliest and most important of these is a series of exquisite original drawings by Daniel Rabel (1578–1637), picturing masked performers in court entertainments.[19] Harvard also preserves broadsides, libretti, engravings, and commemorative volumes concerning early court masques, balls, and festival entertainments. (A number of these are in the Theatre Collection; others may be found in the Houghton Library, the Loeb Music Library, and the Fine Arts Library.) Naturally, masks figure prominently in *commedia dell'arte* and its related forms, all of which are represented strongly in the Theatre Collection, especially through engravings and prints of scenes and performers.

Among the masks in the Theatre Collection are the following:

MODERN THEATER

A pair of masks designed by Lucinda Ballard for the first production of Archibald Macleish's play *J. B.* was given by Robert Ballard, 1993.

A set of masks designed by Robert Edmond Jones for the first production of Eugene O'Neill's early play *The Great God Brown* was given by Elizabeth Jones, 1968.

A group of seventeen masks made of Plexiglas, as well as photographs of masks, used in a 1972 production of Eugene O'Neill's play *The Great God Brown* by the New Phoenix Repertory Company were given by Carolyn Parker.[20]

An unpainted ceramic mask was given by the actress and dancer Katharine Sergava.

STUDENT PROJECTS

The Theatre Collection has a number of papier-mâché masks made for student productions of *The Tempest* at Quincy House in 1977, *The Duchess of Malfi* at Quincy House in 1980, and in mask-making workshops sponsored by the Office for the Arts in 1980; these were all gifts of Laura Shiels, 1981.

There is also a mask made by Dominic Mayman for a Harvard Dramatic Society production of *Gammer Gurton's Needle* in 1986; this was the gift of Arthur Friedman, 1991.

Nine reproduction Noh masks made by John Perkins.

INDONESIAN MASKS

Lion, deer, and two other dance masks, and fourteen other Javanese masks. The gift of John M. Ward, 1991 and 1992.

JAPANESE MASKS

Painted wood masks with hair and movable mouths, four pieces, approx. seven to nine in. The gift of John M. Ward, 1990.

A painted wood mask, approx. six in. long.

Unpainted wood masks, without side holes for cords: one with hair, one with a wooden bit for grasping with the teeth, presumed to have been made for shrines or ceremonies and not for theatrical performance. Three pieces, each approx. six to nine in.

NOH MASKS

Unpainted and painted Noh masks, some with hair, eight pieces, eighteenth and nineteenth centuries, several possibly earlier (five pieces), each approx. seven to nine in. The gift of Dr. Ernest G. Stillman, 1947.

Noh masks made by Yukichi Kodera, four pieces, approx. seven in. each. The gift of Dr. Ernest G. Stillman, 1947.

Fine modern Noh masks, painted, female figures, in wooden boxes and cushioned silk pouches, two pieces, approx. eight in. each, ca. 1965–1975, together with another example of lesser quality. The gift of Ruth N. and John M. Ward, 1990.

NOH MASK NETSUKE ORNAMENTS
Fine unpainted wood netsuke ornaments in the form of Noh masks, eighteenth and nineteenth centuries, twenty-three pieces, approx. 1½ to 2½ in. Some of these pieces were made and signed by members of the noted Deme family of Noh mask makers. There are also examples made from cinnabar-colored wood and ceramic. The gift of Dr. Ernest G. Stillman, 1947.[21]

Asian Performance Instruments

The largest portion of the collection of Ruth N. and John M. Ward includes manuscripts, books, scores, and ephemera documenting the history of the use of music in dance and theater in the Western traditions; but it also includes a large collection of Asian puppetry and theater, much of which is listed earlier. The Ward collection also includes a pair of wooden Kabuki sticks and a Noh drum.

Clockwork Asian Dancer

An animated Asian dancer with a clockwork mechanism, wood and cloth, approx. twelve in.

Japanese Dolls

A pair of Japanese dolls, young man and woman in aristocratic dress, used for display, each doll is approx. eleven in.

Clown Dolls

Dolls representing the circus clown Emmett Kelly, composition heads with cloth bodies, approx. sixteen in. and thirty in. The gift of Herbert Myron, 1978 and 1979.

The Ralph McGoun Collection, described earlier, also contains a significant number of masks.

Access to the Collection

The Harvard Theatre Collection is a department of the Houghton Library, the rare book and manuscript library of the Harvard College Library system. The collection is located in the Nathan Marsh Pusey Library, which is situated in Harvard Yard adjacent to both the Widener and Houghton libraries. The collection is freely available to all scholars regardless of affiliation; positive identification is required for registration.

The Theatre Collection's Robert Jordan Reading Room and Edward Sheldon Exhibition Rooms are open weekdays (excepting university holidays) from 9:00 A.M. to 4:45 P.M. Researchers are strongly advised to make an appointment before visiting the Theatre Collection, particularly if material is desired that has not been located in Hollis. (Some material is stored in the Harvard Depository, some miles removed from Cambridge; this material will necessarily take a day or more to retrieve.)

None of the material in the Theatre Collection may circulate outside of the reading room. All reproductions require the curator's approval. Limited photocopying services are provided by the staff; photographic services are available through the Harvard College Library Imaging Services Studio.

Most special collections are represented in Hollis by a general listing, but more detailed inventories or other descriptive information may be available by application to the curator. Large general series in the Theatre Collection (programs, photographs, posters, prints, printed play texts, clippings, etc.) are generally not catalogued, but can be located by the reading room staff.

The Theatre Collection continues an active acquisition program. Donations of appropriate material are especially appreciated.

Notes

1. This gift was made by a group of Harvard alumni, led by George Pierce Baker, in memory of the college's librarian, Justin Winsor (1831–1897), who had made a special study of the great English actor. There had been in the Harvard library material on the history of theater as well as play texts since the earliest days of the library, which was founded in 1638.

2. The library of Robert Lowe was purchased by the university in 1903 through a gift of the actor John Drew. The collection of Robert Gould Shaw was presented in 1915, and the collection of Evert Jansen Wendell was bequeathed in 1918. The Theatre Collection

received several significant gifts before the arrival of the immense Shaw and Jansen collections. Robert Gould Shaw served as the first curator of the Harvard Theatre Collection.

3. The writer acknowledges the valuable assistance of Elizabeth Carroll-Horrocks, the technical services librarian in the Harvard Theatre Collection, in identifying many of the relevant holdings listed herein.

4. This ballet by François Alexis Blache was published as *Polichinel vampire, ballet-pantomime et divertissemens burlesques en un acte et spectacle. Musique de M. Alexandre.* Paris: Pollet, 1823.

5. The papers and puppet collection of Peter Arnott are described elsewhere in this volume by Annette Fern, research and reference librarian in the Harvard Theatre Collection. The call number of the collection is dbMS Thr 409.

6. The W. A. Dwiggins puppets are described by Dorothy Abbe in *The Dwiggins Marionettes: A Complete Experimental Theater in Miniature* (New York: Harry N. Abrams, 1970). Dwiggins himself described his puppets in *Marionette in Motion* (1939).

7. The Fredric Wertham Collection is described in an article in the *Harvard Gazette*, June 15, 1990. The Busch-Reisinger Museum published a catalogue of the entire collection, *The Fredric Wertham Collection*, in 1990; the puppets are all illustrated and described on pp. 84–90. These puppets are designated HUAM 1987.119.1-26 in the museum's accession records.

8. *Le Théâtre du Merveilleux* (Paris: Olivier Perrin, 1962); English translation published as *The Theatre of Marvels* (New York: Benjamin Blom, 1964).

9. The Bread & Puppet Theater records have the call number bMS Thr 319.

10. The Robert Edmond Jones Papers, given in 1975 by his sister Elizabeth Jones, have the call number bMS Thr 201.

11. Hollis (Harvard On-Line Library Information System) is the Harvard library union catalogue for books, monographs, serials, and manuscripts. It is freely available worldwide via the Internet. The URL is: http://holliscatalog.harvard.edu.

12. Author and title searches are entered from the main searching screen. Author names take the form: *lastname, firstname*. Titles are entered without initial articles. Some other types of searches are explained below.

13. Some of the categories that fall within this range include the following: *Commedia dell'arte*, Harlequin, Harlequinade, Pantomime, Masks, Masque, Mime, 560; Punch and Judy, 561; Shadow Plays, Children's Theatre, Toy Theatre, Puppet Plays, 562. Not always have classification rules been applied consistently. Also in TS 562 are found puppet and marionette plays, many published in uniform series (such as, for example, *Theatre Guignol*, Paris: Librairie Bricon & Lesot), as well as single titles. Some of these plays have attractive wrappers or plates, sometimes printed in color.

14. Thr 151 includes the subject of pantomime, together with a number of pantomime texts. Thr 154 includes shadow puppets.

15. The simplest method to use Hollis to search by class (that is, by call number) is to select one of the three types of call number from the main search screen.

For Theatre Collection books using Library of Congress classification (most recent books, classified as "HTC-LC"), select the Library of Congress Call Number search option and type *PN 1970*, for example, in the text box.

For books originally classified in the Widener Library ("Thr" classes), select the Widener Call Number search option and type *thr 150*, for example, in the text box. Owing to old cataloguing inconsistencies, *additional* books may be located by selecting the Other Call Number search option and using these same call numbers.

For most older Theatre Collection books ("TS" classes), select the Other Call Number search option and type *ts 560*, for example, in the text box.

Certain archives and manuscript collections have a call number that begins with MS, with or without a format prefix such as "b" or "f." These are located using the Other Call Number search option.

Adding the string: *and wsl=the* will limit a call-number search to books held by the Theatre Collection, excluding the holdings of other Harvard libraries.

Further on-line help is available from the Hollis website. One useful option is the key-word search, which will return all catalogue records in which the specified words occur. Type the desired words in the appropriate text box.

All Hollis searches can also be expressed as command strings. From the main search screen, first select Command Search. Then in the text box, type *clc=* for Library of Con-gress Call Number search, *cwi=* for Widener Call Number search, and *cot=* for Other Call Number search; in each case the command is followed immediately by the call num-ber. A complete list of search commands is available from a link at the bottom of the Command Search screen.

16. Subject searches may also be entered from the main search screen by selecting the search option Subject Beginning With. Principal subject headings include PUNCH AND JUDY, PUPPET MAKING, PUPPET THEATER, PUPPET THEATERS, PUPPETEERS, PUPPETRY, and PUPPETS.

17. A case in point is the British Puppet and Model Theatre Guild, an organization for enthusiasts and collectors.

18. These albums are from the collection of Robert Gould Shaw. The call number is TS 946.5.

19. Daniel Rabel's ballet drawings, in watercolor, and highlighted in gold, form a part of the collection of George Chaffée, given in 1952. The Chaffée Collection is one of the most important repositories of pictorial and documentary material related to early dance and court entertainments.

20. The call number of this collection is bMS Thr 308.

21. This collection, together with the collection of Japanese masks, has recently been examined and described in detail by Mrs. Fumiko Cranston of the Fogg Art Museum, to whom we express our gratitude.

Asian Puppets at the UCLA Fowler Museum of Cultural History

ROY W. HAMILTON

The institution now known as the Fowler Museum of Cultural History was founded on the UCLA campus in 1963 as the Museum and Laboratories of Ethnic Arts and Technology. This name reflected the goals of gathering together scattered campus collections of non–Western art and material culture and developing a permanent home for them that would serve campus research and teaching needs, as well as overseeing what was hoped would be a growing collection. Among the items accessioned by the museum in its first year of operation was a group of one hundred fifty-four Turkish shadow puppets, which were transferred to the new museum from the university's Center for the Comparative Study of Folklore and Mythology.[1] Puppetry has remained a subject of interest for the museum ever since.

In the ensuing years, the museum has twice undergone a change of name, becoming in 1971 the Museum of Cultural History and, with the opening of its new building in 1990, the Fowler Museum of Cultural History. The burgeoning growth of the Southern California region in the 1970s and 1980s, and especially its growing embrace of non–Western arts, propelled the museum into its current position as one of the largest and most active university-based ethnographic museums in the United States. The number of puppets in the collections has swelled from the original one hundred fifty-four to over one thousand three hundred.[2]

Although there are some interesting European marionettes, the real strength of the museum's puppetry holdings lies in its extensive collections of Asian puppets.

Table 1 gives a breakdown of these Asian puppets according to type and country of origin. In the museum's records, puppets have been classified into one of four types: (1) string puppets or marionettes, operated usually from overhead with a series of strings; (2) hand puppets operated with a hand placed inside the puppet; (3) rod puppets operated with one or more external rods; and (4) shadow puppets held between a source of light and a screen, to project shadow images on the screen. A fifth category, water puppets, has recently been added to accommodate newly acquired examples of this unique type of Vietnamese puppetry.

Table 1.
Classification and Provenance of Asian Puppets

	String	Hand	Rod	Shadow	Water	Total
Burma	4					4
China	4	427	1	72		504
India	54	3	1	213		271
Indonesia			64	236		300
Japan			1			1
Korea		1	2			3
Malaysia	4	3		8		15
Thailand			7	56		63
Turkey				154		154
Vietnam					7	7
Total	66	434	76	739	7	1322

It is impossible to talk about the museum's puppetry collections without invoking the names of Patricia B. Altman and Melvyn Helstien, which are found over and over in the museum's puppetry records. Pat Altman (b. 1917) and her husband Ralph Altman (1909–1967) owned an art gallery in Los Angeles from 1946 until 1964 that is still remembered as a seminal gathering spot for scholars and students of non–Western arts (Birney 4–5). When the museum was founded in 1963, Ralph Altman was appointed chief curator, a position he filled until his death in 1967. Pat Altman continued her association with the museum and served as curator until her retirement in 1994. Her lively interest in many types of folk arts, including puppetry, helped shaped the museum's collecting interests during those formative years.

Professor Melvyn Helstien (1920–1990) was a leading force in UCLA's Department of Theater from 1948 until his retirement in 1986. An extraordinary puppeteer, Professor Helstien designed, produced, directed, or performed in more than eighty productions during his career and developed one of the nation's leading puppet theater programs at UCLA. He traveled throughout Asia researching and collecting puppets and became an authority on the puppetry traditions of south and southeast Asia. He eventually narrowed the focus of his research to the Karnataka region of India, and he was working on a book about Indian shadow puppets at the time of his death. Professor Helstien's research files are now housed at the museum.

Altman and Helstien were the organizers of the exhibition "Asian Puppets: Wall of the World," held at UCLA in 1976. A book with the same title was published the same year to accompany the exhibition and featured illustrations of many of the most interesting puppets in the collections. Readers interested in more details are advised to consult the publication. The exhibition proved popular with the public, and there were frequent requests over the years to showcase the puppets again. In 1997 the museum mounted a smaller installation of a selection of the shadow puppets, entitled "In the Play of Shadows: Puppets from Asia," this time with no published catalogue. Over the years there have been numerous Asian puppetry performances at UCLA, some organized by the museum and others by the World Arts and Cultures Department or UCLA Performing Arts. These have included Balinese *wayang kulit* shadow puppetry, Sundanese *wayang golek* rod puppetry, Chinese shadow puppetry, and Vietnamese water puppetry.

The museum's shadow puppets deserve particular mention, as they constitute one of the principal resources in the United States for the study of this uniquely Asian form. Shadow puppet plays may have been performed as early as 200 B.C.E. in India, and they subsequently spread with other elements of Indian culture throughout southeast Asia. The plays are mostly based on the great Indian epics, the *Mahābhārata* and the *Rāmāyana*. The shadow theater is a rich and enduring tradition of great cultural importance. The puppet master is by turns a teacher, an historian, and a philosopher, as well as a consummate entertainer. At the highest level of interpretation, the screen on which the shadows move serves as a metaphor for the cosmos. Seated behind it, the puppet master breathes life into heroes and villains alike, invoking the cosmic struggle between good and evil.

In the Indian state of Andhra Pradesh shadow puppet masters come from a caste that includes shamanistic performers, while in Kerala they are granted an honorific title meaning "scholar" (Museum of Cultural History [MCH] 1976:41). In Java the shadow puppet master, or *dalang*, commands dozens of stories and hundreds of characters, each with its own voice and personality. He performs from dusk to dawn, sometimes without stirring from his position behind the screen. The long pre-dawn hours, normally outside of daily human experience, give the shadow theater a special aura, and it is no wonder that the *dalang* is sometimes an awe-inspiring figure. The connection between the puppet master and divine power is explicit, as the puppet master is seen to animate his characters in a way that is analogous to the divine force that animates humans in the universe. According to the *Bhagavad Gita*, the Indian text that relates Krishna's counsel to Arjuna in time of war, "The Lord is present inside all beings / Moving them like puppets by his magic power." At the level of folk interpretation, a Javanese description of the shadow theater is equally telling: "[F]rom the *dalang* side the [*wayang*] figures show their bodies, their outsides, but from the shadow side they show their souls, their inside" (Geertz 1960 269).

The highlights of the museum's Asian puppetry collections are further described below in country-by-country summaries. Some of the puppets are general in the sense that the puppeteer can use them for a range of nonspecific characters: a princess, a warrior, a demon, and so on. Others represent specific named characters. The appendix lists by name the known characters that can be found in the collections, to the extent that they can be identified using the museum's records.

Burma

Two of the Burmese marionettes were purchased by Helstien in Rangoon in 1965. They were old puppets obtained from a puppeteer who had used them in his performances.[3] One of the two, a male puppet with a turban and red costume, is identified as the standard Burmese magician character (*zawgyi*) who appears in most performances. The other is a princess character in a beautiful green dress. The other two marionettes are from different sources. One is a female character and the other a horse described as a "toy" puppet.

China

The most compelling Chinese material in the collection is a group of four hundred twelve hand puppets representing an extraordinary range of characters, many of them beautifully painted and clothed. These puppets could not have all originally been part of a single set, as some are from Fukien and others from Taiwan, although it is likely they were brought together and used as a set on Taiwan. The best of them are extremely expressive, with special symbolic features in the faces or clothing that convey the puppet's character.

Blind scholar (hand puppet), Taiwan. The face of the blind scholar is emblazoned with a passage from a well-known Chinese schoolbook, *The Book of Three Character Phrases*. (Photograph by Don Cole, © UCLA Fowler Museum of Cultural History.)

The other highlight of the Chinese collection is a shadow puppet master's set, including his traveling chest, over five hundred puppet pieces, and thirty-nine volumes of handwritten scripts. The set belonged to a puppet master named Lung-hsi Ts'ai of Kaohsiung County, Taiwan, up until the time of World War II (P. Altman, handwritten collection notes). The museum purchased it in

1965 from a Santa Fe art gallery. Chinese shadow puppets have separable heads, and this set is typical in that it contains many more heads (220) than bodies (38). Because of this complication, the individual pieces in this set are not included in the chart given above. The puppeteer could simply make new characters by re-using the limited number of bodies with new heads. The puppet pieces vary in their styles and dates, which are estimated to range approximately from 1900 to 1930. The manuscript volumes contain the scripts for eighty plays.

A smaller set of shadow puppets is also of interest because it is associated with a known story, called the "Feast of Peaches." The puppets in this set include the Eight Immortals, each carrying a different symbolic object that serves to identify the character. Even more inventive are two puppets with human bodies and crustacean heads, identified as the Shrimp Guardian of the Dragon Princess and his counterpart, the Crab Guardian of the Dragon Princess.

India

The Indian puppetry collection represents several distinct traditions from different parts of India. The string puppets come from Tamilnadu, Rajasthan, and Karnataka. A group of sixteen puppets from Bangalore, collected by Helstien, are the most interesting of these. The Bangalore style of puppetry is based on the Yakshagana dance theater (MCH 11). The names of the puppeteers who used the puppets are recorded in many cases.

The strength of the collection, however, lies in the large number of shadow puppets from the southern states, notably Karnataka and Andhra Pradesh, but also with smaller numbers from Kerala and Orissa. Mel Helstien collected most of these puppets in the field in India, and many are accompanied by his documentation regarding the character portrayed and the puppeteer who made or used them.

Helstien investigated several local schools of shadow puppetry, with variations in the size and style of the puppets. In general, the Indian shadow puppets are much larger than their counterparts in China or Southeast Asia, with many of the figures life-size or larger. The puppets are not as intricately cut as Javanese shadow puppets and, therefore, do not cast the finely detailed shadows that are the hallmark of shadow puppetry in Indonesia. Instead, the Indian puppets rely on color for much of their visual impact. The hide they are made from is translucent and brightly dyed so that the puppets cast colored "shadows" upon the screen; strictly speaking this is actually a type of transparency projection rather than shadow casting. Indonesian shadow puppets are brightly painted, too, but they are opaque, and the color does not show on the screen.

The familiar cast of characters from the *Mahābhārata* and the *Rāmāyana* is well represented among the museum's puppets, including Bima, Arjuna, Rama, Siti, Ravana, and Hanuman. Other puppets depict even more iconic characters from the Indian pantheon, such as a four-headed Brahma seen riding on his vehicle, the *hamsa*, or Ganesha, the elephant-headed son of Shiva and Parvati, who is worshiped as the remover of obstacles. There are more obscure figures as well, such as Ganda Berunda, the state symbol of the Vijayanagar Empire.

One style of Indian shadow puppet is not articulated and shows an entire scene rather than a single character. In fact, the scene may contain several characters. The puppet master projects the scene and tells the accompanying story. A scene of a man worshiping a Shiva lingam is one of the examples of this type; another is a hunt scene with a group of dogs bringing down a stag. Many of these complex puppets depict scenes deeply rooted in Indian mythology, such as Krishna surrounded by snakes in Naga Loka, or the Mahishasura-Mardini scene of Durga slaying the demon Mahish.

Brahma (shadow puppet), Andhra Pradesh, India. Brahma, the first deity of the Hindu triad, is identifiable by his four heads. Hindu deities are typically depicted astride their animal vehicles; Brahma's is the goose known as the *Hamsa*. (Photograph by Don Cole, © UCLA Fowler Museum of Cultural History.)

Indonesia

Java is one of the most developed centers for shadow puppetry, and shadow plays, or *wayang kulit,* have been well-known features of all levels of Javanese society, from the royal courts to rural villages. Village performances are often held to celebrate weddings or other family events. The play begins in the evening and concludes with a climactic battle scene just before dawn. Because the host family must pay the performers and feed the guests, sponsoring a shadow play adds to the family's prestige in the community.

There are twenty-eight shadow puppets from Java in the collections, but these were accessioned a few at a time and are not all members of a single set. Interestingly, six of them are Chinese in style, rather than Javanese, and must have come from a puppet theater established in overseas Chinese communities. Chinese puppet performances can still be seen in small towns, such as Tuban, along the north coast of Java. A group of thirty-seven beautiful color plates illustrating different named *wayang kulit* characters is also maintained in the museum's archive; it was published in Batavia (now Jakarta) in 1930 by the *Commissie voor de Volkslectuur* of the Dutch colonial administration.

The collection additionally includes two of the Javanese wooden rod puppets known as *wayang klitik* and two unusual puppets that resemble shadow puppets in their form, but are made of plant straw gathered in the wild. These puppets have been called *wayang rumput* (grass *wayang*) and are featured in art exhibitions in Indonesia, but they are not really intended for use in *wayang* plays. They are the creation of Kasanwikrama Tunut, who was born in Purbalingga, Java, in 1905 and is commonly known as "Pak Gepuk"; this has also led to the name "Wayang Gepuk" (Oetama 1997 3–16).

The western third of the island of Java is the home of the Sundanese people, who have their own form of puppet theater based on elaborately dressed three-dimensional rod puppets called *wayang golek.* Among the sixty-two *wayang golek* puppets in the collection are one group of seventeen and another of twenty-seven that appear to have come from single sets. Unfortunately, there is no documentation of the original source.

Bali maintains a tradition of shadow puppetry related to that of Java but with an even more inventive cast of characters. While the Javanese supplemented the original Indian characters, most famously with the

addition of the four Javanese clowns, the Balinese
populated their shadow
theater with many char-
acters drawn from uni-
quely Balinese stories
that are not found in
shadow puppetry else-
where. Other Balinese
characters, like the
demonic goddess Rangda,
have Indian roots, but
were made into some-
thing uniquely Balinese.
The museum's 206 Bali-
nese shadow puppets rep-
resent a tremendous
range of characters from
Sanghyang Widhi (Bali's
ultimate and abstract
"high" God) to gross
deformed demons. Many
of the puppets' character
names are known, either
from the museum's rec-
ords or based on the
experience of Balinese

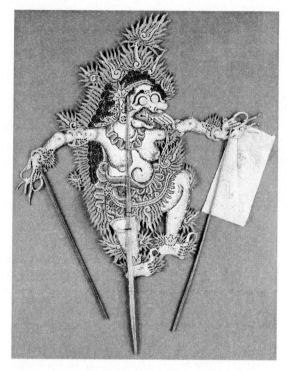

Rangda (shadow puppet), Bali, Indonesia. Rangda
appears only in plays unique to Bali called the
Calon Arang stories. The cloth she holds in her
hand contains her magic power, and she kills her
victims by touching them with it. (Photograph by
Don Cole, © UCLA Fowler Museum of Cultural
History.)

puppeteers who have viewed them.

A group of sixteen Balinese shadow puppets is of particular interest because they were collected by the Mexican painter Miguel Covarrubias when he lived in Bali during the 1930s. As a group, these puppets
are even more imaginatively designed and vividly colored than the rest,
suggesting that Covarrubias may have purposefully chosen them as such
or perhaps even commissioned them.

Japan

Japan's *bunraku* puppetry is unfortunately represented by a single example. The puppet was made by a Japanese puppet maker, Yurahiro Hishida, and purchased by Helstien. The character is Osono, wife of Hanshichi, from the play *Hadesugata Onna Maiginu*. As with all *bunraku* puppets, it has no inner body structure and takes its shape from the costume. Manipulation of the puppet requires three puppeteers. The puppet's arms and articulated hands are manipulated by rods and cords attached to the lower arm. Female *bunraku* characters have no legs; the puppeteer simulates the movement of walking by manipulating the puppet's kimono.

Korea

The museum has three puppets from the Korean puppetry tradition known as *ggokdukgagsi*, which consists of stories revolving around the key character Pak Ch'om-ji. The puppets in the collection represent Pak Ch'om-ji, his nephew Hong Dong-ji, and the serpent I Si-mu. All three are illustrated in MCH's *Asian Puppets* catalogue (141).

Malaysia

Shadow puppetry in Malaysia is confined to the east-coast state of Kelantan, a center of traditional Malay culture where other Malay crafts such as kite making and cloth weaving still flourish as well. The eight shadow puppets in the collection were made in the 1960s by the puppet master Nik Abdul Rahman in Kota Bharu, the urban center of Kelantan. Malaysian shadow puppetry shows the influence of the same forces that have shaped Indonesian and Thai shadow puppetry. The stories are primarily based on the Indian epics, but there are added clown figures similar to those found in Java. Many of the puppets in the collection wear distinctly Thai styles of headgear, suggesting that Thailand may be the more important influence; indeed, this style of Kelantan shadow puppetry is called *wayang Siam* in Malay.

The four string puppets and three hand puppets were purchased by

Helstien in Kuala Lumpur in 1965. The hand puppets are described as toys rather than performing puppets. One of the string puppets is the Chinese character Pigsly from the novel *Journey to the West*. Pigsly is the companion of a Chinese monk who travels to India to study Buddhism. The other characters are unknown, but several of them are distinctly Chinese in appearance. It is likely then that they belong to a tradition of Chinese puppetry established among the overseas Chinese population of Kuala Lumpur.

Thailand

Thai shadow puppetry has two different forms: *nang yai* and *nang talung*. *Nang yai* is a courtly genre that uses large, nonarticulated puppets. Some of them depict single characters, but many are multicharacter scenes. The puppet master displays the scene and dances both behind and before the screen (MCH 79). *Nang talung* is a folk tradition using the more familiar articulated puppets representing single characters. Both theaters draw upon the *Rāmāyana* for their stories, but the *nang talung* has added *Jataka* stories (stories of the Buddha's childhood) and also clown characters, as used in Java or Bali.

The seven rod puppets were made in Bangkok by the puppeteer Khun Wa Piak and purchased by Mel Helstien. They were newly made at the time and never used. Helstien noted that this style of puppet was used only in Bangkok. The characters are from the *Rāmāyana*.

Turkey

The set of one hundred fifty-four Turkish shadow puppets was apparently acquired by the Center for the Comparative Study of Folklore and Mythology when Turkish folklore professor Ilhan Basgöz was a visiting faculty member in the early 1960s. According to the museum records, they were made by an Istanbul puppeteer named K. Ali. As the puppeteer was from Istanbul, one could argue that this is a European rather than an Asian theater acquisition. However, as the rest of the collection so well demonstrates, shadow puppetry is a quintessentially Asian form. Compared to the fine filigree work of the Indonesian shadow puppets, the Turkish versions are crudely cut, yet they are carefully painted in bright colors and exhibit a lively sense of design. Although the genre may be Asian, the stories are similar to other series of European folktales revolving around comic characters, such as Punch and Judy. The central character in the Turkish shadow plays is Karaghöz, whose name literally means "black eye." His antics and troubles are depicted in many versions. The puppets include the Karaghöz character in many humorous plights: freshly circumcised, for example, or disguised as a minstrel, a madman, or a bride.

Vietnam

Water puppets are found only in Vietnam and are intimately associated with the flooded rice-field landscape of the Red River Delta. Originally they were a form of village entertainment, associated with post-harvest or New Year festivities and performed in a local pond. Today the main venue is a new theater in the center of Hanoi. The team of puppeteers stands knee-deep in water behind a curtain or other barrier. The puppets are controlled by long rods that run underwater and they appear to magically float on the surface several meters in front of the operators. There is no "story" per se, but just a series of entertaining vignettes of rural life. Although Vietnamese water puppetry thus lacks some of the philosophical depth of southeast Asian shadow puppetry, the puppets are often remarkably inventive. Dragon puppets may spout fireworks from their nostrils as they dive across the pond, for example, or a whole team of dancing maidens may pirouette together across the surface.

The puppets became popular tourist souvenirs as international tourism expanded in Vietnam in the 1990s. The museum recently commissioned a set of seven puppets illustrating the various stages of rice agriculture: drawing a harrow behind a buffalo, irrigating with a water scoop, transplanting seedlings, scaring birds, harvesting, transporting the crop by boat, and milling with a foot-powered mill. The puppets were made by Hanoi puppet maker Dang Van Thiet.

Appendix

The lists below give the specific names of known characters repre-sented in the puppet collections. There are many puppets for which this information is not known. No attempt has been made to re-check the identifications or to standardize the spelling of the names in English. General characters such as a soldier, a servant, a monkey, etc., are not included unless a specific name is associated with it, such as Nandi, the bull of Hindu mythology. In some cases even shadow puppets repre-senting complex ideas have specific names, such as Agni, the Balinese shadow puppet representing fire, or the Ashavamedha, a puppet inspired by an Indian vedic ritual.[4]

Burma, string puppet: Zawgyi.

China, hand puppets: Blind scholar, Boddhisattva of the Thou-sand Eyes, Buddha, Ch'eng Yao-chin, Chi Kung, Hsiao Sheng, Kuan Yü, Lei Kung, Pao Cheng, Shou Hsing, Sun Wu-k'ung.

China, shadow puppets: Chang Kuo-lao, Chia Kuan, Chia-kuan, Chiang Shih (and wife), Chiao Ting-kui, Chung Li-ch'üan, Dragon Princess (and her crab and shrimp guards), Erh-lang, General Kang Hsuch (and mother), General Ting-kui Chiao, General Tsung-pao Yang, Han Hsiang-tzu, Ho Hsien-ku, Hsüeh Kang (and mother), Hung Pang, Lan Ts'ai-ho, Li T''ieh-kuai, Lü Tung-pin, Marshal Ching Ti, Meng Hsiang Hsuch, Shiih Chiang, Ti Ch'ing, Ts'ao Kuo-chiu, Western Queen Mother, Yang Tsung-pao.

India, shadow puppets: Abhimanyu, Ankusha, Apsara, Arjuna, Ashavamedha, Bangarakka, Bharata, Bharatha, Bhima, Brahma, Brah-min, Chamundi, Chandra, Dasaratha, Deva, Dharmarata, Dhobi, Drau-padi, Duryodhana, Ganda Berunda, Ganesha, Garuda, Gatotkaca, Hanuman, Hanuman in the form of Marjala Rupa, Hidimbi, Indrajit, Jambava (or Jambavan), Jambulmali, Jatayu, Kali, Kalyan, Kalyani, Kamadhenu, Kapalika, Karna, Kartikeya, Kausalya, Kicaka, Killekyatha, King Janaka, Krishna, Laksmana, Mahish, Mandodari, Maricha, Nandi, Narada, Purushambriga, Rama, Ravana, Rsyasringa, Sami, Sarasvati, Sat-urgna, Shikandin, Shiva, Sita, Sugriva, Surpanaka, Surpranike, Vali, Vanara, Vayu, Vina, Vishnu, Vishwamitra, Visnu Nagaloka.

India, string puppets: Arjuna, Bhima, Brahmin, Ganesha, Hanu-man, Krishna, Laksmana, Rama, Ravana, Sarasvati, Shiva, Sita.

Indonesia, Balinese shadow puppets: Abimanyu, Abiyasa, Agni, Arjuna, Baru, Bayu, Bhisma, Bima, Bonaspati, Celeng, Citraska (?), Condong, Cupak, Delem, Dewi Uma, Drupadi (or Draupadi), Durga, Durna, Duryudana, Dusansa (?), Gajah, Ganesha, Garuda, Grantang, Hanuman, Harada, Jogormanik, Kala, Karna, Krishna, Kunti, Laksmi, Mandodari, Marica, Merdah, Nakula or Sadewa, Nala or Nila, Pamurtian, Prahasta, Rama, Rangda, Rawana, Rewang, Sakuni, Saliya, Samba, Sanghyang Widhi (Sanghyang Tunggal), Sangut, Setyaki, Siva, Sugriwa, Twalen, Vagawan Vyasa, Yudisthira.

Indonesia, Javanese *wayang klitik* puppets: Arjuna, Sabda Palon.

Indonesia, Javanese *wayang kulit* shadow puppets: Arjuna, Buta Raja (?), Drona, Gatotkaca, Semar, Srikandi.

Indonesia, Sundanese *wayang golek* puppets: Antaboga, Bima, Gareng, Gatotkaca, Gustur, Indrajit, Krishna, Nakula, Sadeva Subadra, Udel, Umarmoyo.

Japan, *bunraku* puppet: Osono.

Korea, hand puppet: I Si-mu.

Korea, rod puppets: Pak Ch'om-ji, Hong Dong-ji.

Malaysia, string puppet: Pigsly.

Malaysia, *wayang Siam* shadow puppets: Hanuman, Lakshamana, Maha Risi Kala Api, Maharaja Rawana, Pak Dogol, Seri Rama, Siti Dewi, Wak Long.

Thailand, *nang talung* shadow puppets: Buk Borng, Hanuman, Kinnara Apsara, Nung Sidah, Phra Bun, Phra Nalai, Phra Ram, Pipek, Queen Nang Laveng, Rishi, Sida (Sita), Suwanmajcha, Tosakan.

Thailand, *nang yai* shadow puppets: Hanuman, Maiyarap, Tosakan, Wironhok.

Thailand, rod puppets: Hanuman, Rama, Sida (Sita), Tosakan (Ravana).

Turkey, shadow puppets: Arnavut, Atli Acem, Bahce Bekcisi, Bebe Ruhi, Bekci, Bekir, Calgi Cilar, Celebi, Ciplagi, Demeli, Didigibi, Dilenci, Egyptian slave seller, Esek, Ferhad, Gidiyor, Greek doctor, Hacivad, Hain Kethuda, Hamamanasi, Hasan, Havan, Heduye Goturen, Himmet Dayi, Hinzer Deli, Karaghöz (in many disguises), Kaynana, Kerem, Kilci, Kulhanci, Laz, Matiz, Mayisoolu, Merjan Agha, Mison, Muslu, Nargileh, Rabis Hanim, Salomon, Sarkici Kiz, Seymen, Tahir, Tiryaki, wrestler from Roumelia, Zuhre.

Notes

1. After the development of the museum, folklore studies were reorganized into the Folklore and Mythology Program, an interdepartmental degree-granting unit of the university. As of 2001, this program is again being reorganized as part of the Department of World Arts and Cultures, which will grant doctoral degrees in cultural performance with a specialization in Folklore Studies.

2. The problem of counting puppet parts precludes any definitive exact count. The figures given here and in the accompanying chart omit incomplete puppets (such as puppet heads or garments) and most stage setting pieces. Also omitted is the museum's largest set of Chinese shadow puppets, which consists primarily of hundreds of separable puppet body parts (described in the text of this article).

3. There seems to be contradictory evidence about who the puppeteer was. Notes made from an interview with Helstien in 1967 record the name of U Shwe, but a caption (MCH 1976 113) gives the name U Thun Ye.

4. The Ashavamedha puppet is a horse. In the stories, the king's *asva*, or horse, is sent to wander for a year. During this period of wandering, another king that encounters the horse must send tribute to the horse's owner or go to war. After the year is over, there is a ritualistic coupling of the horse and the king's wife, after which the horse is sacrificed.

Works Cited

Birney, Barbara Ann. 1984. *The Mosaic Image: The First Twenty Years of the Museum of Cultural History*. Los Angeles: Museum of Cultural History, 1984.

Geertz, Clifford. 1960. *The Religion of Java*. Glencoe, Ill.: The Free Press, 1960.

Museum of Cultural History (MCH). 1976. *Asian Puppets: Wall of the World*. Los Angeles: Museum of Cultural History, 1976.

Oetama, Jakob, et al. 1997. *Wayang Gepuk Wayang Alternatif.* Jakarta: Bentara Budaya, 1997.

The Center for Puppetry Arts Museum Collection

NANCY LOHMAN STAUB

The Center for Puppetry Arts (CPA) of Atlanta, Georgia, is the largest organization in the United States whose total focus is the art of puppetry. Its mission is to build recognition of the art form, as well as to increase awareness of puppetry's aesthetic and educational aspects. Its primary goal is to present productions by America's leading puppetry artists and international guests. Because puppetry is the unique performing art that focuses on objects rather than actors, exhibitions of puppets are essential to enhance understanding and appreciation of performances.

The CPA officially opened to the public on September 23, 1978. Many of the one hundred fifty puppets I lent to the CPA were on display when Kermit the Frog and Jim Henson cut the ceremonial ribbon. I later donated those puppets, and the collection has grown to over nine hundred puppets and one thousand posters and other graphics. A complementary research library now contains files of numerous photographs, clippings and periodicals, over fifteen hundred books and over one thousand videotapes. There are two large climate-controlled storage rooms with state-of-the-art cabinets, a large gallery of several rooms for long-term installations and a smaller gallery for rotating exhibits that visit for six months to a year. Puppets and posters are also displayed in the huge main theater atrium and throughout the facility. Over 350,000 people visit the CPA annually. All of them see some part of the collection.

The mission of the CPA Museum Program is to introduce the

American public to the diversity and universality of the art of puppetry. The objective is to amass a collection of puppets which exemplifies myriad types, styles and social functions of puppetry from every continent of the world. There is virtually no culture without some form of puppetry. The historical significance of a particular tradition or artist is always a consideration. The ultimate goal is to demonstrate the universality underlying the diversity of puppetry and, through it, of humanity itself.

I began collecting because David Nixon, an elderly artist and puppeteer in New Orleans, fell down on his luck. When he needed money, he would ask me to buy some of his antique puppets. I felt I should save them for the puppet world, rather than for decorators or dilettantes. My occasional support for Nixon grew into something more substantial when, to supplement my collection, I could no longer resist puppets for sale in shops and galleries. I put them in cases at my own theater, the Puppet Playhouse of New Orleans. In 1978, when I left Louisiana and my theater to organize the 1980 World Puppetry Festival in Washington, DC, I decided to transfer the collection to the new CPA. I realized it would become a major regional attraction and, eventually, a national institution, due to the vision and business acumen of its executive director, Vincent Anthony.

CPA expanded its holdings considerably through donations of two major collections. Following the exhibitions of the Caroline Lutz collection from the University of Richmond in "Puppetry in China" and the Ilhan Basgöz collection of Turkish puppets from the University of Indiana in the "Turkish Shadow Theatre" at the CPA, the institutions recognized that CPA would be an excellent repository. This significantly increased the breadth of the CPA museum. Sometimes individual artists have also donated puppets they lent for temporary exhibits, as Winnie Wilson did after the "African and African-American Puppetry" showing. Some companies bestowed puppets immediately following performances at CPA, like Les Zygomars of Belgium and the Velo Theatre of France. Some art dealers that the CPA had patronized for years made donations, including Joan Walker-Abrams, who gave numerous Asian shadow puppets. The CPA became the beneficiary of individual collectors, including Allelu Kurten, former general secretary of the American Center of UNIMA, the international union of puppeteers, and Caroly Wilcox, former head of the New York puppet-building workshop for Jim Henson Productions. Jane Henson and Jim Henson Productions contributed

Karaghöz (left) and Hacivat (right) (shadow puppets). (Photograph by Richard Termine, courtesy the Center for Puppetry Arts.)

several Muppets and have been generous supporters of the museum. The estates of Donald Cordry, Mel Helstien and Marjorie Batchelder McPharlin placed objects at CPA. A few puppets were specifically commissioned at my request, such as the Kathakali hand puppet that U.S. puppeteer Theodora Skipitares secured while on a Fulbright Study Grant trip to India. Prominent Atlantans have offered puppet treasures because they felt they would be appreciated at CPA. Edith Hills donated several Taiwanese hand puppets. Henri V. Jova gave a fabulous Sicilian rod marionette acquired by his ambassador brother in Argentina. Ruth and Don Gilpin, of local television fame, entrusted CPA with many of their famous string puppets. One morning, two Burmese marionettes appeared mysteriously on the doorstep, followed by a phone call from an anonymous source who said that CPA was welcome to them because his lover felt they had bad karma. The museum now has a priority list detailing the pieces desired to fulfill its encyclopedic vision. Through a modest acquisition fund, it seeks to purchase or commission new works and waits hopefully for the next wonderful and unexpected gift.

The first full-time museum director, Diane Kempler, began the arduous process of documenting the collection, improving the storage facilities, and arranging important consultancies and self-study grants. She organized several excellent exhibitions, and the collection grew substantially under her tenure. Among the museum directors to follow her, Kerry McCarthy stands out for her diligence and efficiency as she expanded the museum program in both space and activities, as well as multiplying the size of the collection. The current museum director, Susan Kinney, and her professional assistant and volunteer docents work closely with a museum board of advisors and with the CPA education program staff.

The collection serves as the resource for CPA exhibitions and loans to other institutions. Long-term installations, such as "Puppetry: Echoes of Society," present an overview of the art form. Temporary exhibits focus on specific cultures, such as "Puppetry of India"; techniques, as in "Trick Puppets"; themes, like "Fools, Jesters, and Gods"; the work of individual artists, such as Bil Baird; and related arts, exemplified by "Masks." The CPA reaches larger audiences for its collection by touring special exhibitions to other venues regionally and nationally, and tours have lasted as long as three years. The CPA hosts travelling exhibitions as well, including the blockbuster "Art of the Muppets."

The CPA has examples of the four main categories of puppets: shadow, rod, hand, and marionette. Shadow puppets are designed to cast a shadow on a screen and are generally controlled by rods from beneath or behind. Rod puppets are also worked from below or behind, generally with a central rod and often additional rods and sometimes srings. Hand puppets fit directly on the hand. Alternately called glove puppets, they are sometimes actually gloves. Marionettes are worked from above with strings or a central rod, sometimes a combination of rods and strings. Of course, there are hybrid forms, such as the hand-and-rod puppet, in which the head rod is short so the controlling hand is inside the puppet. Some hand puppets have rods on the hands or feet. There are several additional types of puppets, including finger puppets and body puppets. Related forms in the collection include toy theaters and masks. Of course, according to Bil Baird in his book, *The Art of the Puppet*, "A puppet is an inanimate figure that is made to move by human effort before an audience." This means almost anything could become a puppet.

The collection includes examples from most of the culturally significant styles of puppetry. Puppets naturally reflect their diverse creative cultures so they have very different styles around the world and even within one nation. Puppet face painting may simulate theatrical makeup. The figures may resemble sculptures or paintings. Puppets' movements may imitate dancers or actors and vice versa. The stylistic diversity makes puppetry ideal to stimulate study of artistic codifications and traditions, as well as reflections on their sources. Underlying the differences in culturally determined stylistic appearances and movements of puppets is the basic human concept of animism, the belief that natural objects and phenomena and the universe itself possess souls or consciousness. Children instinctively accept manipulated objects as alive, and adults can be manipulated to accept them as they once did instinctively as children. Puppeteers can exorcise demons, perpetuate myths and legends, promulgate religious and social values, and celebrate the human condition with tears and laughter. I have tried to find examples from all over the world that serve various universal functions and seem, to me, to have souls.

Photographs and slides of puppet performances, puppeteers and their audiences augment the inanimate objects. When certain important puppetry forms are unobtainable or have not yet been acquired, photographs are incorporated into the exhibitions and enrich the collection. Hundreds of posters and other graphic materials add another dimension. Videotapes of performances and documentaries of specific traditions are indispensable and available for viewing in the library and in the galleries. These materials all serve to aid the viewer in his or her experience with a static performance object. They place the puppets within performance context and remind visitors and scholars that the puppet is meant to move and be seen in motion.

While CPA's museum professionalizes its operation and expands its collection, it continues to move toward its achievement of long-range goals. The creation of a CPA Study Center is one such objective. Through this program, the entire collection would become accessible worldwide by placing digitized photographs and detailed accession records and information on the history of each puppet tradition in an on-line database.

We are grateful to our many patrons and contributors, including individuals, national foundations and corporations, and local and national government agencies. As the CPA nears its twenty-fifth anniversary, the museum program continues to set new goals and seek out new puppets for its growing collection.

Collection Descriptions

Africa

The strength of CPA's African collection of over twenty-five objects lies in the range of figures from sub–Saharan Africa. While this section is small in number, it is one of the richest in sheer aesthetic quality. In sub–Saharan Africa, sculptures are often carried by a dancer, worn on the body or head, or mounted on a mask and pulled by strings. These performing objects can be called puppets, and some still appear today in rituals and ceremonies, in addition to articulated figures more commonly classified as puppets. The CPA has examples from traditional performers of the Bamana and Bozo of Mali; the Ibibio, Ibo, and Yoruba of Nigeria; the Kuyu of the Republic of the Congo; as well as from a modern marionettist from Togo. The North African collection includes puppets from Egypt and one from Tunisia.

The Kuyu-sculpted head may be the most beautiful carving in the collection. It is held above a dancer's head, with raffia grasses disguising the dancer's legs; therefore, the dancer's body becomes the puppet's body in the *kyébé-kyébé* dance honoring the snake god and creator, Dyo.

The body puppet from the Yoruba, a culture located in Benin, as well as in Nigeria, may be the most unusual in the collection. A Yoruba Géléde Society mask was mounted on a barrel, which serves as the upper torso. The puppeteer within could manipulate the arms, seeing through screened openings in the chest. The performances are both spectacle and ritual honoring the power of women, especially the elderly, who are traditionally a force that rivals that of the gods and ancestors.

The Americas

From the Americas, the collection includes over three hundred fifty objects. From Latin America, there are puppets from Argentina, Brazil, Cuba, Mexico and Venezuela. Bernal Diaz, who accompanied Cortez to Mexico in the sixteenth century, described performance objects, as did conquistadors in Peru. The two clay figures from the Hausteca people of Mexico in the collection have been verified to date from 1200–1500 A.D. The articulated arms are missing, but the assumption is that the puppets were used in a ritual or ceremony. New puppetry forms arrived in the New World along with the colonizers. The Cortez expedition to the Yucatán included a puppeteer to amuse the troops. Guignol hand puppets from France and string marionettes date back to the mid-eighteenth century in Mexico, where the French Emperor Maximilian ruled. Sicilian rod marionette troupes appeared in Argentina in the early twentieth century.

The American collection includes an example of the folk tradition called *mamulengo,* which evolved in northern Brazil. Its hand puppets have carved wooden heads and hands similar to Pulcinella, but take on their own characters, melding indigenous, African, and Portuguese influences.

From Mexico there is a papier-mâché hand puppet of a simple farmer with a straw hat and sandals, made by Roberto Lago, a beloved performer, historian, and supporter of puppetry. He toured shows internationally that promoted cultural heritage, as well as national touring productions that fostered educational and health-related issues. He wrote a book about the small clay folk marionettes from Puebla; the CPA has a set of these puppets from the play *Don Juan Tenorio.*

Several of the best puppet companies in the Americas and the world today are Canadian. While the CPA's representation of the Canadian tradition of puppetry is small, it has showcased the range and breadth of this nation's work in a temporary special exhibition. One of the most imaginative puppets of the collection is Canadian, Trixie la Brique, from Toronto's The Puppetmongers production of *Brickbrothers' Circus.* Trixie, a tightrope walker, is a brick wearing only a tutu. Ann and David Powell, a brother/sister team dressed as brick masons, create an entire circus with bricks, a few pieces of cloth and string, and a wheelbarrow that becomes the stage.

The United States shares with Canada indigenous groups of the Northwest coast — Native American and Inuit cultures — that still carve and use articulated masks and figures in their rituals and ceremonies. Obtaining examples is a high priority for our collection. Massive immigration into the United States included puppeteers, who brought Mr. Punch by, at least, the end of the eighteenth century, and variety marionettes by the nineteenth century from England. Contemporary Americans borrow from world culture and draw on the latest technology, using puppetry to teach, satirize and entertain.

Television and film have spread American puppetry around the world. The most significant hand puppets from television in the collection are Jim Henson creations, Link Hogthrob and Dr. Strangepork, from Muppet Show skits called "Pigs in Space." Thanks to new light plastic materials, Jim Henson's Workshop could create large sculpted heads, whose mouths could be well synchronized. This kind of "mouth" puppet is often called a Muppet, although that is actually a trademark name. The Muppets were designed for the television camera, so precise "lip sync" was essential to the success of "The Muppet Show." Internationally, millions of people viewed it weekly from 1976 to 1984. The Muppets on "Sesame Street" still teach reading and mathematics daily to viewers all over the world.

"Madame" of television and nightclub notoriety is our most famous hand-and-rod puppet. Created by Wayland Flowers, her mouth was articulated, but Flowers stayed in full view, interacting with her, though making no effort at ventriloquism. It's a tribute to his artistry that audiences accepted his characterization. Frank W. Ballard, founder of the University of Connecticut puppetry program and Ballard Institute and Museum of Puppetry (BIMP), designed the most magnificent rod puppet in the collection. It is Abu Bakr, the Orange Merchant, from the 1975 student production of *Kismet*. Ballard designed and taught for nearly thirty years, influencing a generation of puppet artists.

Abu Bakr, the Orange Merchant (rod puppet). Designed by Frank W. Ballard for *Kismet*, 1975. (Photograph by Richard Termine, courtesy the Center for Puppetry Arts.)

Tony Sarg is considered the father of marionette popularity in America during the twentieth century. The collection includes The Mad Hatter from his touring show of *Alice in Wonderland.* For many children and their families, a marionette performance with an elaborate stage and scenery was their first experience, not only of puppetry, but also of live theater. A Ralph Chessé marionette of King Lear exemplifies his work for beautiful adaptations of Shakespeare's plays. The collection's Harry Burnett clown from the Turnabout Theatre of Los Angeles has a coffee-mill control so he can be swirled around at breathtaking speed, epitomizing the gravity-defying attribute of the marionette. The most famous marionette at CPA is Clyde from the Broadway show *Flahooey* by Bil Baird, which has his characteristic articulated big eyes and eyelashes. Baird's company performed not only on Broadway, but also on TV, and in films, World's Fairs, and his own theater in New York City.

Mad Hatter (marionette). Designed by Tony Sarg for *Alice in Wonderland,* c. 1920. (Photograph by Richard Termine, courtesy the Center for Puppetry Arts.)

The collection includes two puppets representing extreme scale differences from tiny to enormous. The smallest is a dancer finger puppet by Mollie Falkenstein, once a ballerina herself with the Ziegfeld Follies. The puppet's body was attached to Falkenstein's hand, and her fingers became the dancing legs. The most gigantic is the Population Rod Puppet.

It has a huge papier-mâché sculpted head, with human figures on its forehead and surrounding its face and beard, as well as enormous papier-mâché hands. It required at least three puppeteers to control it, who were concealed under an attached cloth. This was one of several large puppets from *The Pageant: Our Domestic Resurrection Circus* of 1994 by the Bread & Puppet Theater of Vermont. Known for political satire and participation in public demonstrations, the company performs during summers in Vermont and tours regularly in the United States and Europe, under the direction of Peter Schumann.

Bruce D. Schwartz, a MacArthur Grant recipient, donated his delicately sculpted Elizabeth the Queen, whose modeled composite head and hands appear to be porcelain. Schwartz developed a unique technique in which he directly held the neck between his fingers but used rods on the hands, in a manner reminiscent of Indonesian rod-puppet manipulation. He performed in the open, as in Japanese *bunraku*. His puppetry reflects Asian influences, as does the work of many contemporary Americans.

Modern artists have been attracted to the theater of the inanimate by the poverty of theatrical realism and its replacement by the electronic media. Hanne Tierney explores materials, light, and movement to create abstract images that interpret the essence of her ideas and interpretations of the work of other playwrights, including Chekhov and Lorca. She invented an elaborate grid system, through which strings are mounted from various objects to counterweights on a precise painted control panel. Her work is represented in the collection by Anita Loos, draped purple cloth, and Picasso, flexible silver tubing, from her version of *A Play Called Not and Now* by Gertrude Stein. Julie Taymor is represented by an abstract figure, The Angel of Death, made entirely of twigs, for the New York Public Theater production of *The Haggadah* by Elizabeth Swados in 1979. Taymor has gained international acclaim for her production of *The Lion King*, currently playing on Broadway and in several cities in the United States and abroad.

Paul Zaloom animates objects from the trash to satirize our throwaway culture. He has donated several of his cast-off "junk" performances to us, including *Acid Rain*. Trinkets and trophies become characters; sheets of plastic and cloth, egg cartons and cardboard boxes become scenery.

Asia

CPA's collection also includes over four hundred twenty-five objects representing the major puppetry traditions of Asia. The wide variety of techniques and fascinating cultural codifications make this a rich resource for understanding puppetry and its communal roles. Objects from Borneo, Burma (Myanmar), China, India, Indonesia, Japan, Malaysia, Sri Lanka, Thailand and Vietnam are supplemented by Asia Minor examples from Turkey and Israel.

Writings as ancient as the *Bhagavad Gita* part of the Hindu epic, the *Mahābhārata*, make references to puppetry. Scholars place the origin prior to 500 B.C., and episodes are still enacted with puppets today. In Indonesia some *dalang* (puppeteers) continue to perform rituals, in addition to scenes from epics, and are considered to have spiritual powers. Sponsored by royal courts, shrines, and temples, puppet shows also became popular entertainment in private homes and public places throughout Asia. The various performing arts of narration, drama, song, and dance were reflected in the puppet performances, and, conversely, their live counterparts often imitated the puppets.

The most seminal Asian acquisition is a contemporary four-part panel of a *wayang beber* (play scroll) from Indonesia. Some scholars consider *wayang beber* to be the oldest form of *wayang* (play) preceding cutout flat figures and dancers that move like them. As the narrator unrolls the paintings on cloth to show the audience, he tells the story of the legendary hero, Panji, along with musical accompaniment. The painted figures resemble the Javanese *wayang kulit* puppets, which are carved from opaque buffalo hide and designed to cast intricate patterns of light on a screen. The rich colors, often gold, can only be seen by those seated on the puppeteer's side. The puppets are controlled by rods on the body and (an) articulated arm(s) from beneath. Balinese clown characters have hilarious moving mouths pulled by strings. The collection includes two rare Thai *nang yai* figures carved from hide, representing scenes or characters with no moving parts. They are held by their two rods over the heads of dancers, who appear in front, as well as behind, a back-lit screen, as a narrator tells tales from the other major Hindu epic, the *Rāmāyana*.

Marionettes from Rajasthan in India serve as models for the essence of puppetry. The puppet torsos are carved of one piece of wood, the arms are stuffed with cloth, and there are usually no legs. Manipulated with as few as one looped string held in the hands of the puppeteers, these puppets can amaze with transformations, such as changing from male to female, by flipping around and performing tricks, including juggling. The CPA has an authentic cloth stage in which to display the several examples in the collection.

A water puppet from Vietnam is the most unusual puppet in the Asian collection. Villagers still create wooden dolls to imitate their daily life: planting rice, fishing, and boating. The puppets are controlled by ropes and pulleys mounted on long horizontal rods hidden under the surface of murky water that becomes the stage. The puppeteers stand waist-high in the water, concealed from the spectators on the shore by bamboo screens or more elaborate scenery in a kind of stage house. With music, the puppets perform a series of entertaining vignettes at communal celebrations, including battles, and a spectacular dance of a floating dragon, with fireworks spurting from its mouth. There is now a government-sponsored national troupe of water puppetry that tours internationally with a plastic pool to represent a pond.

Australia

The CPA library offers an excellent history of Australian puppetry, which has flourished in the past thirty years. The Australian aborigines are one of the few cultural groups that apparently have never used performing objects that could qualify as puppets, although some may be found among the Maori of New Zealand and on other South Pacific islands, including New Hebrides, examples of which we would like to add to the collection. The CPA has only one puppet from Australia, a black silhouette of a hippo by the world-renowned artist Richard Bradshaw. Contextual videotapes of his work available in the library demonstrate how a cardboard cut-out can come to life through the expertise and humor of a master puppeteer.

Europe

The European collection includes over one hundred twenty-five puppets from Belgium, the Czech Republic, France, Germany, Great Britain, Greece, Hungary, Italy, Poland, Russia, and Spain. Museum curators have classified some Ice Age sculptures as puppets, and puppetry in

Europe was recorded as early as the fifth century B.C., in the writings of Plato. The hand-puppet tradition, derived from the Italian *commedia dell'arte*, was spread across Europe by wandering showmen. One of the most popular folk puppet heroes from that development is Pulcinella, the Italian ancestor of Punch, who was first witnessed in London in the seventeenth century. In the twentieth century, puppetry enjoyed a renaissance in eastern Europe, with state subsidies under Communist regimes, and in western Europe by intellectuals and artists.

The CPA already possesses a marvelous Mr. Punch and plans to commission a Pulcinella soon. Additionally, the collection includes a number of their cousins who have taken on their own cultural characteristics: a Kasper from the Hohnstein Theatre of Germany; a Polichinelle from Marseilles; a Guignol from Lyons, France; and a Petrushka from the former Soviet Union. The puppet museum of Chrudim in the Czech Republic donated the most recent addition, an authentic Kasparek.

The European collection includes an example of the simplest form of rod puppet called a marotte. It is operated by one central rod, with the movement of any body parts being incidental. It is from the Gulliver Theatre of Poland. The puppet's head is a wooden oval with no features, and she wears a Polish ethnic folk costume. From the Central State Puppet Theatre in Moscow, CPA has a beautifully crafted puppet from *The Dragon* by Eugene Schwartz, directed by the legendary Sergei Obratzsov. His company brought the rod puppet to new heights of technical development, with three or more manipulators using mechanical controls to accomplish very complicated maneuvers with a complex articulated figure. This state-subsidized theater is one of over one hundred in the former Soviet Union.

A phoenix, which serves as a metaphor for creativity, rises out of a trash can at the entrance of the current CPA collection exhibition, "Puppets: The Power of Wonder." The spectator triggers it by stepping on an electronic control. This phoenix is classified as an automaton, differentiated from a puppet because it is manipulated by mechanical means. In his Oregon studio, Michael Curry creates many automata with electronic activation for the Walt Disney Company and other prestigious clients. Curry generously contributed a great deal of time to the current exhibit of the permanent collection, which was the brainchild of guest curator

Michael Malkin. Professor Malkin teaches theater in California and wrote many books and articles about the art of puppetry, including the catalogue essay. "Puppets: The Power of Wonder" is a state-of-the-art installation, with over 50,000 visitors per year since it opened in 1995.

The Bread & Puppet
Theater Company Collection

ELKA SCHUMANN

Some twenty miles south of the Canadian border, Vermont Route 122, a two-lane road, winds west from Lyndonville, crosses a watershed between the Connecticut and St. Lawrence river basins and merges with Route 16 just south of the little town of Glover (pop. 820). Half-hidden behind a hedgerow of burdock and chokecherry bushes growing along the road stands an old New England barn. Its vertical board siding is darkened and eroded with age; its west gable towers a good fifty feet above an overgrown pasture; its east end runs into a woodshed, which connects to the rambling farmhouse and garage/workshop. A shuttered cupola graces the barn's ridgepole; worn basement doors swing in the wind.

But when you cross the threshold you enter another world: a vast, unearthly realm populated by hundreds and hundreds of puppets, masks and pictures. Here, tucked away in the Green Mountains of Vermont's northeast kingdom, is the Bread & Puppet Museum, one of the largest collections of some of the biggest puppets in the world.

The first floor once housed the fifty or so dairy cows of Jim and Daisy Dopp, who farmed here for half a century until the mid 1960s, when age forced them to retire, albeit reluctantly. The wooden stanchions are mostly gone now, but the stalls remain, offering display areas. The ceiling here is low, crisscrossed with hefty beams, the floor patched and uneven. Down the length of the one-hundred-foot-long barn run three aisles crowded with puppets grouped by theme, chronology or simply by color or size, like the hand puppets clustered by the center door, an assortment of Punches and Judys, Shakespearean characters and oddballs. Some of the larger puppets are familiar dramatic characters: a cardboard cut-out King Lear addresses his cardboard daughters under the eyes of a herd of cows; boldly painted rod puppets from *Carmen* flaunt their wire arms in a wild Spanish dance; closer to the entrance, an authentic Sicilian marionette in golden armor confronts a motley crew of shabby but undaunted warrior-peers with olive-oil can bodies, coffee-can heads and rough-sawed lathe appendages.

But the majority of the figures do not come from the world of theater, but from one man's daydreams and nightmares: a faceless soldier in a spiked helmet straddles an ungainly beast (part steer, part hippopotamus); a black woman leans over a hand-chiseled pine trough, patiently kneading invisible dough; crude figures robed in shreds of black plastic struggle and torment one another in scenes reminiscent of Goya's *Disasters of War*. In another corner, matronly figures busy themselves with household tasks, one bending over a wood-fired Glenwood cookstove, another adjusting a treadle sewing machine, a third turning a barrel butter churn, their weary, good-natured faces the epitome of Mom (or Grandma) and apple pie.

Not only figures are on display here — almost every inch of wall surface is covered with bright papier-mâché reliefs, painted backdrops and pictures large and small. They tell stories too, either independent of the life of the creatures surrounding them or else echoing the motifs of the nearby puppets and masks. The aisles are narrow; the puppets surround you, invite you into their space.

Upstairs is completely different. The cramped intimacy is gone — the ceiling soars, the walls expand. This used to be the haymow, and teams of horses once pulled wagons piled high with fragrant hay up the stone ramp (now replaced with a smaller wooden one) and down the twenty-foot-wide center aisle. The hay was pitched over rails into the windowless bays; above, another rickety floor held sheaves of flax and tangles of dried beans. The slender rafters slant up to the ridgepole, disappearing into the cathedral-like gloom. Hand-hewn, eight-by-eight-inch beams tie the structure together, their joints fastened with wooden pegs.

On this floor the puppets are giants: superhuman effigies looming fifteen, twenty and more feet into the air. Huge faces stare down or gaze off into space; enormous hands point, hail or clench into fists. A whole gallery of archetypal characters is on view: fierce generals, beatific saints, gorging gluttons, impassive bureaucrats, playboys, monsters, and martyrs. Colossal sisters of the downstairs matrons gather by the grand double doors, aloof and remote, a hint of archaic Greek smiles on their lips, paired off with their eighteen-foot-tall rustic swains. Across from them, a mob of scarlet demons conspires some dastardly deed. The biggest objects, two heads, each almost twenty feet tall, are barely noticeable amidst the array of figures. A small army of life-size garbagemen, their homely faces as familiar and comforting as baked potatoes, slouch together in a friendly, beer-guzzling gang. Chalky white herds of spirit deer, horses, and fanged beasts surge across an invisible tundra. A group of clowns holds court over doll-size subjects. And at the far end of the aisle are the earliest large puppets, monolithic shapes draped in ochre and umber burlap — the Last Supper on Easter Island. Once giants in their own right, they have shrunk over the years, dwarfed by the latest behemoths to emerge from the papier-mâché workshop.

Overhead, between the rafters, there are more reliefs, some glowing with color, others barely distinguishable from the browns of the aged wooden interior. Lanterns of fabric over wire frames and globes of papier-mâché covered with figures hang the length of the barn. Masks of every description, including casts made directly from actual faces (life-masks), adorn the upright posts. And in between everything, populations of tiny figures go about their business, some cheerily occupied with daily chores, others caught up in scenes of mayhem as executioners, victims, and bystanders. If any one principle reigns in this museum, it is *horror vacuii*— the fear of empty space.

The contents of this unique museum are only a small part of the creations and accumulations of the Bread & Puppet Theater. In the cavernous upper reaches of the museum there is one floor of backdrops, banners, and costume storage, and higher still, the loft is filled with little-used artifacts. Down below, in the basement, are stored sets of multiples of cardboard and masonite cut-outs: life-size beds, oversize chairs, open hands, and clenched fists, sheaves of wheat, meadow flowers, and panels and panels of connected landscapes. Here an ongoing battle rages against dampness, especially in the spring, and slowly but surely all the stored objects succumb to the moisture emanating from the earth.

Across the road, the red storage shed is tightly packed with the masks, puppets, flags, and theater effects most constantly in use. Big

Indian chiefs and horses. (Photograph by Alex Williams.)

white birds, their fringed cloth bodies wound around their poles, rest across rafters, while cardboard bluebird heads are strung up like beads on a string. There are colorful dragons, hordes of different animals, sheep, horses, cows, caribou, apes, donkeys, squads of goon-like Uncle Fatsos, and, resting in boxes, duplicates of some of the popular puppets in the museum, prepared to sally forth at a moment's notice to join a jolly parade or an anti-globalization rally.

In 1995 a brand-new building named, somewhat unoriginally, the New Building, was erected behind the museum, mainly to provide a covered rehearsal space, but by its very size also affording an expansive attic, again, quickly filling up.

(At the time of this writing, Bread & Puppet has two major exhibits on the road. One is called "The Papier-mâché Cathedral" and fills a room of six hundred square meters. The exhibit was made of mostly preexisting, plus some made-to-order, works for the Basic Needs Pavilion at the EXPO 2000 World's Fair in Hanover, Germany. Another selection of B&P Theater effects fills six large rooms of the Art Museum in Fort Lauderdale, Florida.)

The Bread & Puppet Theater was founded in New York City in 1963 by Peter Schumann, a young sculptor and dancer from Germany. He had experimented earlier in Munich and then on the Lower East Side in New York City choreographing masked and unmasked dancers, sometimes in combination with clumsy chicken-wire and papier-mâché effigies, and had worked with a series of very short-lived companies. For a year he taught art in a Vermont village school, and there he hit upon the idea of moving sculpture — sculptures dancing, or puppets. After seeing the Manteo Brothers' Sicilian marionettes at a Puppeteers of America festival and being impressed by their roughneck virility and *Orlando Furioso* passions, he discovered puppet theater. Schumann described it as "applied and socially embedded sculpture." In a manifesto from the mid–1960s, he writes: "Puppet theater is the theater of all means. Puppets and masks should be played in the street. They are louder than the traffic. They don't teach problems but they scream and dance and hit each other on the head and display life in its clearest terms…" (Schumann 1964).

Returning to New York in '63, Schumann worked for the first few years in a loft above a gypsy bar on Delancey Street; when neatened up, it also served as a small performance space with wooden milk-crate seating. He made a precarious living for himself, wife Elka, and a growing family as a housepainter and moving man. Later, as the B&P Theater began to earn fees, his job as sexton of the Spencer Memorial Church in Brooklyn provided more room for work and shows, and in the late '60s Bread & Puppet settled, rent-free, in an empty, city-owned courthouse on Second Street and Second Avenue.

Three main elements shaped the style and content of B&P shows in this decade: working with children in the slums of the city; a growing political awareness resulting in massive participation with puppets and masks in protests against social injustice and war; and the profound influence of Schumann's European background and education — folklore, folk art and medieval art, and the art of the Dadaists and German Expressionists. In his first years in the United States Schumann was also drawn to the work of Merce Cunningham, the Living Theater, and Claes Oldenburg, Red Grooms, and the early Happenings.

The shows that Schumann and his company created were as varied as the influences around them. Short, powerful street pieces, like *The King Story* (1963) and *A Man Says Goodbye to His Mother* (1966), were developed alongside the *Christmas Story*, a lively mix of traditional and innovative puppetry, the Biblical tale and the *Daily News*. Puppets and masks slipped from one sphere to another: the cigar-puffing landlord from the *Pied Piper of Harlem* (1965), a community-created protest against poor housing, became a brutal-fisted Uncle Sam in anti-war rallies; the ten-foot Christ puppet wears a sign saying "Vietnam" and is crucified on a shark-nosed bomber; impassive, ghostly life-masks from the show *Fire* (1965) are worn by white-robed women in long sidewalk processions mourning the war dead. The protests grew in size and moved from downtown churches and side streets to Fifth Avenue, St. Patrick's Cathedral, Madison Square Garden, and to the seats of power in Washington, DC. The ranks of masked demonstrators swelled as dozens and scores of volunteers joined B&P to make political statements in strong visual and visceral terms.

Fire, a full-length chamber music–like play of almost excruciating stillness, dedicated to three Americans who immolated themselves in protest to the Vietnam War, was the first B&P show to receive critical recognition and acclaim. In 1968 the company was invited to present it at the International Theater Festival in Nancy, France, where it was widely commended. As a result, for the next dozen years, B&P regularly toured Europe, frequently attending theater festivals and receiving some prestigious awards like the *Prix di Roma* in 1963 and The Erasmus Award in 1978. B&P attained a certain celebrity in alternative and radical circles, sometimes on the level of a rock band.

During those same years, alongside the anti-war activity and festival hopping, B&P ran several summer-long open workshops in city parks, involving whole neighborhoods of kids and adults. They came out of curiosity and to make their own puppets and masks, and stayed on to communally build a family of giant mythic figures; Mother Earth and the God of Heaven Uranus each required four to six people to move them. The body of the crocodile-headed dragon needed a file of children a block long to parade.

By then, Schumann could give up his day jobs and eke out a livelihood from performance and workshop fees, and B&P slowly became able to support a small number of full-time puppeteers. But for many of its productions the theater depended heavily on volunteers, some of whom have become deeply involved in the work, and this is still true today. On the other hand, many come to B&P (or call or write) and want to join, whether out of political solidarity, love of performing or pure goodwill. Over time, great heaps of group puppets, objects, cut-outs and masks were made to accommodate the participants: cows and computers, flags and frogs, to name a few. This symbiotic relationship, this interdependency of B&P and volunteers, has become regulated. That is one reason there is so much of so many things. (Another reason is the artist's exuberance!) Yet this relationship is always unpredictable, fraught with uncertainty: will only three turn up instead of the needed — and promised — sixty? Will forty hands reach for twenty-five flags?

In 1968–1969 a new show was developed that merged many aspects, both physical and thematic, of earlier work. *The Cry of the People for Meat* had giant puppets and dragons, tiny figures, and masked and unmasked performers. It compressed the entire Bible into three hours and updated the Parables of Jesus into guerrilla theater. Fragments of it were shown at the 1968 Newport Jazz Festival to a mostly bewildered audience, and then, in response to a flood of invitations (still generated by *Fire*), *The Cry* and four other shows launched a nine-month-long European tour. The crew numbered between twenty and forty as groupies joined up and dropped out, and it included three families with small children. In bus and truck they crisscrossed the continent, performing in streets, parks, train stations, universities and theaters. But when the theater returned to New York City in December 1969, it found itself evicted from its Second Avenue courthouse home. A temporary place was found, an unheated bank under the Brooklyn Bridge, but the high rent plus ordinary urban living expenses ate away the tour savings. The seven-person-strong Schumann family was growing out of its two-and-a-half room railroad flat on Sixth Street and Avenue A. When an invitation came from Goddard, a small liberal arts college in central Vermont, to be the theater-in-residence, it seemed like a godsend. B&P moved there, bag and baggage, in June 1970, fulfilling a long-held, vague but strong yearning for the country life. The amenities at Goddard were considerable: exclusive use of Cate Farm, which included a large brick farmhouse and a roomy remodeled barn, half of which was a *heated* workshop, the other half a decent May-through-June rehearsal area. Each new piece created over the next four years premiered in Goddard's Haybarn Theater. Students came to watch or help, and a handful became full-time and valuable members of the company. Along the way, B&P became a nonprofit tax-exempt corporation, with a board, an annual meeting, a bookkeeper and a payroll on which every full member received the same low salary.

The first summer on Cate Farm was an exciting and prolific time. Immediately, with the sky being literally the limit, a bunch of giant puppets were built, including the Peace Hand and two large heads. One, calm and harmonious, was mounted on a twelve-foot pole, robed in flower-printed cloth, and named the Constitution. (Later, as the Godface, this puppet became the central figure of the yearly pageant.) The other face, painted blue, became the prow of a boat, the Ark for All, the first of a veritable fleet of cloth boats, some with huge painted sails. A group of tall white puppets named the Indian Chiefs, a flock of white birds mounted on tall sticks, and a set of banners printed with big, bright daffodils and roses were also made early that summer. These, and many puppets brought from New York, marched in several local parades that year and every year thereafter. B&P continues to this day to participate in such parades, in Hardwick, Barton, Cabot, Lyndonville and other nearby towns, with occasional forays to more distant cities for political parades (or for Halloween).

The Cate Farm years gave birth to many productions, whose puppets constitute some of the major exhibits in the museum. *The Birdcatcher in Hell* (1971) at the top of the stairs is easily the most spectacular: big demons in scarlet and pink frame a red curtain, which is the body of Yama, the King of Hell. His gargantuan visage is a composite of creatures — bird, beast, and human — and every inch of his face and giant outstretched hands is covered with delicately painted plants and animals. *Birdcatcher* was conceived and performed outdoors on the green of the Winooski River floodplain just below the farmhouse, but it translated well into theaters and toured successfully abroad, together with *Gray Lady Cantata No. 2* (1970). These shows were a study in contrasts: shrill reds vs. muted grays; screeching and incessant drumming vs. barely audible scrapes and whispers; orgiastic dance vs. slow motion; and a text consisting of a medieval Japanese Kyogen, fragments of the *Iliad* and a speech by then President Nixon vs. a nursery rhyme–like round by Thomas Tallis. The themes, however, were linked: Nixon's pardon of Lieutenant Calley of the My Lai massacre on the one hand, a son going off to war and the bombing of hapless innocents on the other.

The *Gray Lady* sisterhood (1965–1966) was built as a chorus, rising and falling and rising yet again to J. S. Bach's *Wachet Auf Cantata*, performed during the Week of the Angry Arts in New York City. In the 1970s they were the protagonists in five more Cantatas, and in 1999 *Cantata No. 2* was briefly revived. Now they cover one wall at the far end of the museum, hanging in rows with downcast heads, their dirty mop hair falling over their mournful faces. Arching above them and on the next wall, layered like shingles, are the puppets from *That Simple Light May Rise Out of Complicated Darkness* (1973–1974), large, beautiful faces sculpted as shallow reliefs with bodies of voluminous black plastic. That show also traveled to Europe, but its abstract theme, wordless bulk, and mutinous volunteers made it a difficult and often thankless undertaking.

The floor in this bay is also home to the foot-high Johnny (as in "When Johnny Comes Marching Home Again…") puppets. Quickly and sloppily mass-produced in the mid–1960s for burning at an anti-war rally, enough of them survived to demonstrate on a tabletop stage how banal everyday life intersects with the suffering and destruction of war.

But the most important and far-reaching creation to come out of Cate Farm was *Our Domestic Resurrection Circus*. The flat verdant meadow below the farmhouse bluff was Schumann's inspiration to create *Circus* in the broadest sense, meaning a spectacle-in-the-round with an all-embracing theme: the cycle — of day and night, summer and winter, life and death. Work on this project began the first summer, on a reasonably small scale, with a few newly made giant puppets ambling in a circle, some performers going through ritual-like motions, donning and doffing masks, watched by a few dozen curious onlookers. By 1974, B&P's last summer at Goddard, a definite basic structure had emerged, which was retained for the next quarter-century. The Circus began informally with an audience wandering among small scattered shows, music making and clowning; next came a puppet circus with papier-mâché animals, fake tricks, political commentary and a funky brass band; a serious piece followed, in a different location, often in conjunction with a piece of solemn music (in 1974 it was the seventeenth-century oratorio *Jephthe* by Giacomo Carissimi); and, as evening fell, a pageant unfolded all over the landscape, depicting the struggle between Good and Evil.

That same year, B&P left Goddard; Cate Farm had become too crowded for the growing number of both puppets and puppeteers. At the same time, in an undreamed-of stroke of good luck, a large, uncommonly well-situated farm up in the northeast kingdom of Vermont became available through the generosity of Elka's parents, John and Maria Scott.

At first it seemed an unlikely location for an experimental theater, but it turned out to be ideal for the company's many different projects. There was fertile land for substantial gardening, well-kept fields, a pine plantation, a former gravel pit in the shape of a natural amphitheater for outdoor performances; indoor space for (some) building and rehearsing, and a beautiful, solid old barn. The barn had not been used for almost a decade, and, although it was chock-full of chaff and debris, it was the perfect place for a puppet museum. Crews of puppeteers shoveled and swept for weeks, and still the dust and dried manure sifted down, the whitewash flaked, and the cobwebs billowed (as they still do, but not as much). The theater's sixty-passenger school bus made countless trips to Goddard, hauling back load after load of puppets and materials. Finally the barn was pronounced cleared out and the mounting of the exhibits began. For the first years only the upstairs was used for display, and the cow stalls below were reserved for storage. But every passing summer brought new building projects; expanding the museum to the ground floor and moving storage to ever bigger quarters could not keep pace with the output of the Claypit.

To the viewer of the puppets and masks, Schumann's singular artistic vision is inescapable and all-pervasive. His style, a prodigious mix of the Romanesque, Cycladic Minimalism, German Expressionism and potato-nose Naturalism, gives the museum a distinct aesthetic unity. But the actual making of the puppets and masks, sometimes with painstaking care, other times in slapdash assembly-line fashion, has been done over the years by literally hundreds of hardworking, enthusiastic men and women, teenagers and children. The achievements of this creative community of coworkers reflect not only their skill and dedication, but also their lively engagement with both the how and why of the task. A core of experienced puppeteers, assisted by scores of helpful friends and neighbors, builds the puppets from Schumann's sculpted clay models. From the mid–1960s through the early 1980s the material of choice was celastic, a synthetic fiber, which, when dipped in acetone, becomes pliant and self-adhering, hardening quickly into a light, resilient, waterproof shell. As the price rose, and, as workers became more aware of the safety and health hazards linked to the chemicals, a switch was made back to papier-mâché; its strengths and refinements were rediscovered and carried to new heights in the building of bigger-than-ever puppets. The puppeteers and helpers designed and executed mounting systems, costumes and accessories that transformed layers of paper and glue into supernatural beings.

Although the results can be extraordinary, the means and materials were almost always simple.

> Puppetry is conceptual sculpture true to its popular origins, uninvited by the powers-that-be, its feet in the mud, economically on the fringes of existence, technically a collage art combining paper, rags and scraps of wood into two-and three-dimensional bodies... [Schumann *Radicality* 1990].

The clay used to sculpt the faces and figures came from nearby riverbanks and is piled in old bathtubs in the front yard of the museum in the Claypit, where most of the building takes place. Found materials make up the bulk of the construction: industrial-strength brown paper and paste made of cornstarch bought in fifty lb. bags; damaged cardboard from the local furniture factory; cedar and poplar poles cut in the nearby thickets; baling twine unraveled and dyed for manes and wigs; rummage sale leftovers for costumes.

Clay has another important use in the B&P Theater: the three outdoor, wood-fired, Quebec-style bread ovens are made of clay. The largest oven in the Circus Field is the size of an igloo. Since bread is one-half of the theater's name, a description of its role is warranted. Schumann wrote in the 1984 B&P booklet *Bread* that he comes "from a stretch of land where bread meant bread, not a pretense for a hot-dog nor a sponge to clean up sauces with, but an honest hunk of grainy, nutty food which had its own strong taste and required a healthy amount of chewing."

To Schumann, bread baking is intrinsic to his work, art and life. He grinds the rye berries in a hand mill, mixes warm water and sourdough from the previous batch, and bakes from twenty to forty loaves in the smaller ovens, up to three hundred in the large one. He learned to bake bread as a small boy from his mother in pre-war Silesia, and he continued to do it regularly, sometimes daily, all his life. Describing his work in the early years in New York City, Schumann wrote that, "The bread part was no problem; bread is necessary, good bread is hard to find..." ("Lecture").

Schumann made bread as a student in order to live cheaply and ever after for the same reason and out of a conviction bordering on the religious. In his manifesto Schumann wrote

> We sometimes give you a piece of bread along with the puppet show because our bread and theater belong together. For a long time the theater arts have been separated from the stomach. Theater was entertainment. Entertainment was meant for the skin. Bread was meant for the stomach. The old rites of baking, eating and offering bread were forgotten. The bread decayed and became mush.... Theater is not yet an established form, not the place of commerce you think it is, where you pay to get something. Theater is different. It is more like bread, more like a necessity.

The bread baking continues even on tours, and the grain, mill, plastic baby bathtub, and baking sheets are part of most packing lists. At first, local bakers were persuaded to share their ovens for the B&P loaves; then, in the 1980s, a simple brick oven design was invented and sponsors for shows were asked to provide the four hundred fifty bricks needed and a fire permit, if required. Such ovens were built on tours in Poland, France, Germany, the Soviet Union, Taiwan, Brazil, Nicaragua, Sarajevo, and in many places in the United States.

The first building project in the new location in Glover was a monochromatic relief series that told the life and death story of a white horse. This story was translated into other media and became a book of woodcuts and a show, *The White Horse Butcher* (1976). A scene from it is mounted in the museum, surrounded by the original reliefs and a multitude of expressionless butcher masks.

The good-natured, slow-moving maintenance men at Goddard College served as models for a B&P archetype. The Garbageman, invented

Life-size Washerwomen. (Photograph by Alex Williams.)

as a solo stagehand and gofer for Cate Farm shows, was replicated in Glover into a small army. After the originals retired to the museum to gossip and guzzle away their days, a duplicate set replaced them in shows and parades. Soon the need arose for female companionship, and in 1978 a chorus of Washerwomen angels appeared on the scene in *Oswald von Wolkenstein* (1978), the main show of that summer. Clones of this titular medieval one-eyed troubadour lord it over a table of awards upstairs in the museum. The Washerwomen were a cheery, bustling, buxom presence thenceforth, and a whole show, *Ah! Or the First Washerwoman Cantata* (1979) deals with their stalwart battle against nuclear arms. These friendly angels were a new and welcome ingredient in B&P parades, a counterweight to the monsters, dragons, and oppressive types dominating the scene. Then a puppeteer suggested that it would be nice to have a giant pair. The 1979 summer was devoted to the making of big faces, hands, and feet, and the sewing of giant overalls and aprons and other garments. Finally an interracial octet was born, four couples — so they could do a square dance. They were designed to come apart and collapse,

Giant Washerwomen and Garbagemen and life-size Garbagemen. (Photograph by Alex Williams.)

and can be reassembled in short order, and thus they have had their share of national and international travel. For several seasons *The Washerwoman Nativity* (1979–1983), a variation of the *Christmas Story*, was presented at Judson Church in New York City; these giants also make guest appearances in fare as varied as soap operas and Greek tragedies.

Another set of august oversize puppets comes from the show *Masaniello* (1977), named for a Neapolitan revolutionary. The Blue General who quashed the rebellion glowers from the north wall of the upstairs, while an elegantly tuxedoed Duke of Naples offers a cabbage-size rose to a majestic Queen of Spain. (She later starred in *Josephine or the Mouse Singer* [1984], based on a story by Kafka, flying over the audience on an intricate pulley system.)

In the early '80s the themes of B&P shows moved in new directions. The threat of nuclear weapons and the need to disarm them became central to a number of shows, like *Swords and Plowshares* (1981) and *The Story of One Who Set Out to Study Fear* (1981). The million-strong anti-nuclear parade on June 12, 1982, in New York City included a thousand Vermonters carrying and wearing Bread & Puppet puppets, masks and flags in a Fight-the-End-of-the-World contingent — the largest number of B&P artifacts ever to appear in public.

In those years U.S. policy in Central America became increasingly the focus of other shows: *The Door* (1984), its Indian-faced effigies reminiscent of *Fire*, and *The Birth, Crucifixion and Resurrection of Archbishop Romero of El Salvador* (1984), replete with papier-mâché crucifixes and skeletons.

With fewer trips to Europe, touring turned to this hemisphere, to Cuba, Puerto Rico and Nicaragua for solidarity reasons, and to Venezuela and Colombia, in response to invitations to prestigious theater festivals.

Nature and the environment were also calling for attention. One of the upstairs museum bays is full of characters representing these concerns. A green company of St. Francises was built to honor his eight hundredth birthday. Green Men, nature spirits who somehow survived the Middle Ages, their heads a tangle of plant life, clothed in leaf-covered ponchos, replaced the Washerwomen and Garbagemen in many parades and shows. Dark-featured rubber tappers from *The Same Boat: The Passion of Chico Mendes* (1989) celebrated this champion of Brazil's rain forests. Brown papier-mâché trees with kindly faces demonstrated on Montpelier's State House lawn against toxic spraying programs in the north woods.

The Queen of Spain from *Masaniello*— or "Josephine the Mouse Singer." (Photograph by Alex Williams.)

Many of these puppets and shows saw their first light of day at one or another of the Circuses, which took place one weekend every summer (except 1980, when B&P did a similar program in Lyons, France) in the twenty-four-acre meadow across the road from the museum. Starting in 1975 with a few dozen performers and a hundred or so spectators, the event grew steadily in all directions. By the late 1980s, tens of thousands came to wander among the simultaneous sideshows, sit around the gravel pit amphitheater for the Circus, and, as twilight fell, perch precariously on the southern bank to watch the mysterious pageant ebb and flow across the expanse of meadow, ending with the burning of the symbol of evil.

For the lighting of the final fire, the two largest active puppets were regularly employed to carry the torch: white Domestic Insurrection and brown Mother Earth (both housed permanently in the museum), would take turns with the one-hundred-foot-long gown and the gigantic pair of hands (painted to match the face), in order to swim over the field, animated by forty to fifty puppeteers and embrace many in her long arms. (A second bonfire, after the final cleanup, consumed piles of signs, flimsy structures, and heaps of worn-out, poorly made or second-rate puppets — so there was less storage to worry about!)

Growth brought with it many problems and difficulties, as well as the exhilaration of performing to vast crowds. After a tragic death in a nearby campground in 1998, Schumann and B&P decided to stop *Our Domestic Resurrection Circus.* A much smaller program of shows, spread over the summer, has supplanted the one huge performance.

As we try to make sense of this vast collection, some words of Schumann come to mind — that all the things here

> ...are ordered by a strange ambition, namely: to provide the world with an unfragmented and uncontrollably large picture of itself, a picture that only puppetry can draw ... which praises and attacks at the same time, a *theatrum mundi,* What is this *theatrum mundi?* It is certainly more than its encyclopedic massiveness and more than the beautiful megalomaniac wholeness of the world and more than all the bedrooms and kitchens ... and it includes the precious cabbages and the precious witchgrasses and the noble antelopes and the noble cockroaches. This puppet *theatrum mundi* which is made possible through the special talents of puppets and the special grace of things, this puppet *theatrum mundi* derives from the magicians,

from the time when art was votive art ... (it) never quite succeeded
to be what it wanted to be ... (and) is as unfinished as it is ancient
[*Old Art*].

Earlier Schumann wrote this specifically about the museum:

The barn is full to the brim; its population density is an expression
not only of the accumulations of time but of the urgencies which
inspired the making of so much stuff: the poverty of the poor, the
arrogance of the war-mongers, the despair of the victims. And naturally all this will decay in due course.... So why does this Museum
have to be?
    I guess the answer is an admission of failure. First of all, we never
succeeded in our aspirations to make that all-encompassing puppet
show which would employ all these celastic and papermache [*sic*]
forces. And secondly, the reason for the gigantic size of such a show
escapes us more and more. Some things simply go as they will: the
puppets have established their own right in the old cow stalls. Like
donkeys, they don't mind not to be moved [*Bread and Puppet Museum*].

A final postscript from the museum brochure: "...since this Museum
replaces the traditional museum's ideal of preservation with acceptance
of more or less graceful deterioration, consider making your visit sooner
rather than later."

Works Cited

Schumann, Peter. The Puppet Christ. Program note to the 1964 Spencer Memorial
    Church Easter show.
_____. "Bread." "Pamphlet published by the Bread & Puppet Theater, 1984.
_____. "A Lecture to Art Students at SUNY/Purchase." Glover, VT: Bread & Puppet
    Theater, 1987.
_____. "Bread & Puppet Museum." Brochure published by the Bread & Puppet The-
    ater, 1989.
_____. *The Radicality of the Puppet Theater*. St. Johnsburg, VT: Troll Press, 1990.
_____. "The Old Art of Puppetry in the New World Order." Bread & Puppet Press, 1993.

Puppets and
"The Iconography of Drama":
The Brander Matthews
Collection at
Columbia University

JOHN BELL

It has always been a matter of pride for theater scholars at Columbia University that Professor Brander Matthews (1852–1929) was, as he put it himself, "the occupant of the earliest chair to be established in any American university specifically for the study of dramatic literature" (v). Columbia's pride of place — to have been the initiator of serious academic study of theater in the United States — is legitimate and is a competitive dig at Harvard and Yale's own professor of dramatic literature, George Pierce Baker, although Baker's playwriting classes had a far more influential effect on the shape of modern American drama. Matthews's vision of the theater was different from Baker's: it was centered not only on dramatic literature, but on the theater experience as a whole, in all its varieties. Matthews, a millionaire's son and a New Yorker from the age of seven, felt the range of theater experience from "the genius of Sophocles and of Shakespeare, of Molière and of Ibsen," to "the minor arts of the dancer and the acrobat, ... the conjurer and the negro minstrel, ... the principles of pantomime and the development of scene-painting," and, we can confidently add, puppet and mask theater (v).

Matthews's childhood included extensive trips to Europe (where he saw and began to collect French and Italian puppets), as well as frequent exposure to New York's theater scene. In a move that must have raised some Manhattan eyebrows, Matthews married an English actress, Ada Smith (her stage name was Ada Harland), in 1873, and, when his father's fortune dwindled after the economic panic of the same year, Matthews began writing articles, and then books, about literature and the theater. Matthews's writing, while centered on a classic sense of theatrical hierarchy crowned by Greek tragedy, also always included some sense of "the minor arts," an appreciation (and, one suspects, sheer enjoyment) of the wide spectrum of theater forms that would necessarily lead him to the worldwide traditions of puppets and masks. Matthews's writings centered on such traditional dramatic subjects as *The Theatres of Paris* (1880) and *French Dramatists of the Nineteenth Century* (1881), but he also wrote a comedy, *Margery's Lovers* (1884), which was performed on the London stage. In *A Book About the Theater* (1916), Matthews displayed his wide-ranging interests by writing about such underappreciated subjects as pantomime, "Women Dramatists," acrobats, variety theater and magic, as well as a brief history of world puppet theater, and special chapters on Punch and Judy shows, toy theater and its relationship to melodrama, and the shadow theater of the *Chat Noir* cabaret in Paris (which Matthews had experienced firsthand). Matthews's sense of theater as popular, commercial entertainment was typically American and led Edward Gordon Craig, Europe's pioneer of puppet-oriented art theater, to scorn Matthews. Craig read an interview with Matthews from the *American Review* (April 1, 1911) in which the professor proposed that budding playwrights pay close attention to box-office successes in order to learn how to write successful dramas, opining that Shakespeare and Molière also followed this rule. Craig had nothing but contempt for Matthews's sense of box-office success, writing that Matthews represented "all that is unpractical, unoriginal and impotent in America" (19).

Matthews began teaching at Columbia, his alma mater, in 1891, was appointed professor of literature in 1892, and then received the innovative title of professor of dramatic literature in 1900, a position he held until he retired in 1924. What is quite startling to realize at the beginning of the twenty-first century, when it appears as if the study of puppet theater has only recently become "legitimate," is that Matthews consistently articulated his interests in "the subordinate subdivisions of the art of the stage" a century ago. Matthews's unabashed inclusion of puppets into his sense of essential theater led him (as it has so many other students of the form) to a pan-cultural awareness of global theater traditions, many decades before a multicultural sensibility took hold in the American academic consciousness.

Matthews not only understood, collected, and analyzed puppets and masks, but he also championed their study as a legitimate part of any theater education. Moreover — again different from Baker, and quite radical even now — Matthews proposed that the best way to study theater history is from an analysis of its artifacts. To this end, Matthews set up the Brander Matthews Dramatic Museum and Library on the third floor of Columbia's Philosophy Hall, a multimodal assemblage of sources that, in Matthews's mind, would augment the study of dramatic texts with the visual presence of theater models, set models, illustrations, and masks and puppets. In 1911, the year the museum was created, Matthews described his new endeavor by first defining "the drama" as an art that combined "music and dancing, epic and oratory, painting, sculpture, and architecture," and he argued for a multidisciplinary approach to theater study centered on collections like his museum.

> Insofar as drama is within the limits of literature it can be studied in a library, but, insofar as it is outside the limits of literature, it needs, for its proper understanding, a gallery and a museum, containing the graphic material that will help the student to reconstruct for himself the conditions under which the masterpieces of the great dramatists were originally performed.
>
> It should be the duty of such an institution to collect, to set in order, and to display to advantage the iconography of the drama. It should place at the disposal of the student all the graphic materials likely to be of use to him,— materials which the historians of the drama have not yet realized to the full [quoted in Mazer and Bell].

"No museum of precisely this scope," Matthews went on to point out, "has yet been established anywhere either in America or in Europe."

Matthews's wider definition of theater differed fundamentally from George Pierce Baker's central focus on the mechanics of playwriting. But Matthews's appreciation of high and low culture, of international performance traditions, and of the importance of learning from sources not limited to play texts also made him in many ways a precursor to late twentieth-century modes of performance studies, which pursue similar goals from a differently theorized background. In this way, Matthews's contribution to theater studies is not simply one of chronological priority (Baker was made a professor of dramatic literature at Yale five years after Matthews's position was created), but of a substantially different focus: one that above all leads to a sense of global performance traditions as an international heritage, including not only western dramatic literature, but even such omnipresent forms as puppet theater.

The Brander Matthews Dramatic Museum and Library, according to its 1930s curator, Jean F. Spaulding, became "the nucleus of the Columbia Library theater collection" (Gilder and Freedley 33). Matthews's initial assemblage of five thousand theater books was the literary core of the collection, whose treasures by 1936 also included "models of Greek, Japanese, French, Elizabethan and mystery play stages as well as modern sets ... English playbills, ... photographs, prints, and extra-illustrated books on the theater," and "English, French, Javanese and Italian marionettes and shadow figures" (McPharlin 33). The expansive range of the collection inspired hundreds of Columbia students in their studies of theater, such as Paul McPharlin, the puppeteer, writer, publisher, designer and producer, whose exposure to Matthews's collection as a Columbia undergraduate helped spur him to help define the American puppet revival of the twentieth century. Matthews's museum was displayed in rooms 305 and 306 of Philosophy Hall for a number of decades, and then moved to Low Library, where parts of it were on display through the 1960s. Matthews would probably be surprised to learn that the Dramatic Museum, which he envisioned as an accessible learning tool for theater study, is now difficult to visit. Closed off from the public on the top floor of Columbia's Butler Library, as part of the Rare Books and Manuscripts Library, Matthews's collection of over five hundred puppets, masks, and related items is rarely ever seen.

The Puppet Collection

The puppet collection of the Brander Matthews Dramatic Museum is based on objects Matthews himself collected, as well as pieces Matthews's friends collected for him. (The Dramatic Museum also includes over one hundred masks from Japan, Africa, India, Bali, Europe, and the United States.) The collection's scope is eclectic, rather than exhaustively thorough, but marked by unusually vivid examples of world puppet traditions. The puppets in the collection represent Japan, China, Burma, Thailand, Java, India, Turkey, England, France, Africa, Haiti, Mexico, and the United States, and each puppet is listed in a card catalogue in the Rare Books and Manuscript Library. However, specific information on the puppets and their provenances is often scandalously brief, inconsistent, or entirely missing. Innovative research on the collection's holdings will make them much more useful to scholars and students.

African Puppets

Although Matthews's interests went far afield, they did not focus on African puppet traditions (although a few quite interesting African masks are part of the collection). The collection's catalogue does list a hand puppet from northern Africa, about which further information is lacking, as well as a wooden puppet from Ghana, whose articulated arms were also moved by rods. Again, further identification of this intriguing puppet is missing.

Puppets of the Americas

The collection's representatives of puppet theater in the Americas are not extensive, but feature some intriguing examples. For instance, there are three wooden puppets attributed to Haiti, which provenance would be quite interesting if true. The trio includes a twelve-inch father puppet, wearing a top hat, as well as a mother figure and a child. The Dramatic Museum also includes twelve pieces from Mexico, eleven clay "jigging" puppets and one marionette giraffe, which may represent the prolific Mexican marionette traditions established by the extensive Rosete Aranda family in the late nineteenth and early twentieth centuries.

The Brander Matthews Collection does not include many puppets from the United States. There is a marionette of a young boy in blue clothes, and a set of ten cards representing circus figures, to be cut out into flat puppets called pantins.

Asian Puppets

The Dramatic Museum's Asian puppets include a small variety of Japanese puppets, including what the card catalogue describes as a "very old" sixteen-inch-tall rod puppet, perhaps an Awaji-style figure, and two tiny marionettes of a man and a dragon. There is only one *bunraku* figure, from the early nineteenth century, but it is stunning: an elegant woman in a red silk kimono, whose head and arm mechanisms are all intact. There is a small set of Chinese shadow figures, twelve in all, and a remarkable mechanical theater featuring eight automaton musicians. There are three many-stringed Burmese marionettes, but there is little information about them.

An interesting part of the museum's Asian holdings is a collection of forty-seven puppets from Thailand. These include twenty-two *nang yai* shadow figures, the large, one-piece leather figures of characters from the Ramakien epic, set in action poses within the objects' filigreed borders, and operated by two wooden handles by dancers holding the puppets above their heads. According to the catalogue information, at least one of these figures is seven feet tall.

The museum's Javanese puppets, all collected in the 1920s, offer a modest example of three different forms of *wayang*. There is one wooden relief *wayang kletek* figure, and four *wayang kulit* shadow figures, including an unidentified male epic hero, a Garuda bird, and a *kayon*, the tree-of-life icon that demarcates a *wayang kulit* performance. In addition, there are seven three-dimensional *wayang golek* rod puppets, whose remarkably lifelike movements and gestures literally and figuratively added a new dimension to the flat figures of *wayang kulit*. The Museum's *wayang golek* figures are important, of course, not only as examples of Javanese theater, but also because *wayang golek* puppetry played an important role in America's modern puppet revival, immensely impressing such American puppeteers of the early twentieth century as Marjorie Batchelder (Paul McPharlin's wife), who radically changed American puppet theater when she made rod puppets influenced by the *wayang golek* style in such productions as Maeterlinck's *Death of Tintagiles* (1937).

A great treasure of the Brander Matthews's Dramatic Museum Collection is twenty-three *tholu bommalata* shadow figures from Andhra Pradesh in south India. They represent a full array of characters from the *Rāmāyana*, including the ten-headed demon ruler Ravana. Like all *tholu bommalata* puppets, these are translucent, lusciously multicolored leather figures four to five feet tall, and feature one or two articulated arms. The extensive set of *tholu bommalata* figures would greatly benefit from further research.

Another remarkable feature of the collection is a set of nine Karaghöz shadow figures from Turkey. Said to have been collected in Istanbul in the nineteenth century, the set also includes fourteen pieces of scenery and accessories from a Karaghöz show. The shadow puppets are of relatively thick hide, and all feature a central hole through which the perpendicular operating stick was inserted (which is to say, these seem to have been used in performance). Karaghöz differs from the Indian and Javanese traditions represented in the collection because it features the largely comic, often ribald and scatological escapades of the clownish Karaghöz and his friend, Hacivat. Two of the figures in the Turkish set are clearly Karaghöz and Hacivat, who, in this particular tale, have both been transformed into donkeys with human heads and animal bodies.

European Puppets

Another richness in the Brander Matthews Collection is its set of Italian marionettes. Matthews had a real affinity for marionettes, and, when he wrote feelingly of them in *A Book About the Theater*, he echoed Heinrich von Kleist by remarking upon "the advantages possessed by the dancing puppets over the dancers of more solid flesh and blood" (295). The collection includes marionette rod puppets identified as Orlando (the Christian knight whose adventures against the Moors and other foes are performed in the *Orlando Furioso* epics once performed in four-hundred-day cycles by Sicilian marionette theaters) and his fellow knight, Rinaldo. They were acquired, according to the collection's records, in the "late nineteenth century" in Sicily, and are less than one foot tall, which would seem to link them to the puppet traditions of Palermo in northern Sicily. (Southern Sicilian puppets are usually about four times taller.)

From Italy also come eighteen six-inch-tall marionettes representing *commedia dell'arte* characters, including Arlecchino, Brighella, Pantalone, and Il Dottore. There is also a skeleton marionette, and one of the puppets is identified as "Pinocchio." According to catalogue records, these marionettes were collected in "Paris 1925, Naples 1926," a time when *commedia* characters and puppets were inspiring avant-garde artists throughout Europe. Finally, a third element of the collection's Italian pieces is a "17th century *praesepe* [crêche] from a church in Rome."

It is understandable that Matthews, with his affinity for and lifelong familiarity with French theater, would have collected French puppets, and the Brander Matthews Dramatic Museum does indeed reflect that interest. In fact, during his first trip to France in 1867, Matthews, aged sixteen, bought a set of eleven Guignol hand puppets with wooden heads, together with, as Matthews put it, "the manuscript of half a dozen of ... little plays, written out (in all the license of his own simplified spelling) by the incomparable performer who was in charge of the leading Guignol in the Champs-Élysées in 1867" (282). Another set of hand puppets has more fragile papier-mâché heads, and these are quite personable and full of character. According to Shirley O'Donnol, who interviewed Dr. Henry Wells, then the curator of the Dramatic Museum, for a 1961 issue of *The Puppetry Journal,* the puppets are from "Anatole, who gave shows on the Champs-Élysées, and who personally turned over his papier-mâché actors (including a caricature of Sarah Bernhardt) as an outright gift to Brander Matthews, who was his friend" (13). If O'Donnol and Wells are correct, the connection is important because Émile Labelle, who took the name "Guignol Anatole," was one of the most important French puppeteers at the turn of the century, performing in outdoor booths in the gardens at the Champs-Élysées, and then in the park at Buttes-Chaumont. It was for the "celebrated Anatole," in fact, that Alfred Jarry wrote *Ubu sur le Butte,* a raucous two-act version of *Ubu Roi,* which Anatole performed in 1901 (Jarry 447).

The Dramatic Museum's French puppets also include over eighty marionettes "from 1870–1925," which, according to Jean Spaulding, were acquired by Brander Matthews in Paris in 1925, from "De Vere, a famous dealer over 80," who was "closing out his business" (McPharlin 26). These include a rather remarkable violin-playing marionette and other variety show characters, reflecting the succession of trick puppet acts that then characterized popular European marionette theater. Matthews, like many theater historians of the early twentieth century, was interested in the medieval roots of European theater, and four marionettes he acquired in Paris must have fascinated him because they represented characters from traditional puppet Nativity plays: Mary, Joseph and two Magi. According to the collection's records, the puppets' origins are in eighteenth-century Provence. Matthews would later write that "we need not be surprised when we discover that the marionette has long been allowed to appear in religious drama. Indeed, it appears probable that the very name *marionette* is directly derived from the name of the Virgin" (300).

A rather unusual puppet that Matthews acquired in France is a "ledge type" puppet "worked by strings" (McPharlin 26). O'Donnol describes this as a "very interesting French rod figure, dressed in the costume of an eighteenth-century gentleman, wigged and ruffled, ... made of carved wood (costume and all) and intricately jointed with a spring in the neck to control head action. Head and arms are operated by fine wires" (13). Although the collection's records date the puppet to the eighteenth century, the figure seems to reflect the style of the mechanical rod puppets invented by Henri Signoret, whose productions of classic literature were popular Parisian puppet attractions from 1888 to 1892.

Brander Matthews visited the *Chat Noir* cabaret on Montmartre during his visits to Paris. The *Chat Noir*, in addition to being an early nexus of bohemian social life in the last decades of the nineteenth century, was the site of some of the first intensive artistic experiments in puppet theater: epic shadow-theater spectacles that Matthews describes with a kind of enthralled awe in *A Book About the Theatre* (313). O'Donnol, basing her information on Henry Wells, wrote that "the famous *Chat Noir* café has contributed a cast of Parisian hand-puppets," to the Dramatic Museum, but this seems unusual, if not unlikely, because shadow puppets, not hand puppets, were far more typical of *Chat Noir* productions. This area of the collection also seems ripe for inspired research. In 1925, according to Spaulding, Matthews did collect a set of fifty shadow figures and set pieces from the Parisian dealer De Vere, together with a scenario and score for an eleven-piece string orchestra. These figures, including a man with a pickax, are not as sophisticated as those made by Caran d'Ache and Henri Rivière for the *Chat Noir*, and instead seem like characters from the popular French shadow show *The Broken Bridge*, which Matthews describes in *A Book About the Theater* (308–309).

Matthews seems not to have collected puppets from Germany or Spain, but he did accumulate a number of interesting English puppets. These include a seven-piece Punch and Judy set, apparently given to the Dramatic Museum by the British actor George Arliss in 1925. The Punch and Judy set is interesting because it marks the way English puppet theater reflected popular actors' theater: in addition to the venerable characters of Punch and Judy, the set's various antagonists include "Jim Crow the Negro," a character from nineteenth-century minstrel shows. A set of flat "jigging puppets" is also part of the English collection. These simple figures would likely have been operated by a single rod, or a string running through the torso, and made to dance to the accompaniment of the puppeteer's music. One of these figures, "The Magic Nigger," also reflects the era's fascination with race and ethnic archetypes. Two puppets remain from a five-piece set of English marionettes, the most popular form of nineteenth-century English puppet spectacle, as practiced by "Middleton's Royal Automaton Figures" or "Holden's Marionettes," both of which featured brief melodramas and astounding transformation puppets. The English marionettes in the Brander Matthews Collection include a milkmaid carrying a yoke and two pails.

Matthews also collected a substantial number of English toy theaters, the amateur home performance medium whose popularity extended across Europe and into the eastern United States. The Dramatic Museum appears to include two actual toy theater stages, and, in addition, a whole range of toy theater sheets, the mass-produced images of characters and scenery to be cut out, colored in, and mounted on cardboard for toy theater performances. The toy theater sheets (by such celebrated toy theater publishers as Skelt), as well as the truncated scripts which accompanied them, reflect quite clearly the popular successes of the London stage: melodramas such as *The Flying Dutchman*, *The Miller and His Men*, and William Thomas Moncrieff's exotic *Cataract of the Ganges; or the Rajah's Daughter*. The Brander Matthews toy theater collection also includes toy theater versions of the British pantomime tradition such as *Harlequin Whittington Lord Mayor of London*. This particular toy theater print might bear further scrutiny because, according to the collection's records, it is said to be designed "possibly by Blake." It is sometimes rumored that William Blake designed toy theater plates in early nineteenth-century London, and, although toy theater historian George Speaight has been skeptical about such hearsay, he has also written that such ascriptions remain "a possibility about which there is doubtless more to be said" (72).

Remo Bufano

The most surprising, and perhaps most valuable, aspect of the Brander Matthews Collection's modern puppets is a small collection of puppets by Remo Bufano (1894–1948), perhaps the most remarkable pioneer of modern puppet theater in the United States. Bufano had grown up in New York's Greenwich Village and was a part of the theatrical experiments of the Provincetown Playhouse and other elements of the Little

Theater Movement, which in the early twentieth century sought to create an American theater based on art, not commerce. But Bufano was
also influenced by the many Sicilian marionette companies that then
populated New York's Italian neighborhoods, and Bufano's innovative
work took inspiration from both traditional puppet theater and the avant-
garde. For example, there is a flexible, somewhat goofy, cloth-sewn green
dragon marionette for Bufano's own version of *Orlando Furioso*, which
he performed (in Italian and English) at numerous points in his career.
There is also Bufano's life-sized marionette of Don Quixote, from his
production of *El Retablo de Maese Pedro*, the operetta by modernist composer Manuel de Falla (based on the puppet episode from Cervantes's *Don
Quixote*), which the League of Composers produced at New York's Town
Hall in 1924. The production of *El Retablo de Maese Pedro* (in which,
incidentally, modernist stage designer Mordecai Gorelick worked as a
puppeteer) was not only the premiere of a new modernist music work,
but one of the earliest moments when Broadway audiences saw how puppets could create modern theater. The revelation of puppet theater's
potential made Bufano a celebrity (his caricature was featured in *The
New Yorker's* "Talk of the Town"), and his following productions were
highly anticipated. Bufano, like most puppeteers, kept his hand in children's theater with such productions as *Jack and the Beanstalk* (1926),
whose four-foot-tall Giant marionette is part of the Brander Matthews
Collection. Bufano made a real breakthrough for modern puppet theater
with his over-life-size marionettes for Stravinsky's opera *Oedipus Rex*,
which Robert Edmond Jones designed for the Metropolitan Opera in
1931. Two of Bufano's *Oedipus Rex* puppets are part of the collection: a
nine-foot-tall Jocasta and an equally large Oedipus (the rest of the set is
part of the Detroit Institute of Arts's puppet collection). The over-life-
size figures were operated above the floor of the Met, while the chorus
sang onstage underneath them, and puppeteers such as Bil Baird pulled
control ropes backstage. Such oversize puppets seemed to catch an audience's eyes, and Bufano continued in such a scale with a forty-foot-tall
expanding clown for Billy Rose's Broadway production of *Jumbo* in 1935.
The actual puppet for this production most likely no longer exists, but
Bufano's model for it resides in the Brander Matthews Collection.

    The puppet collection in the Brander Matthews Dramatic Museum
is modest, but it is of historical significance because the United States'
first professor of dramatic literature fully believed in the importance of

Oedipus and Jocasta puppets, over ten feet tall, built by Remo Bufano for Robert Edmond Jones's 1931 production of Stravinsky's *Oedipus Rex* at the Metropolitan Opera House in New York. (Photograph by Richard Termine.)

puppetry as a significant theatrical art form. In addition, particular elements of the collection offer historically salient examples of a wide variety of puppet forms throughout the world (although a good deal of research could be done to identify many of the puppets more clearly). Matthews also fully believed that the puppets in his Dramatic Museum would be most valuable if large numbers of people could see them. At present this aspect of Matthews's vision is almost nonexistent, but perhaps renewed interest in the collection and in puppetry in general will bring more people in contact with Matthews's puppets.

Works Cited

Craig, Edward Gordon. [Published under the name "Allen Carric."] "Fiddle-De-Dee, or Professor Brander Matthews's Infallible Receipt for Making an Omelette Without Eggs." *The Mask* 4 (1911–1912): 19–21.
Gilder, Rosamond, and George Freedley. *Theater Collections in Libraries and Museums.* New York: Theatre Arts, 1936.
Jarry, Alfred. "Ubu sur le Butte." *Tout Ubu.* Paris: Le Livre de Poche, 1962, 445–492.
Matthews, Brander. *A Book About the Theater.* New York: Charles Scribner's Sons, 1916.
Mazer, Sharon, and John Bell. "An Exhibition of Puppets and Masks from the Brander Matthews Dramatic Museum" (catalogue). Low Library Rotunda, Columbia University, February 1989.
McPharlin, Paul. "Marionettes in Museums in the United States." *Puppetry: A Yearbook of Puppets and Marionettes, 1930*, Ed. Paul McPharlin. Detroit: Inland Press, 1930, 25–27.
O'Donnol, Shirley. "Historians and Collectors: The Brander Matthews Collection." *Puppetry Journal* 12.5 (March-April 1961), 12–13.
Speaight, George. *The History of the English Toy Theatre.* London: Studio Vista, 1969.

The Ballard Institute and Museum of Puppetry Collection

PHYLLIS T. DIRCKS

The Ballard Institute and Museum of Puppetry, housed at the University of Connecticut, preserves, documents and displays thousands of puppets of all kinds: marionettes, glove puppets, rod puppets, shadow puppets and body puppets, as well as puppetry stage materials. Named for renowned puppeteer Frank Ballard, who founded the first undergraduate and graduate degree program in puppetry in the country, the Institute has become one of the three largest puppetry collections in the country and is expected to be named Connecticut's state museum of puppetry soon.

The origin of the Ballard Institute and Museum of Puppetry (BIMP) can be traced to 1987 when a small group of alumni established the Puppet Preservation Trust in order to find suitable storage space for the hundreds of puppets that had been created by Professor Ballard and his students for productions at the University of Connecticut. The puppets, which had been widely acclaimed and had garnered numerous awards for Ballard and his students, were beginning to deteriorate because of lack of personnel to care for them and inappropriate storage facilities. Realizing that each puppet had been meticulously researched and that each rendering was truly a work of art in itself, advocates argued for a permanent internationally recognized puppet museum. After years of dedicated volunteer work on the part of its supporters, such a museum opened its doors in April 1996 in an eight-room cottage near the University of Connecticut. Today, BIMP has expanded to four buildings, adding one to house the Institute library with its collections of papers and photographs, and two for puppet conservation and storage.

At the center of this dynamic activity has been Frank Ballard, a puppeteer wholly devoted to his art. Ballard believes that "a puppet is the artist's soul set free," and that belief created the vision that also brought puppetry to the classroom. Since the establishment of the puppetry program in 1962, Ballard's students have gone on to creative careers on stage and in movies and television. Today other universities, such as the University of Hawaii and the University of West Virginia, offer training in puppetry, but the University of Connecticut is the only university where a student can work at three different degree levels: B.F.A., M.A., or M.F.A., and it is the largest puppet arts program in the English-speaking

An exhibition room at BIMP.

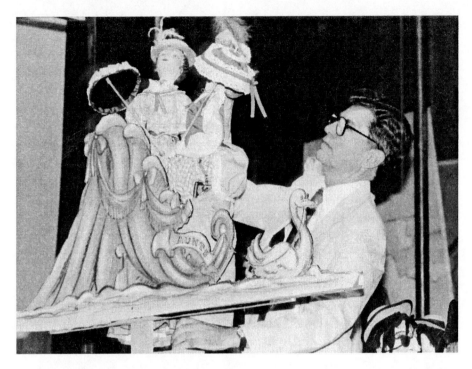

Frank Ballard adjusting puppets of *H.M.S. Pinafore*, 1989. (Courtesy the Ballard Institute and Museum of Puppetry.)

world. In a couple of basement dormitory rooms crammed with molds, masks, tools and puppets-in-progress, graduate and undergraduate students learn to design, build, and manipulate puppets.

Ballard, a charming and gracious man who is now retired, has always challenged his students to stage large and spectacular productions, unlike the small-scale productions that usually identify the work of students. As Ballard recently told me, "Due to economic restrictions, the majority of puppet productions in this country are performed by small companies consisting of two or three puppeteers. Productions at the University of Connecticut are much larger for three reasons: to capitalize on the puppet's flair for the theatrical, to show the public that puppet theater productions don't have to be modest, and to give as many of our students as possible the rare opportunity to perform on a grand scale." Indeed, Ballard has been a superb role model. For his 1975 production of *Kismet,* Ballard engaged twenty-seven student puppeteers, while another eighteen student stagehands shifted sets and operated the lights

The Caliph and Princess Samaris from *Kismet*, 1975. (Courtesy the Ballard
Institute and Museum of Puppetry.)

and sound equipment. For this production, Ballard created two hundred fifty-three puppets. His favorite scene from that play is the wedding procession; the grand entourage, led by the Caliph on his white horse, featured dancing girls, standard bearers, musicians, lantern carriers, the royal white elephant, monkeys and peacocks preceding a long line of silvery women carrying a tinsel garland. Another hugely successful production was *H.M.S. Pinafore* in 1989; for this, he created a chorus of sisters and cousins and aunts in hand-sewn Victorian outfits, a shipload of sailors in their regulation white shirts and straw hats, an elaborately costumed, monocled old Sir Joseph Porter and a chorus of fish puppets peering out of portholes. Ballard modestly notes that his many successes have been peppered with occasional problems and mishaps. Perhaps his most notable crisis occurred during a performance of *Carmen* when Don José's knife

became stuck in his sash during the stabbing scene. The vigorous tugs of the anxious student puppeteer caused the puppet to fly into the air feet first before his encounter with Carmen. One reviewer wryly noted that this was the first time he had seen Don José stomp Carmen to death.

Ballard was succeeded as head of the puppetry arts program at the University of Connecticut by Bart Roccoberton, his one-time student, who is now widely recognized as a master puppeteer. Roccoberton established and has directed the Institute of Professional Puppetry Arts at the O'Neill Theatre Center in New London, Connecticut, and has toured with the Pande-

Hajj, the Beggar from *Kismet*, 1975. (Courtesy the Ballard Institute and Museum of Puppetry.)

monium Puppets, a puppet company that he founded. He has
created and performed characters for television programs, New
York theater productions and has
worked extensively in China.
When pressed, Roccoberton will
admit that he led China into
the world puppet organization.
"When I went to China in January [1999] to give a small seminar, I arrived to find the entire
leadership of Chinese puppetry
there for my seminar."

In a recent interview, Ballard told me that the BIMP collection, which developed from
his own vast assemblage of puppets, now includes several thousand puppets. The collection is
comprised of marionettes, masks,
and hand, finger, shadow, rod
and body puppets, as well as life-
size puppets. The BIMP puppets
document puppet activity in
many cultures and periods, from

Captain Corcoran on bicycle, from *H.M.S.
Pinafore*, 1989. (Courtesy the Ballard
Institute and Museum of Puppetry.)

Asia to the Americas and from the eighteenth century to the present. The
BIMP collection includes four hundred twenty-seven puppets created by
Paul McPharlin, a famed early twentieth-century puppet artist, and it
offers a rich variety of puppet specimens, ranging from rare tiny Floren-
tine Fabrini porcelain marionettes to one of Jim Henson's Muppets, the
stage manager, Scooter.

These days Ballard is excited about the acquisition of the puppets
of Rufus and Margo Rose, popular puppeteers from the 1930s through
the 1970s, who were once billed as "America's foremost artists of the Marionette Theater." Thus far BIMP has accessioned 195 puppets, not quite
half of the collection. The Rose acquisition also includes props, correspondence and maps of the nationwide tours taken by the Roses. Another

Various characters from *H.M.S. Pinafore*, 1989. (Courtesy the Ballard Institute and Museum of Puppetry.)

recent acquisition is the intricate puppetry of Sidney Chrysler, consisting of three-inch puppets fabricated from pipe cleaners and crepe paper, with heads crafted of popcorn covered with modeling paste. The Chrysler collection includes puppets from nine operatic productions, including *Tosca, The Marriage of Figaro* and *La Traviata*. A brand-new acquisition is the puppetry of Leonard Suib, well known to New Yorkers for his work in the puppet theater in Central Park. This collection, like the Rose acquisition, includes stage props and lights.

BIMP is also proud of acquiring Marjorie Batchelder's production materials for Aristophanes' *The Birds,* including notes, designs, and music. Legendary early twentieth-century New York puppeteer Tony Sarg is also well represented at BIMP; the holdings include the Fishfootman from *Alice in Wonderland* and Friday from *Robinson Crusoe.* And the Tony Sarg Archive containing his papers and correspondence offers extensive research possibilities to the student of puppetry. BIMP also holds other notable correspondence, including that of composer Foreman Brown, who was one of the three founders of the Turnabout Theatre for Puppetry in Los Angeles; and personal letters of Eugene O'Neill to Jero Magon, a modernist puppeteer who undertook a puppet production of *The Emperor Jones* in 1933 and *Marco Millions* in 1938, as well as Magon's

Set and puppets from *Tosca*. (The Chrysler Collection. Courtesy the Ballard Institute and Museum of Puppetry.)

designs and posters. Among the museum's rare jewels is a note from George Bernard Shaw to Rufus Rose concerning the staging of Shaw's puppet play, *Shakes Versus Shaw.*

The Ballard Puppets

Since the puppets of Frank Ballard, which include marionettes, hand puppets, hand and rod puppets, rod puppets, papier-mâché masks, mouth and body puppets, and shadow puppets, form the basis of the BIMP collection, I list here some of the most characteristic pieces in Ballard's seminal contributions to the collection.

Marionettes

Samson. 18 in., white pine, *Samson and Delilah*, 1969.
King of Clover. 30 in., styrofoam and papier-mâché, *The Love for Three Oranges*, 1970.

Queen of the Night. 30 in.,
    neoprene and white pine,
    The Magic Flute, 1986.
Josephine on Bicycle. 30 in.,
    neoprene, *H.M.S. Pina-
    fore,* 1989.
Captain Corcoran on Bicycle.
    30 in., neoprene, *H.M.S.
    Pinafore,* 1989.
Sir Joseph. 30 in., neoprene,
    H.M.S. Pinafore, 1989.
Sir Joseph on Bicycle. 30 in.,
    neoprene, *H.M.S. Pina-
    fore,* 1989.
Sir Joseph on Bell. 30 in., neo-
    prene, *H.M.S. Pinafore,*
    1989.

Princess from *The Love for Three Oranges,*
1970. (Courtesy the Ballard Institute and
Museum of Puppetry.)

Hand and Rod Puppets

Hajj the Beggar. 24 in., latex
    rubber, *Kismet,* 1975.
The Imam. 24 in., latex rub-
    ber, *Kismet,* 1975.
The Caliph. 24 in., latex rubber, *Kismet,* 1975.
Czar Dodon. 72 in., celastic, *The Golden Cockerel,* 1977.
The Queen. 72 in., celastic, *The Golden Cockerel,* 1977.

Rod Puppets

Princess Samaris. 24 in., latex rubber, *Kismet,* 1975.
Pooh-Bah. 48 in., plastic wood and celastic, *The Mikado,* 1968.
Church Procession. Six puppets, each 30 in., styrofoam and cloth,
    Petrouchka, 1971.
Kangaroo. 36 in., cloth, *The Carnival of Animals,* 1971.
Lion. 36 in., cloth, *The Carnival of Animals,* 1971.
Rhinoceros. 36 in., cloth, *The Carnival of Animals,* 1971.
Hippopotamus. 36 in., cloth, *The Carnival of Animals,* 1971.

Body Puppets

Happiness of Being Rich. 36 in., mouth and body puppet, foam rubber, *The Blue Bird*, 1984.

Happiness of Satisfied Vanity. 36 in., mouth and body puppet, foam rubber, *The Blue Bird*, 1984.

Happiness of Drinking-More-Than-Necessary. 36 in., mouth and body puppet, foam rubber, *The Blue Bird*, 1984.

Happiness of Eating-More-Than-Necessary. 36 in., mouth and body puppet, foam rubber, *The Blue Bird*, 1984.

Happiness of Understanding Nothing. 36 in., mouth and body puppet, foam rubber, *The Blue Bird*, 1984.

Happiness of Hearing Nothing. 36 in., mouth and body puppet, foam rubber, *The Blue Bird*, 1984.

Happiness of Doing Nothing. 36 in., mouth and body puppet, foam rubber, *The Blue Bird*, 1984.

Happiness of Sleeping-More-Than-Necessary. 36 in., mouth and body puppet, foam rubber, *The Blue Bird*, 1984.

Hand Puppets

Horrible Henry. 18 in., plastic wood, *Carnival*, 1966.

Penguins. Three puppets, 18 in. each, papier-mâché and cloth, *Babes in Toyland*, 1982.

Masks

Sugar. Papier-mâché, *The Blue Bird*, 1984.

Bread. Papier-mâché, *The Blue Bird*, 1984.

Milk. Papier-mâché, *The Blue Bird*, 1984.

Fire. Papier-mâché, *The Blue Bird*, 1984.

Water. Papier-mâché, *The Blue Bird*, 1984.

Light. Papier-mâché, *The Blue Bird*, 1984.

Night. Papier-mâché, *The Blue Bird*, 1984.

Paul Mcpharlin and Puppetry at the Detroit Institute of Arts

John Bell

Puppetry — the telling of stories in theatrical or ritual events combining humans and pieces of the surrounding physical world — is arguably
the most widespread form of performance. Puppets can be traced as far
back as ancient Egypt, Greece, and Rome and are found today in cultures worldwide, across the Americas, Europe, Africa, and Asia. The task
of making this ancient art of puppetry work in the modern era is an
ongoing endeavor. In the twentieth century puppeteers sought to expand
the role of puppet theater in modern society in many different directions:
as a means of making popular entertainment, as art theater, as an educational tool, and as a means of persuasion. At different times and places
puppeteers pursued various combinations of these goals, making "serious" drama, children's theater, promotional shows, commercials, political spectacle, films, and television shows.

At the turn of the twenty-first century, a renaissance of puppet theater appears to be underway. In the United States during the 1990s, a
theatrical production of Disney's *The Lion King* showed that a mask and
puppet spectacle could become a runaway hit on Broadway, and the Jim

---

The text of this chapter has been excerpted from John Bell's Strings, Hands, Shadows: A Modern Puppet History *(Detroit Institute of the Arts, 2000), pp. 7–11, 53–58, 66–75, 107.*

Henson Foundation's series of biannual International Festivals of Puppet Theater began to expose new audiences to the richness and variety of innovative theater based on puppetry. Generations of children had grown up watching and learning from Jim Henson's Muppets on television, and a new appreciation of puppetry as a theater capable of conveying profound artistic, social, and political ideas, stories, and emotions had developed from the influence of Peter Schumann's Bread and Puppet Theater, which had begun in the 1960s. But the appearance of a puppet renaissance is somewhat deceptive, for puppetry is an art that sees fit to renew itself continually, as new generations of performers, sculptors, painters, writers, and audiences discover the possibilities of playing with material objects in performance. There is an uncanny similarity, in fact, between sentiments expressed in the 1920s and the current sense of a puppet revival. In 1926 puppeteer Remo Bufano, flush from the success of his own triumphs with puppet theater on Broadway, predicted a "renaissance of the marionette" in American theater. In fact, Bufano's prediction was quite correct, and the 1920s puppet renaissance was the first in a series of modern discoveries of the possibilities of puppet theater. Our sense of the nature of those first modern puppet renaissances is valuable for our sense of the current one.

A fine record of this perpetual rebirth is the puppet collection at the Detroit Institute of Arts, based largely on the accumulation of puppets and related materials put together by Paul McPharlin during the years in which he was a major participant in the first puppet revival. The museum's collection has continued to grow as further elements were added during the more than fifty years since McPharlin's death. The collection lays out clearly and in rich detail the complex paths followed by puppeteers in the twentieth century as they redefined traditional forms from Europe and around the globe in order to reflect the changes brought about by the modern world.

McPharlin was more than an interested observer of the puppet phenomenon — in fact, he was a major player in its development and in the first half of the twentieth century perhaps the most important single force in establishing puppet theater's legitimacy and continuing presence in American culture. Like many puppeteers, he was a multi-talented individual: not only a performer, but a designer and builder as well. He was also a writer, editor, historian, curator, and organizer. From the moment he discovered puppets as a college student at Columbia University, to his untimely death from brain cancer in 1948 at the age of forty-four, McPharlin was a tireless proselytizer for the cultural importance of puppet theater, not only as a viable means of making contemporary theater but as a world-wide cultural treasure. Together with Marjorie Batchelder, another puppet enthusiast who was his long-time friend and colleague, and whom he married the year before his death, McPharlin articulated his vision of the modern importance of puppet theater. He published books and articles; organized exhibits, conferences, and festivals; helped found the Puppeteers of America; and above all built and performed puppet shows of remarkable artistic integrity and beauty.

McPharlin's collection, and the pieces added later, stand as one of the United States' important physical records of the development of puppetry worldwide. But perhaps even more than that, the collection stands as a remarkable testament to the ingenuity and inspired skill hundreds of people applied to the task of making beautiful, comic, serious, and mostly humble theater out of wood, paper, cloth, metal, and plastic, as well as their own bodies and voices. That work, often by little-known or anonymous women and men, can still inspire us, as it so obviously inspired McPharlin and Batchelder.

Innovations of Puppet Modernism

The birth of modern American puppet theater dates to the early twentieth century. The sense that the twentieth century would redefine the concept of "modern" had its roots in European cultural currents of the nineteenth century, which sought to temper the seemingly inexorable development of the West as an industrial, urban society based on realism, rationalism, and capitalism. There was a search for and idealization of traces of the non-rational, the non-realistic, the non-western, and the pre-industrial as a kind of spiritual salve for the inexorable hardness of the encroaching machine age. Beginning with the Romantics in the early 1800s, who saw emotion and intuition as the equal of reason; continuing through such developments as the Arts and Crafts Movement, which championed the role of traditional crafts in an age of industrial design; and culminating with the late-nineteenth century Symbolists, who emphasized interior states of mind over naturalism; writers, philosophers, and artists began to respond to the modern age with artistic

methods and theories that inevitably (and perhaps contradictorily) combined technological achievements with ancient aesthetics. Puppet theater was central to such experiments, from Heinrich von Kleist's
metaphysical treatise *On the Marionette Theater* in 1810 to Alfred Jarry's
outrageous assertions (with his 1896 play *Ubu Roi*) that puppetry should
be the model for all modern theater. Jarry was not alone in his turn-of-
the-century rediscovery of puppet theater. Maurice Maeterlinck, Arthur
Schnitzler, William Butler Yeats, Hugo von Hofmannsthal, Paul Claudel,
and other Symbolist playwrights also saw a kind of artistic truth in the
physicality of marionettes and masks — especially in the face of the
astounding realism becoming possible through photography and film.

The western rediscovery of puppet theater in the early twentieth
century — or its "revival" as Paul McPharlin put it — began in Europe
and involved a number of factors: a newfound valuation of the traditionally low-culture art of European puppet theater; an appreciation of
Asian, African, and Native American puppet performance as models for
western artists; a renewed sense of puppet theater not only as commercial entertainment but as a cultural, spiritual, and educational element;
and a sense that these older practices and purposes of puppet theater
could be pragmatically combined with any machine age innovations yet
to come. This is not to say that all modernist puppeteers agreed with
each other about what twentieth-century puppet theater should be; but
they all had a sense of new and exciting possibilities for this centuries-
old art form.

The primary European exponent of modern puppet theater as a
legitimate art form equal or superior to actors' theater was the English
artist, actor, director, and writer Edward Gordon Craig. Craig was not
unusual in proposing a romantic alternative to the mass, industrialized
culture developing across western Europe and (especially) in the United
States, but he was a bit uncommon in espousing non-realistic, ritualized
performance with masks and puppets as the "theater of the future."

Throughout the early twentieth century, a succession of avant-garde
movements in different European countries — Futurism, Expressionism,
Dada, Constructivism, the Bauhaus — all followed Symbolism's effort to
define modern culture specifically through art and performance. As modern industrial societies created that culture, with or without those movements' assistance, the United States was a constant image of what
modernity looked like. So it is only fitting that American puppet theater

of the early twentieth century fulfilled a variety of modernist ambitions, and that Paul McPharlin, a puppeteer from the United States's most important industrial city, Detroit, would be at the center of that modernism.

Puppet theater did not re-emerge simply in the arena of educated western artists. Equally modern were the ways in which highly traditional popular art forms adapted themselves to and reflected change in the societies in which they existed. After all, an ability to adapt to changing circumstances was a necessary survival method for such living art forms. We have seen how nineteenth-century dress and machines could be reflected in the apparently rigid and centuries-old image system of Chinese shadow theater. Similar reflections of modern change could be found in the appearance of western clothing on Javanese *wayang golek* puppets. The McPharlin Collection also has some interesting examples of Japanese hand puppets created by K. Udriyama in the 1930s. These puppets, although they represent traditional characters, are created in a form and style different from the traditional design aesthetics of Japanese puppet forms of *Bunraku* and rod puppet theater — almost as if they reflected the aesthetics of Western realism.

A different kind of adaptation occurred throughout Europe in the early decades of the century as artists turned to traditional European puppet forms in order to pursue new purposes. This was the case in Russia, after the 1917 Revolution, which energized a generation of modern Russian artists to apply the radical aesthetics of Futurism and Constructivism to the creation of a modern revolutionary society. Toward this end young artists turned to the traditions of Petrushka hand puppet theater, first as a means of spreading the revolution, and later as a method of mass education. The recalcitrant underdog Petrushka was a hero of popular theater, a working-class trickster in continual conflict with authority — a perfect revolutionary, it would seem.

A "Red Petrushka" collective began in 1927; the "Red Army Petrushka Group" started the next year, and various other Petrushka companies sprang up in factory clubs. All of these groups, according to a Soviet historian, "carried out idiosyncratic and extremely useful educational work in schools, clubs, and pioneer camps." The use of traditional Russian puppet theater for education and propaganda was relatively well known in the United States, in part because of McPharlin's 1935 English translation of *The Adventures of a Russian Puppet Theatre* by Nina

Efimova. Efimova was a visual artist who, together with her architect husband Ivan Efimov, adapted the techniques of the fairground Petrushka theaters to perform short hand-puppet plays like *How a Peasant Fed Two Generals* in factories, clubs, libraries, theaters, barns, barracks, union halls, railroad stations, parks, business co-operatives, and hospitals in provinces as well as in big cities. One of the most important aspects of the Red Petrushka theaters is that the title character's eternal problem with any authority soon led the Soviet state to suppress the rebellious and anarchic Petrushka in favor of a more benign and bland Petrushka, whose main purpose was to educate children. This conception of the form and purpose of puppet theater came to epitomize the active state-supported puppet theater in Eastern Bloc countries during the Cold War, but it also had clear parallels in children's-oriented puppet theater in the West, which became equally devoted to the tasks of education and advertising — the western version of propaganda.

Puppet Visionaries and the New World

In the first decade of the new century, a California painter, Michael Carmichael Carr, and his Dutch wife worked with Edward Gordon Craig in Italy, as Craig experimented with new staging and lighting designs. Carr built scale-model sets for Craig, and his wife translated Dutch documentations of Javanese *wayang* performance, which texts Craig would later use in his magazines *The Mask* and *The Marionette.* Carr built a number of unpainted papier-mâché marionettes for Craig that show a typically modern combination of interests: abstract geometrical form (in the torso and limbs) and Asian design motifs (in the head and headdress). Of course, the whole idea that "experiments" in some kind of scientific method might be conducted in puppet or any other type of theater was also a modern concept. Carr later made more such puppets for Cleveland puppeteer Helen Haiman Joseph, who popularized Craig's concepts of puppet theater in her 1920 *Book of Marionettes.*

In a way, the strongest impression Craig's theater ideas made in the United States was in the Midwest. Carr seems to have worked there after his experience in Italy, and scenic designer Samuel Hume, an early and important Craig collaborator, pursued his own work in Detroit upon his return from abroad. McPharlin himself corresponded with Craig with some frequency and was clearly inspired by the letters Craig sent him. These included Craig's idealized expectations for puppet theater, as articulated in a 1933 letter to McPharlin: "Puppetry is a true art — the true art of the theatre-in-little, theatricals having got their deserts and become a false kind of photography enlarged."

The rediscovery of puppet theater represented an aspect of artistic regeneration for modern European artists and audiences, and in the Craig/Carr connection it found open and receptive ears in the New World. But puppet modernism meant something quite different in the United States, where the oldest theater traditions were Native American performance forms, the commercial showmanship of melodrama, circus, minstrelsy, and vaudeville, and the quasi-underground array of African-American performance forms of dance, music, and theater. Most of the Americans involved in American puppet modernism were not yet ready to attempt an understanding of Native American culture; continued to see African-American forms through the haze of nineteenth-century racism and paternalism; and felt ambivalent about commercial theater traditions focused solely on entertainment and the bottom line of economic success. Inspired by the stirring (and often utopian) ideals of the European avant-garde, modernist American puppeteers wanted to create new forms of puppet theater that would answer social, political, educational, and economic needs in the twentieth-century democracy of the United States. In other words, they wanted to create modern puppet theater as an art form fully integrated into American society. The shift, as puppeteer Bil Baird put it, was from the "traditionalism" and "vaudeville tricks" of the "wandering showmen" to "a new premise — that the best puppetry derived from the highest artistic and creative effort."

The elevated and somewhat ambiguous goals Baird defines could obviously be interpreted a number of different ways, and they were. Modernist American puppeteers in the early twentieth century engaged in a wide variety of significant cultural projects. Although they saw puppet theater's value as a highly entertaining and effective medium of show business, they also considered it a serious art form suitable for the performance of classic dramatic texts of high cultural value. It was also seen as a means of enriching different forms of education, therapy, and recreation; and as a means of engaging in the persuasive performance discourses of politics or advertising products to a growing consumer society. Some American puppeteers in the early twentieth century focused on one or two particular aspects of these wide-ranging goals, while others sought to explore the full range of possibilities now apparently available to them. Paul McPharlin termed this nexus of new puppet theater methods "the artistic puppetry revival," and wrote that "by 1915 American amateurs were thinking seriously of the aesthetic and educative possibilities of puppetry." By 1920, he continued, "they had brought about a revival of puppetry as an artistic medium and explored new applications for it."

Puppet Modernism in the Midwest

While New York City was a whirling center of commerce, art, and education, the Midwest persisted as a center for making, thinking about, and writing on puppet theater as a modern cultural treasure. A marker of this high-mindedness is the effect of Edward Gordon Craig's romantic idealism on Michael Carmichael Carr, Samuel J. Hume, Ellen Van Volkenburg, Helen Haiman Joseph, and Paul McPharlin, who contributed articles to Craig's journal *The Mask*. But the interest in puppetry as high culture did not at all mean that midwestern puppeteers remained aloof from advertising, publicity, and other forms of commercial life in Chicago, Detroit, Cleveland, and other cities. Successful professional puppet companies grew and prospered there, and puppeteers consistently found outlets for their work in a variety of commercial contexts. However, the high ideals proposed by Little Theater institutions in the century's second decade continued in the Midwest through the creation of puppet shows as art theater; through work in all levels of the region's educational system and in community theaters focused on puppet theater; and, above all, in McPharlin's dynamic writing, organizing, and theater-making.

Although the Chicago Little Theater's development of modern puppet art theater basically ended with World War I — after which director Ellen Van Volkenburg moved to the West Coast — Helen Haiman Joseph of the Cleveland Playhouse intensified her puppet work from the twenties onward. She started her own professional puppet company in 1925 and created over fourteen different productions for it, ranging from *Robin Hood and His Merry Men* to *The Life and Death of Doctor Faustus*. According to Paul McPharlin, by 1942 she had nine troupes performing in all parts of the United States. In addition, the resourceful Joseph developed a commercial line of puppets and puppet-building kits for mass distribution.

Paul McPharlin was clearly the most prolific figure in the midwestern puppetry scene; he was active in all areas of its development, and continually built, performed, wrote, and organized for the development of modern puppet performance. Born in Detroit in 1903, McPharlin played with traditional English toy theaters in his youth, and as an undergraduate at Columbia University he studied the international puppet collection amassed by Professor Brander Matthews and took part in puppet productions of French farces directed by a Columbia faculty member, Mathurin Dondo. But his work as a puppeteer began to blossom when he returned to the Midwest after graduation. He formed a "Marionette Fellowship," first in Evanston, Illinois, and then in Detroit, in order to support his puppet shows.

From the outset, McPharlin's puppet productions show the range of styles and subject matters typical of modernist puppet art theater. Although his first Marionette Fellowship production was Shakespeare's *Taming of the Shrew* (1928), McPharlin quickly turned to more exotic materials. His 1929 *Drum Dance* was an experiment in Chinese-style shadow theater, using the script of a traditional Chinese shadow play by Tsou Ku Chan Mien, which McPharlin had translated from Berthold Laufer's 1915 collection *Chinesiche Schattenspiele (Chinese Shadowplays)*. In *Drum Dance*, a prince's jealous wife and his concubine compete for his attention by attempting to dance flawlessly on a set of drums, but the wife turns out to be a witch who uses her magic powers to defeat the concubine. Instead of traditional leather puppets, McPharlin built lacquer-painted celluloid puppets and sets that reflected both Chinese design motifs and McPharlin's own sense of modernist minimalism. Some of the advice McPharlin gave on constructing such shadow puppets (in his 1938 edition of Benjamin March's *Chinese Shadow-figure Plays and Their Making*) is an interesting example of practical, inventive modern methods of approaching an ancient puppet tradition. After describing how to construct celluloid shadow figures, McPharlin wrote: "For control sticks umbrella rods are light and strong. They have an eye at one end through which they may be attached with tough cord to holes bored in the hands, necks or feet of the figures. Attach a small battery clip at the end of the rod, rivet leather tabs to the figures where they are to be supported, and catch the tab in the clip for manipulation." It is important to note that

McPharlin's approach to Chinese puppet theater was quite novel — even revolutionary — especially in comparison to the nineteenth-century European and American marionette traditions of presenting Chinese characters as clownish circus oddities. McPharlin, benefiting from the increasing volume of new scholarship on Asian theater, took a Chinese play and attempted to do it justice, not by using traditional Chinese shadow puppets, but by building his own in a manner that at once respected Chinese techniques and styles but also translated them into a modern American idiom.

Also in 1929 McPharlin produced *Noël, or the Mystery of the Nativity*, a medieval-style Christmas play written in 1888 by Maurice Bouchor for Henri Signoret's rod-puppet theater in Paris, an important early example of European puppet art theater. Again, McPharlin translated the text into English, and as in *Drum Dance* he employed a relatively novel puppet technique for the American puppet stage: rod puppets. McPharlin's finely crafted *Noël* rod puppets show his talents as a sculptor and painter. The Three Kings are quite grand figures realized in a stylized modernist aesthetic, but the shepherds and holy family are, as Bouchor suggested in his planscript, realistic figures in contemporary dress, in this case rural midwestern farmers of the 1920s. McPharlin's sculptures succeed as puppets because their effectiveness can only be felt by viewing them from a variety of angles; in other words, they are only fully completed by movement. In addition to using the relatively uncommon technique of rod puppets for *Noël*, McPharlin also used a procession of European-style shadow figures to represent the caravan of animals on which the Three Kings rode. This combination of rod puppets and shadow puppets, like the puppets from *Drum Dance*, marked a real change from the European-style marionettes that had dominated American puppetry. McPharlin was initiating a new sense of world puppet-theater consciousness that would come to dominate western puppet theater as the century progressed.

McPharlin, however, did not at all turn his back on the European puppet traditions, which had until then defined American puppet theater. His version of Hans Christian Andersen's *Chinese Nightingale*, also from 1929, was a familiar European fairy tale performed in a familiar marionette style. This was also the form he used for *Mozart in Paris*, an eighteenth-century variety show and period piece, which McPharlin's Marionette Fellowship performed at the Detroit Institute of Arts in 1934.

The production combined marionette scenes, featuring Mozart and a female pupil, with a period ballet, *Les Petits Riens*, and Mozart's 1768 pastoral operetta for puppets, *Bastien and Bastienne*. The latter piece featured the title characters, two shepherds, and Colas, a village magician who brings them together.

Like Remo Bufano's production of *The Little King*, McPharlin's marionette version of *Krazy Kat* (1930) took its inspiration from mass-media, in this case, George Herriman's celebrated comic strip of the same name. Also similar to that of Bufano, McPharlin's eclectic repertoire grew to include a shadow-figure Purimspiel, in this case written by puppeteer and novelist Meyer Levin in 1932. McPharlin also created a 1934 production of *Dr. Faust,* again using shadow puppets as well as marionettes. He also created "an advertising show for Old English Floor Wax" with hand puppets in 1936, and such oddities as *Lincoln and the Pig*, a comment on the Emancipation Proclamation performed with marionettes by the Detroit Fellowship in 1934, which has surprisingly racist overtones. McPharlin's 1936 *Punch's Circus* was a hand- and rod-puppet variety show featuring such familiar characters as a Ringmaster, and a stereotyped Chinaman, but also an almost futuristically modern goggled motorcycle Policeman.

Mozart and his pupil, 1930–1932, Paul McPharlin. Gift of Mr. and Mrs. W. H. J. McPharlin and Marjorie Batchelder McPharlin. (Photograph © 2000, The Detroit Institute of Arts.)

Motorcycle policeman, ringmaster, Punch, 1936; created by Paul McPharlin.
Gifts of Mr. and Mrs. W. H. J. McPharlin and Marjorie Batchelder McPharlin.
(Photograph © 2000, The Detroit Institute of Arts.)

McPharlin was the State Supervisor of the Michigan Arts and Craft Project of the WPA from 1941 to 1942, and this work was followed by two years of wartime service with the Army Air Force in Mississippi. In addition to designing posters and literature for the troops on the air base, McPharlin also made a "Rookie Joe" marionette for camp show entertainment and safety instruction.

Part of McPharlin's innovative approach to puppet performance was the way he presented his shows. While he took part in the growing demand for school performances and productions for businesses, McPharlin was also quite concerned with defining puppet theater as relatively high culture. His introduction of puppet classes at Wayne University (now Wayne State University) in Detroit from 1931 to 1938 helped define puppet theater as an intellectually valuable cultural resource. And the Marionette Fellowship itself (as the word "fellowship" suggests) was something more than a simple puppet company. Instead, it reflected McPharlin's desire to combine the integrity and artistry of Old World craft traditions with the mass-production style of modern life so prominent in Detroit. For McPharlin, the puppet productions of the Fellowship were an example of what he once termed "handicraft in the Machine Age"—the possibility that artistic craftsmanship could not only survive in the twentieth century but thrive, despite the omnipresence of manufacturing and machines. This was something McPharlin himself reflected not only in his continuing work in puppet theater but also in his active work in graphic design, typography, and in his designs for shops, storefronts, and manufactured products.

Marjorie Batchelder, McPharlin's friend, partner, and — ultimately — wife, first became interested in puppet theater at the age of twenty-one, when she was asked to paint sets for a marionette production of *Bluebeard* at a summer art camp in western Massachusetts. Batchelder's involvement only increased, and she pursued puppet theater in the various academic environments central to her later work. Her first performances were in 1931, with students at Florida State College for Women, and her later work grew out of her activities at Ohio State University. This included a marionette production of Aristophanes' *The Birds*, which she created for her Master of Arts degree in 1934. She later formed a company, Marjorie Batchelder's Puppet Players, which performed her puppet productions on tours throughout Ohio and surrounding midwestern states.

Batchelder's 1937 production of Maurice Maeterlinck's *Death of Tintagiles*, besides acknowledging the most prominent European playwright for puppet art theater, shows Batchelder's abiding interest in rod puppets. A relatively novel puppet technique in the United States, rod puppets came to characterize the wide-ranging interests of twentieth-century puppet theater. In a 1936 essay on rod puppets, Batchelder noted their broad cultural history, ranging from Chinese, Javanese, and European traditions to such modern applications as Bufano's giant puppets for *Oedipus Rex*, contemporary parading figures used in urban processions, and McPharlin's *Noël*. The design of Batchelder's wooden rod puppets for *Death of Tintagiles* is closer to Javanese *wayang golek* than to popular European traditions, an interesting indication of the international character modern puppetry was coming to assume. Her continuing connection to puppet art theater led her to produce puppet plays by Edward Gordon Craig and Argentinian puppeteer Javier Villafañe, and her persistent exploration of rod puppetry led to such productions as *Baba Yaga*,

Cleopatra, 1940, Martin T. Stevens. Gift of the artist. (Photograph © 2000 The Detroit Institute of Arts.)

created in 1947 for the Columbus Community Theater in Ohio. That was the same year her book *Rod-Puppets and the Human Theater* appeared; it is still considered a central resource on this particular puppet form.

Other midwestern puppeteers included Martin and Olga Stevens of Middlebury, Indiana, who beginning in 1934 developed a repertoire of local and nationwide touring shows that focused primarily on adult audiences. This was unlike most companies, where a desire to reach all ages was tempered by the consistent market demand for children's shows — puppetry having been recognized as an admirable means of entertaining and educating school-age audiences. Although the Stevenses experimented with rod puppets and hand puppets, they focused on marionettes for such shows as *Joan of Arc* (1937) and *Cleopatra* (1940), as well as a Nativity and a Passion Play, straightforwardly religious plays, which they performed annually beginning in 1935. In their prime the Stevenses

Puppets developed into an organization of eight different troupes, and they worked with such puppeteers as Marjorie Batchelder and Rufus Rose. In 1960 the Stevenses created a puppet theater correspondence course, which was popular for over two decades. Romaine and Ellen Proctor of Springfield, Illinois, started making puppet shows with their children in the 1920s but soon developed their work into a professional company performing children's shows, advertisements, and promotional programs. The Proctor Puppets' repertoire in general avoided the high-art aspirations of McPharlin and Batchelder, but the Proctors found regular and consistent audiences for their work.

They converted a Springfield movie house into a puppet theater in 1935, and their regular touring schedule included health education shows at state fairs in Iowa, Illinois, and Indiana. The backdrops and marionettes for *Jack and the Beanstalk* offer an indication of what a typical touring show of the period looked like, with straightforward, colorful props and puppets telling an enthralling fairy tale.

Puppet theater has always been a quirky, mysterious, often subversive, and sometimes peripheral art form, and the fact that it has had to constantly reinvent itself in order to survive is probably a good thing. Its capacity for survival will be a primary resource for its work in the twenty-first century.

The Bil Baird World of Puppets at the Charles H. MacNider Museum

RICHARD LEET

If they weren't "blowin' their horns," they were "pulling lots of strings" in Mason City, Iowa, the River City of Meredith Willson's acclaimed musical, *The Music Man*. That's right, there was trouble of the cultural variety brewing in this modest-sized north Iowa city during the teen years of the twentieth century, and it wasn't all in the pool hall.

A couple of guys, one a little older than the other, were stretching their creative muscles and preparing to take on the world in their related, but different, chosen fields. One, Meredith Willson (1902–1984), became one of America's foremost musicians and composers. The other, Bil ("with one 'L' because nobody ever pronounced the second one anyway!") Baird (1904–1987), was for over a quarter of a century one of the best pup-peteers in the country, if not the best. The topic of conversation for this article is centered on the younger "fella," Baird.

Before reading much further, note that I do not apologize for start-ing off and possibly staying in a lighthearted vein because I know that if this story is told in too serious a manner the man that it is about might not be smiling down on me. Bil Baird liked to have fun, always! That's not a bad trait for a performer, and a very creative one, at that.

In a monograph I authored, which the Charles H. MacNider Museum published in 1988 in conjunction with its "Bil Baird Memorial Exhibition," I said that, though we joke about pulling strings, "Baird was one of those who did it and did it extremely well. He made a career of pulling the strings of thousands of marionettes and pulled himself right up to the very top in his profession and to national and international public acclaim. He was a home town boy who 'made good, real good!'" (7).

Because he took pride in what he came to call his "favorite home town," a major collection of Bil Baird's works now exists in Mason City. It all started innocently enough, but, first, let me fill in a few details about the museum and the evolution of Baird's career. A group of interested (maybe we should say super-enthusiastic) citizens felt the need for and promoted the establishment of an art center in this historic north Iowa town in the early 1960s. By 1964, they had gained the support of another legendary Mason Citian, Lieutenant General Hanford MacNider, and his wife, Margaret, who agreed to purchase a charming old building and gift it to the city of Mason City, if the city, in turn, would accept the responsibility of staffing and maintaining it as a public resource. The city adopted an ordinance in 1964 establishing the museum and appointed a board of trustees. I came on the scene as the museum's first staff member and director in September 1965.

Named in honor of the general's father, the Charles H. MacNider Museum opened near the heart of downtown on January 9, 1966. By October 1969, the die had been cast for the museum's mission in terms of the role and purpose of the permanent collection. Considered to be at the core of the organization and all that it does, the collection had as its objective telling the story of American art and life by obtaining, preserving, exhibiting, and interpreting the best possible examples of different periods and styles of work by American artists. A secondary objective was to include in the collection some representative examples of the art of Iowa and the Midwest.

A very prominent, though small (still under five hundred), holding of paintings, sculpture, prints, ceramics, photography, etc., has been created in this relatively small community. It boasts major paintings by artists like Arthur Dove, Thomas Hart Benton, Jasper Cropsey, Jack Levine, Sam Francis, John Sloan, John Marin, Philip Guston, Adolph Gottlieb, Alfred Thompson Bricher, G. P. A. Healy, and Peter Hurd. The collection is truly a surprise to many who make their first visit to Mason City. To be able to house and show most of these important works most of the time, the museum has gone through four expansion or addition projects since it first opened. The museum was accredited by the American Association of Museums in 1973 — a status it has maintained through two subsequent accreditation reviews.

Now, with that further bit of introduction out of the way, it's back to the Baird collection, which, in reality, must have started with his move with his family to Mason City when Bil was of middle-school age. He was born in Grand Island, Nebraska, but moved a lot because his father worked as an itinerant chemical engineer. "Wherever there was a sugar factory being built, [his] father was there" (Rothman 12). Just prior to coming to Mason City, they'd lived in the Detroit area. A job with American Crystal Sugar brought them to Iowa.

Bil graduated from Mason City High School and the University of Iowa before spreading his wings and beginning a career flight that took him to many different corners of the world. When he was eight years old, his father had made him a simple string puppet. "I got it tangled right away," Baird remembered (Rothman 12). "His dad had also given him a book about puppets written by Helen Joseph. He made good use of it and began to dream" (Leet 7). It was in Mason City, however, that his lifelong work took root and grew.

At age fourteen, Baird started making his own puppets, and, by the time he was in high school, he had built a stage in the attic of the family home and was doing performances of *Treasure Island.* He had taken an old automobile dashboard and remodeled it to create a lighting switchboard. The clincher for his career decision came in 1921 when Bil found himself seated in the auditorium of the old Mason City High School, watching Tony Sarg's touring puppet performance of *Rip Van Winkle.* There was so much action and exhilaration that Baird "decided that night that [it] was the life for [him]" (Baird 179).

Baird landed in New York City in 1928 after spending a year in Paris, where, according to Baird, he spent the better part of twelve months sketching in the afternoons and playing accordion in the cafés of Paris at night (Leet 8). He joined the Tony Sarg troupe and remained an active member of the company for almost five years. Gaining important experience and insight with Sarg, Baird always gave much credit to this man, who served as his mentor and helped develop America's understanding of and appreciation for serious marionette plays.

When Baird formed his own company in 1934, he operated at 50 Barrow Street in New York, locating later to 59 Barrow Street. This was the same year that the Bil Baird Marionettes made their first appearance at the World's Fair in Chicago. "In 1937, Bil met Cora Burlar, an 'up-and-coming' New York actress with Broadway experience in such plays as *Noah* and *Valley Forge,* when an obscure actor named Orson Welles put on Christopher Marlowe's *Dr. Faustus.* Bil created puppets for this production representing the seven deadly sins; they met when Cora turned up as the voice of Envy, Gluttony, and Sloth" (*Bil Baird's Marionettes* 3). They married, and she became a puppeteer and partner in Bil and Cora Baird's Marionette Theater until her death in 1967.

"Before Bil pulled his last string, his marionettes had starred in three Broadway musicals, *The Ziegfeld Follies of 1941, Flahooley,* and *Baker Street;* broken box office records in Broadway theaters with full-length productions of *Ali Baba, Man in the Moon,* and *Davy Jones' Locker;* and appeared in four CBS television series, several movies, and more than four hundred television commercials" (Leet 8). Baird's creations also did TV simulations for some of NASA's early journeys into space; played World's Fairs; traveled abroad on tour under the auspices of various U.S. governmental agencies; starred in films made for private corporations; and had major roles in the TV special, "Art Carney Meets Peter and the Wolf," which was nominated for an Emmy. They did a five-month "gig" with the New York Philharmonic Orchestra, under conductor Andre Kostelanetz in the 1960s; performed regularly in their own theater at 59 Barrow Street in Greenwich Village; and were written up and photographed for articles and pictorial features in national magazines (including for many cover stories) and in newspapers all across the country.

Many honors, too many to list, came to Baird and his company. In 1980, Bil received the Medal of Achievement from the Lotos Club of New York City and was honored, along with Burr Tillstrom, Shari Lewis, and Jim Henson, by UNIMA and the Puppeteers of America, by a performance at the thirteenth World Puppetry Festival at the Kennedy Center. In 1983, Bil was honored, as was Margo Rose, by activities and an exhibition at the Brunnier Museum of Art, at Iowa State University on the occasion of the forty-fourth National Festival of the Puppeteers of America. The University of Iowa in Iowa City presented him with the Distinguished Alumnus Award in 1985.

Now, let's flash back to Baird's Mason City connection and the rekindling or heating up of his link to north Iowa. His parents remained in this community for the rest of their lives, adding substance to the "favorite home town" expression. Bil frequently returned to the city, not only to see his family, but to also see a host of lifelong friends, including his college roommate. He participated occasionally in special community activities, such as when he and wife Cora served as parade marshals in the twenty-first Annual North Iowa Band Festival Parade on June 9, 1959. They were accompanied by their seven-year-old son Peter, their four-year-old daughter Laura, and many of their famous puppets.

Baird and his second wife, Susanna, were in town in 1975 and happened to attend a Mason City Rotary Club meeting as guests of another club member. They were introduced, along with other visitors, at the start of the meeting. At adjournment, I stepped forward to meet them and, in the course of conversation, extended an invitation to come to the Mac-Nider to see what we were creating as a still relatively young arts center. They came that very afternoon for a relaxed and lengthy tour, and, before it was over, I asked Baird whether he might consider letting us do an exhibition of his puppets. One thing led to another, and we presented a very popular show, "The Art of the Puppet: Bil Baird," from August 15 through September 12, 1976. Bil, always sensitive about the handling of his puppets, was exuberant in his reaction to the installation; upon entering the gallery, he grabbed me and hugged me!

Bil and Susanna had come from New York a week early to conduct a puppetry workshop, in conjunction with the opening of the exhibition and the museum's annual Summer Arts Festival. It was also Bil's seventy-third birthday, and, during one of the evening festival activities on the lawn, Bil received the key to the city from the mayor and a birthday cake presented by a Girl Scout Brownie troop. That day, in front of the large crowd, Baird did a complete handspring somersault, akin to the kind he did on the football field as a youthful yell leader at the University of Iowa back in the 1920s!

We maintained communication over the ensuing months, and, when the museum developed plans for a weeklong celebration and dedication of its second and largest expansion project, Bil and some of his company members were engaged to perform as part of the program. On this occasion, in the fall of 1979, Bil gave one of his marionettes to the museum for inclusion in the growing permanent collection of American art. That puppet was Cloon, a leprechaun who had appeared with Art Carney in the TV series, "O'Halloran's Luck." It was a good choice because it seemed to embody many of the master puppeteer's traits and his fun-loving spirit — maybe a personality caricature, if not actually a visual one.

Baird and his company members were genuinely impressed with what had been accomplished in the expansion of the facility since they first set eyes on it in 1975, and they didn't hold back on compliments. We had more than doubled the size of the museum with this much-needed project. Even so, it was a surprise six months later to receive a long-distance call from Bil, during a Sunday afternoon dinner at home with family members, with his pitching this question: "What would you think of having a wing with a collection of puppets?" We were still combing drywall dust out of our hair, cleaning construction fragments from a corner or two of the building, and recovering from many months of fund-raising. The idea didn't include the means to build a gallery, but having such a collection was a morsel worth chewing a bit.

Actually, the first issue to decide was where and how this proposed material fit into our definition of art and our stated mission for the museum and its collection. Once it was resolved that, yes, puppetry was art — a many-faceted, multidisciplined form of creative expression — everything else began to fall into place. The collection, which we now believe to be a national treasure, is the work of one of the most important pioneering American puppeteers of the twentieth century (and one of the city's favorite sons)! We couldn't see ourselves immediately funding a wing, but thought we could muster some local foundation support for renovating an existing space and turning it into a gallery. That was acceptable to the Bairds.

The first shipment of puppets arrived in 1980, with others following in waves not long after. Bil's "little ones" were migrating to their paternal home. The Kinney-Lindstrom Foundation granted the museum money to create the "Bil Baird: World of Puppets" exhibit, and Bergland and Cram, architects of Mason City, designed what proved to be the first phase of a new and special gallery that was dedicated and opened to the public in 1981. The last puppets to settle here came in 1987 as a bequest, following Bil's death in New York. The MacNider Museum created and staged the "Bil Baird Memorial" exhibit in its changing exhibition galleries from July 17 to October 9, 1988, drawing visitors from far and wide.

Now containing nearly six hundred items, including working drawings, props, and costumes, this collection is believed to be the largest holding of Baird's work to be found anywhere. In addition, the museum possesses a wide variety of related archival materials, such as posters, large photographs, newspaper clippings, films, copies of magazines featuring Baird articles, and other odds and ends.

Another building project in 1990 enabled an expansion of the Baird galleries, where there are always 125 to 150 puppets on view (other puppets "sleep" in storage until taking a turn under the lights). This special collection contains examples of Baird's creativity from all periods of his career and represents many different types of puppets, marionettes, materials, and construction methods.

Joining Cloon over the years between 1980 and 1987 was a host of colorful characters that had at one time or another sprung from the fertile mind of the master puppeteer. In the first few shipments of puppets from New York to Mason City, there were also a number of puppets and marionettes collected by Bil. These we have kept and are glad to have, though we do not otherwise collect puppetry material by other artists. Amongst these accessions are works by Tony Sarg, Otto and Caroline Kunze (Austrian), the Salici Company (Italian), Sergei Obraztsov (Russian), old Venetian and French Forain hand puppets, Rajasthani marionettes from India, and Georgian (Russian) hand puppets and marionettes. One special piece is a small hand puppet caricature of a young Bil Baird that was created by Lou Bunin.

As I have already mentioned, Cloon, the leprechaun, has always made me think of Bil because of its ruffle of graying hair and beard, which was almost a trademark of Bil in his later years. Also, Bil was a wiry little man with a spring in his step and a fun, teasing spirit that somehow, for me, is epitomized in the sprightly features of the two-foot-tall marionette in the green suit and hat.

We have a whole cast of characters that were created for *Gawpy Ballet, a Fantasy of Pelican Isle,* a play that was produced as a first venture by Bil, along with Robert and Harold Hestwood, in the late 1920s. The Hestwoods, as the Drury Lane Players Ltd., had left the Tony Sarg troupe to try their hands on their own with some adult puppet theater. Apparently, the world wasn't ready for them, and they beat it back to a safe harbor and the continued tutelage of Sarg. These marionettes, though imbued with a great deal of character, are somewhat crude in construction, compared to the sophisticated, well-crafted works to follow.

The Baird Marionettes, in their early days, toured the nightclub circuit, worked fairs, theaters, and other venues, including the *Shell Oil*

Road Show, where they performed in the streets from a specially outfitted truck-stage. The museum has a Clark Gable caricature marionette from the 1937–1938 Shell Road Show. The likeness is astounding, and the puppet was one of the first of many caricature puppets created by Baird over his long career. Also in the museum collection are Senators Taft and Kefauver; Perry Como; Xavier Cugat as the devil; Stuffsky, a clone of famed conductor Leopold Stowkowsky; and a voluptuous Marilyn Maxwell as Nellie Bly. A wonderful double marionette, Armando and Maxine, a suave, formally dressed, dancing couple, dates from the Bairds' nightclub tour in 1939. It is easy to imagine them swirling about the stage with precision turns and dips, with all the poise and flair that can be seen in championship dancing on television today. Just as with real live dancers, their intensity of expression is very much a part of the performance.

Baird created a number of dancer puppets during his illustrious career, and many of them now reside at the MacNider. Among them are O'Toolova, the Russian ballerina from 1953; Celeste, 1939, and Red Rhumba, a stripper, 1933, both nightclub dancers; Charleston Girl, 1953, from "The Morning Show," CBS-TV; Lady Tango, 1964–1965, from the New York World's Fair show; Paraguay, 1956, a gaucho dancer; and Felice, 1940s, an elegant, almost featureless ballerina, designed to carry well visually in the vast house of the Radio City Music Hall, where she appeared in the Christmas show. Her strings were twenty feet long, another element influenced by the size of the theater and its huge stage. Remember that Cora was also a dancer, and it is thought that some of the dancer marionettes, like O'Toolova and Felice, took on some of her likeness and characteristics. There are even a couple of Dancing Bees and other cast members from the 1944 film *Gardening Is Fun* in the museum's collection. Baird produced that film for the U.S. Office of Inter-American Affairs. It was a Spanish-language film intended to promote better nutrition in South American countries by demonstrating, through a humorous story, how to grow vegetables. Speaking of films, the multitalented puppeteer made a large number of them for many different agencies and companies. The MacNider Museum is fortunate to have copies of many of those films, as well as a quite varied selection of puppets that performed in them.

Puppets King Wheat, Tooth, Iron, Fruit, Milk, Hidden Hunger, Vitamin B1, and others hail from *The King Who Came to Breakfast*, a 1948

Left: Armando & Maxine from a nightclub show, 1939. *Right:* O'Toolova, "The Bil Baird Show," CBS-TV, 1953. (Courtesy the MacNider Museum.)

film about the history of wheat, created for Nabisco. Party Line Piggy and others starred in a 1946 flick for AT&T, encouraging courtesy on telephone party lines, while Always Listen and others appeared in *Adventure in Telezonia* in 1947. The latter, also produced for AT&T, was about the uses of the telephone. A 1945 film, *Wee Cooper O'Fife*, featured Angus, kilts and all, and Lemon in a delightful piece based on an old Scottish folk song. The title song was sung by the late, great folksinger, Burl Ives. We could go on and on, but you get the idea. Baird pulled lots of strings in front of the movie cameras and many of the characters on the other ends of those strings now reside in Mason City.

Baird and his fanciful puppets appeared on television during its early days. He and his little friends were guests on almost every prominent talk and variety show, as well as performers in specials and shows of their own. "Life with Snarky Parker" was a Baird show satirizing westerns (1950), directed by Yul Brynner, that ran fifteen minutes a day, five days a week, for a year on CBS-TV. For this show the Baird troupe used their own prompting device that they called a scriptanola. Bil claimed it as a forerunner of the teleprompter that came into use later on in the evolution of the TV industry. Snarky, Gordon the Ghost, Birdie, Ronald the Rodent, Heathcliff, and the Schnookies aren't on TV anymore, but they are an attraction in our Baird galleries. Heathcliff, the horse that "hangs out" in Mason City, is in disguise as a harem girl! Another series by Baird, "The Whistling Wizard," a half-hour show also on CBS, ran for forty-two weeks in 1951–1952. Our Captain Scorn, originally conceived for the theater production *Davy Jones' Locker,* acted in this one.

Bil appeared regularly on "The Morning Show" on CBS in the 1950s. Some of the characters from those days who have since moved to the Midwest include Honey and the Horn, Hillman, Piccolo Worm, Bugle Boy, Raccoon, and Dancing Couple, Boy, Glockenspiel Player, and Flute Player from *The Swedish Rhapsody* number. Those last four are especially interesting because they were all constructed of cloth and yarn, much in the tradition of the ever-popular Raggedy Ann and Andy dolls. Before completing the list of Baird's TV encounters, it should be mentioned that the museum does not have any of the "Peter and the Wolf" puppets, but it does have some of the space puppets and props used to simulate the Apollo and Gemini flights. Cameras with moving-picture capabilities weren't on those early launches. Any material that could be shaped or controlled in some manner that came within reach of Bil's hands was "fair game" to be used in the building of his puppets and marionettes. There are examples of all types of construction techniques (carving, molding, fabricating, etc.), and examples of all kinds of materials, ranging from wood to paper and cardboard, rubber, cloth, and plastic. Baird's puppets serve as a comprehensive library of how to's when it comes to designing and building any type of puppet.

I've already alluded to Broadway as another "stomping ground" for Baird puppets. They did appear in numerous live shows, as members of otherwise human casts. Shows such as *Flahooley* and *Nellie Bly* are examples, and characters from those productions are housed at the MacNider. Bil produced many shows of his own and staged them in his own puppet theater in New York, as well as in Broadway theaters. They ranged from adaptations of classic children's stories such as *Winnie the Pooh,* to musical revues like *Davey Jones' Locker,* to what could be considered pretty heavy stuff like Stravinsky's *Histoire du Soldat* (*The Soldier's Tale*), a somber version of the Faust legend, and Saint-Saen's *Carnival of the Animals*. The Mac-Nider Museum has almost all of the cast members from *Winnie the Pooh* (1960) and *The Wizard of Oz* (1971–1972). One of the museum's most frequently asked questions is, "Where's Dorothy?" Well, she was probably borrowed, made over a little and cast in some other show, and she just didn't ever get back to "Kansas" or to Mason City. Borrowing and reusing like this was not uncommon. One example of refurbishing puppets in the collection is that of Paw from the "Snarky Parker" shows. He played opposite Aunty Em as Uncle Henry in *The Wizard of Oz*. With his long beard and his overalls, he spends most of his time at the museum "hangin' around" Snarky and his friends.

Paw and Snarky Parker from "Life with Snarky Parker," 1950. (Photograph by Steve Rye.)

The MacNider has puppets from Bil's production created for the Chrysler Show for the 1964-1965 New York World's Fair. These include Nuts and Bolts, Pistons, and Monkey Wrench. We also have a giant body puppet, our largest, as one of the representatives from the Busch Gardens Show Baird and his crew did in 1979. But probably the best-known group in the eyes of the general public is the cast of puppets and marionettes featured with Julie Andrews and Christopher Plummer in the 1965 film *The Sound of Music*. This famous group came to the museum as a bequest following Bil's death in 1987. They are always on view, along with about 120 other characters born of Baird's fertile imagination. Yes, the Goats, Dancing Duos, Bartender, Prince, Mountain Climbers, Goatherder, and the rest still entrance audiences, now in the form of visitors to the Bil Baird: World of Puppets galleries at the MacNider Museum. We are proud of the fact that Bil Baird's legacy and accomplishments are preserved and shared at the Charles H. MacNider Museum in Mason City, Iowa.

Works Cited

Baird, Bil. *The Art of the Puppet.* New York: Macmillan, 1965.
"Bil Baird's Marionettes." Performance program. Dunetz & Lovett, n.d.
Leet, Richard. *Bil Baird: He Pulled Lots of Strings.* Mason City, IA: Charles H. MacNider Museum, 1988.
Rothman, Steve. "Dean of American Puppeteers, Bil Baird: No More Cartwheels, Still Pulling Strings." *Go! Living Well with Arthritis* (Autumn 1983), 12.

The Puppet Collection
of the American Museum
# of Natural History

KATHY FOLEY *and* ANN WRIGHT-PARSONS

Objects in a museum are silent reminders of the results of varied forces. For one, they are reminders of the intellectual discourse of the past: the period of collection in which curators or collectors defined what was important or worthy of acquisition. Other forces include the research focus of a curator or the ever-present pressure to find available funding for purchases. These purchases might be from researchers in the field or from collectors who offer to sell their collections to the museum. Another force influencing the direction of a collection is preparation for an exhibit where gaps in the collection become apparent and pieces are sought to fill them in. All these features converge to create a collection. All of the above inform the collection of puppets in the Department of Anthropology at the American Museum of Natural History.

The first puppets, a Javanese children's set received in 1894, represent the beginning of a collection that now totals more than 3,000 pieces. This puppet collection within the museum is but a small subset of the half-a-million ethnographic and archaeological artifacts of the Department of Anthropology.[1] The range of the puppet collection includes a few pieces from North America, Africa and New Zealand but the majority is from the major performing areas of Asia.

The aim of this chapter is to reveal to scholars and puppet enthusiasts the research possibilities that the collection offers and to explore how these figures born to dance across shadow screens and pop out of puppet booths have come to rest in the climate-controlled cabinets at the museum. Spared the poundings of mock battles, the wear and tear of constant use, and, in more recent years, the exposure to light, dust, moisture and other weathering conditions that they would have encountered in their indigenous contexts, these objects stand as witnesses to the past of puppet genres, some of which have changed significantly, some of which remain virtually unchanged and still others which have disappeared. For those who know the genres as they are performed today, for those who wish to study the history of these arts, or for those eager to widen their understanding of world puppetry, the collection provides an escape into rich arts and older forms.

The types of puppets in the collection represent all the major manipulation techniques: hand, rod, string marionettes, and shadow figures, with the shadow collection being the best developed. The museum is rich in Asian figures with representative pieces from all major traditions, except Japan and Cambodia (Kampuchea). The collection of around 3,006 figures[2] includes extensive holdings from China (1,533), India (928), and Indonesia: Java (452) and Bali (283). Representative figures from Thailand (78), Malaysia (12), Burma (24), Turkey (15), and Taiwan (50) are also found. Additionally, there are two puppets from North America,[3] one from New Zealand[4] and six from Africa.[5]

Of the entire collection, the shadow puppets from China and Bali have the most to offer the researcher due to the care the collectors used in gathering and documenting information about each puppet. The puppets from India are less comprehensively documented, but the shadow holdings are extensive and a significant research resource. Puppets from other areas are sufficient to give some idea of the overall construction of puppets and style, but, lacking complete sets, will not allow an overall sense of the characters and repertoire of the genre in performance.

The development of the collection was a lengthy process and many forces came into play. As with any museum collection, it reflects both focused attention and happenstance. In some cases a collection was the research interest of a scholar in the field who had the funding and mandate to collect what he or she considered of value: both the Berthold Laufer and Margaret Mead collections fit this profile. Also, an acquisition reflects the serendipitous meeting between a collector possessing a good collection who is willing to donate to the museum and a curator cognizant of the value of the collection and interested in obtaining it for the museum. In other cases, available funding for an exhibit allowed the purchase of representative pieces to fill in gaps. In all cases, a key theme that pervades the correspondence in the files, which accompany each acquisition, is funding or lack thereof.[6]

Donor's Gifts

The puppet collection at the American Museum of Natural History (hereafter referred to as AMNH) reveals the vagaries of history. The museum was founded in 1896; the first Department of Anthropology established in 1972. In the early years, there was no overall plan for the acquisition of ethnographic artifacts: objects were acquired primarily for purposes of display ("History of the Department of Anthropology," n.d.). With the hiring of scholars of ethnography, research and study were seen as the primary goal, and collections as a result of fieldwork were encouraged. One of the first significant acquisitions started as an exhibit. Protestant missionaries organized an exhibit of artifacts representative of the ethnic or tribal groups where they worked. Thousands of artifacts from mission posts in Africa, Asia, the Americas and the Pacific Islands were brought to the museum for this exhibit around 1900. Many of these artifacts were acquired by the museum after the exhibit closed. Of this, a group of fourteen marionettes from Burma formed the beginning of puppet theatrical forms.

Puppets continued to be received into the collection but with no apparent intent or overall plan. Travelers to an area in the early part of the twentieth century, upon their return to the United States, offered their acquisitions to the museum (e.g., the Clark collection from Java). In other cases, pieces came to the museum from businesspeople living in Asia who became interested in puppetry and had acquired figures (such as the Rosenblatt collection from Java).

Much of the collection is the result of generous donations from people such as the wealthy financier, George W. Pratt, who gave funding for the acquisition of a large group of puppets, mainly from Cirebon, western Java, in 1927. In addition to shadow puppets from Cirebon, there are masks from the north coast of Indonesia (*topeng*), flat wooden puppets (*wayang klitik*), and a few rod puppets (*wayang golek*). Another generous donation, from India and Thailand, came through donor Kenneth Heuer in 1968. Walter Fairservis, employed in the Department of Anthropology in the 1960s and '70s, recognized the value of a significant collection of puppets from Andhra Pradesh, which were for sale in New York City, and recommended that they be purchased. While lacking good documentation, nevertheless the size of the collection (628 items), provides sufficient examples of the genre for the researcher to make use of.

The puppets from Indonesia reflect the serendipitous mix of such an interest or the lack thereof. Generally, in American collections of Indonesian puppetry, Javanese shadow puppets predominate. However, here instead of a large collection from central Java, there are more examples from Sunda (western Java) and the north coast of Java. (Bali is well represented but this collection will be discussed later.) Perhaps figures from western Java and the north coast predominate because businessmen who promoted the products of plantations, more numerous in western Java than central Java, used these colorful, lively puppets in displays at expositions to attract dealers of tea, coffee or sugar. For example, correspondence in the archives of John Clarke, a dealer in spices with an office on Wall Street, mentions that he had for sale artifacts from the Java Village of the World's Fair in Chicago in 1894. About fifty rod and shadow puppets from western Java and the north coast were the serendipitous connecting of a donor with this spice broker. The connection of trading and artifacts in museums is woven through the correspondence of many donations in the collection, but needs further investigation to give it full dimension.

The fact that there are a number of figures from the decade surrounding the turn of the last century is useful for researchers who are curious to see what changes have occurred. Iconography in the Indonesian frame remains consistent: for example, the wooden rod puppet representing Bima[7], hero and second brother of the five Pandawas from the *Mahābhārata*, is immediately recognizable in this century-old piece. Natural pigments and simpler batik patterns from the past have been replaced by brighter commercial paints, more elaborately sequined costumes, and more detailed carving of hair adornments within more recent decades.

In addition to larger groupings, such as the Pratt donation, other figures have found their way to the collection, including a few marionettes from Burma, a small number of Javanese figures, three Indian Kathakali-style hand puppets (*pava kuthu*), a good number of Rajasthani marionettes (*kathputli*), *Karaghöz* shadow figures from Turkey and Tunis, and Malaysian shadow figures. All these unplanned acquisitions have added to the range of the museum collection, albeit with little information as to their actual origins or their uses.

Research-Oriented Collectors: Berthold Laufer and Margaret Mead

The work of Berthold Laufer and Margaret Mead forms the backbone of the puppet collection and makes it one of the best research resources in the country for information on the past forms of Chinese shadow puppet theater (*pi-ying xi*) and the Balinese shadow play (*wayang kulit*).

Berthold Laufer, born in Köln in 1874, studied Oriental languages at the University of Berlin and also worked at the University of Leipzig prior to accepting the post of leader of research expeditions for the AMNH to the Ainu of Japan in 1898 and then to China in 1901–1904. After his field research he worked briefly at the American Museum of Natural History (1904–1906) in New York City, but fully established his career as curator of Asiatic ethnology at the Field Museum in Chicago. Laufer's research interests ranged widely, from plants to precious stones to "oriental theatricals" (Laufer 1923). His grasp of languages and meticulous attention to detail are reflected in the collections that are his legacy. His monographs and papers address topics as diverse as the history of the rhinoceros (Laufer 1914), the prehistory of flight (Laufer 1928), and the origin of the European dance of death in Buddhist tantric imagery (Walravens 1976).

Laufer, with funding from financier Jacob Schiff, arrived in Shanghai on August 20, 1901, and traveled extensively over the following years, collecting over 10,000 items. His intention was to, as comprehensively as possible, represent Chinese industry and social life, with puppetry falling into the latter category. The bulk of the puppet material was collected in Peking, where he stayed from December 9, 1901 to November 23, 1902 (Walravens 1976, 925).

The Chinese puppets Laufer collected give insight into popular performance in China at the beginning of the twentieth century. For example,

Complex marionette of a lady in a cart pushed by a coolie (even the wheel moves), collected by Berthold Laufer during his China expedition (70/9479). (Courtesy the Division of Anthropology, American Museum of Natural History.)

modest marionettes from Peking in Ching dynasty costumes have two strings running from a clay head to a hoop of willow that served as the control. Although simply made, some of these puppets are quite intricate. One consists of a demure lady holding her fan daintily in front of her while seated in a cart pushed by a coolie. The fact that the wheel of the vehicle can turn as the man's feet march along attests to the intricacy of this particular figure. Clearly, Laufer paid attention to details of manipulation in selecting this example for the collection.

Laufer collected rod puppets with small bamboo controls that move the arms and hands. Familiar characters, such as Sun Wu-kung, the monkey king from the well-known *Journey to the West*, are among the many examples of this collection. The monkey is recognizable due to his white head, mischievous red face and coiled headband by which his monk-master controls his sometimes unruly behavior. Movable eyes make the visage more animated. The delightful rod puppet collection gives a sense of a rough, popular theater genre of the 1900s. An exquisite hand puppet booth stands guard over the puppet cases awaiting the moment that the figures are danced to life once more.

Laufer's field notes record the names of specific characters, sometimes in Chinese characters or romanized Chinese and often with his added notes in a form of German shorthand.[8] The intellectual rationale under which Laufer worked and collected is clear. He achieved a material representation of the social life of China as he found it in the first years of the last century. With the luxury of financial support that Schiff provided, Laufer had the ability to collect methodically and to travel extensively in China. Some of the figures cross-reference other performances that caught Laufer's eye. For example. in his expedition report Laufer spoke glowingly of the *yang-ko*, the stilt walkers of Beijing, detailing the different characters that made up a troupe: "A twelve year old boy wears red silk trousers and

A small boy, an example of the stilt walkers, is part of the extensive collection of shadow puppets collected by Berthold Laufer (70/10118). (Courtesy the Division of Anthropology, American Museum of Natural History.)

blue silk great coat embroidered with flowers and butterflies.... In one hand he holds a flower basket and in the other a horsewhip" (Walravens 1976, 925). In the AMNH collection stilt walkers are available in shadow form (70/10118). The stilt-walker figures correspond almost exactly to Laufer's written description of actual street performers. The stilt-walking man looking back, presumably to catch a kiss from his stilt-walking wife, the comic fisherman, the gong beaters and drummers (70/1016-

10124)—all the characters Laufer described in a *yang-ko* troupe are represented in the deftly cut and delicately colored shadow figures of the Beijing shadow puppet tradition.

Laufer noted that what the Beijing opera stage lacked in scenery was amply made up for by the plethora of set pieces in shadow theater. The figures he acquired bear out his assertions: "Here all the traverses as sea, cloud, rivers, large palaces and temples, carts, sedan chairs and boats, gods, demons and monsters [or] ... the torments of hell are reproduced in a most realistic way" (Walravens 1991, 104). View one tray of figures and you dive into the netherworld of Buddhist hells where figures roast over fires or are sawed into pieces. Open the next case, and you are transported to the heavenly abode of the Jade Empress or see the eight Taoist immortals as they float upon their clouds. All that the artist could envision seems to have been assembled for the shadow stage.

The delicate, translucent figures cast light on this important theater from the beginning of the century. Those versed in Beijing opera will be able to identify the characters from painted-face (*ching*) figures such as Sun Wu-kung, the wily monkey king, to delicate *tan* (female) figures like White Snake. While a number of U.S. museums boast Chinese shadow theater acquisitions, this is one of the most carefully collected, documented and preserved collections.[9]

As an example of the use of this resource for scholars working on Chinese theater, I mention Josephine Humphrey (1980), who advised and assisted in puppet exhibitions in the 1970s, then established her own New York-based company, Yueh Lung Players, for Chinese shadow performance based on the inspiration this material and research gave her. Another well-known scholar in the puppet world is Roberta Stalberg, who researched the figures for her 1984 book on Chinese puppetry.

The vast majority of the shadow puppet figures are "eastern city" (*luanchou*), the more transparent and delicately incised figures of the east side of Beijing. This style of shadow puppetry was patronized by the Ching Dynasty aristocrats. A few of the larger figures from Hangchow, which are considerably taller than the petite Beijing-style puppets, are part of the collection. Less refined painting and the lack of incisions is characteristic of Hangchow figures, which may be completely opaque and up to 22 in. tall.

Laufer's collection is a major research resource for Beijing puppet performance and the pieces give insight into the turn-of-the-century genres. While the marionettes and the rod puppets have deteriorated, they show that the typology of character of traditional Chinese theater was consistent from genre to genre. The shadow figures made of durable leather have aged gracefully. For background on these figures one can usefully look at Laufer's *Oriental Theatricals* (1923).

According to Roberta Stalberg, Laufer reported difficulty in initially finding figures in Beijing, and, when he tried to order a set he was told it would require a year and a half of waiting. Instead he purchased what he thought was the last set in the city from a working theater company noting, "So the *ying hsi* shadow theatre will soon be a matter of the past in Northern China, and I think I saved them in the last hour" (Stalberg 1984, 90). Stalberg notes this comment was an exaggeration as there were still four active troupes in Beijing in 1912, but the purchase, which included musical instruments, stage curtains, dramatic texts and more than five hundred figures, was an important acquisition in which he attempted to show the scope and repertoire of the company. Laufer even recorded three popular plays of the company's repertoire on wax cylinders (Stalberg 1984, 90).[10]

Artifacts Laufer collected, such as Peking opera costumes, Lamaist masks, wood-block prints representing scenes from various operas or even an extensive collection of kites, which show popular theater characters, may have interest for researchers who wish to compare how puppetry relates to iconography used in other popular entertainments. Examples of research that demonstrate the collection's value to scholars is found in Stalberg (1984), Humphrey (1980), Erda (1975 and 1979) and Hirsch (1998).

Another collection that is well documented was made by Margaret Mead while carrying out field research in Bali from 1936–1937. Mead's acquisition of examples of theater arts during her time in Bali may have been influenced by the experience and knowledge of a number of foreign resident artists who were studying and applying their arts in Bali during the time Mead was there.[11] Of these, Mead's notes record meetings with the Russian-German painter Walter Spies, dancer Beryl de Zoete, and Canadian composer Colin McPhee and his wife, Jane Belo, whose interest in trance and performance meshed with Mead's research interests; subsequently, Belo became Mead's assistant. Mead's understandings were expanded further by dancer Katharane Mershon, who was engaged in a study of Balinese religion, and dancer Claire Holt, whose background was in Indian art and culture; these women gave Mead a greater appreciation of Hindu-influenced rituals and arts. In reminiscing some thirty years later about what it was like to do research amidst a group of like-minded scholars, Mead states, "I think it is a good thing to have had such a model, once, of what anthropological field work can be like, even if the model includes the kind of extra intensity in which a life time is condensed into a few short years" (1972, 240).

Arriving in Bali with such a group of artist researchers already in residence, Mead, with husband Gregory Bateson, drew on their knowledge for their own comparative work (Bateson and Mead 1942, xiv). Mead's funding, in part, for this fieldwork came from the Committee on Dementia Praecox and her notes mention that she was interested in comparing stylized arts forms and spontaneous productions (accessions notes 1938–1942). She says she made a collection of *wayang*[12] (shadow) puppets "to use as control material in an investigation of the relative usefulness of highly stylized and spontaneous art productions in the study of character formation with special references to symbolism" (accessions notes 1938–1942). Later she states that "the collection contains all the principal characters used in wajang, but is numerically short in the number of traditional gods and demons which would appear in an ordinary dalang's (shadow play operator's) box, and is very high in the number of comic characters, as the traditional characters show very slight variations, being distinguished principally by details of colour and headdress, while the comic characters are for the most part free improvisations of individual dalangs."

Mead goes on to say that "the collection was made with two points in mind: 1. To provide one set of traditional artistic forms with which to compare the modern art forms — Batuan painting and Sebatu-Taro-Let carving with a view to determining which type of material, traditional, highly stylized forms or modern partly stylized forms, yielded most valuable psychological material [and] 2. To provide a representative collection of shadow play puppets to meet the many requests that come into the Museum from schools, etc."

Mead lists the various *dalangs* she encountered or from whom she purchased shadow figures. Mead records each puppet character or weapon, the maker from whom it was purchased and the name of the village. All of this information is available to researchers on the Asian Collections database on the public Web site of AMNH.

In her essay in *Balinese Character*, Mead mentions seeking out other researchers who were carrying out studies in other areas of Bali for comparison to the village of Batuan where she and Bateson were working (xiv). Mead's research interests — child development, mental illness such as madness, sexual behavior played out in drama, and art as a means of expressing inner emotions — were in concert with exploration of the psychological realm of the individual carried out by anthropologists of the time, and were issues that captured the popular imagination as well. Although her research project in Bali was partially funded as a cross-cultural study of schizophrenia, Mead delved into other areas of research while she was there. However, one can surmise that Mead's interest in the demonic and erotic exemplified in the folk character *rangda*, the widow or witch (1942, 275, 176), and consequent publication of her research results magnified the significance of this character in the eyes of westerners to a greater extent than was typical to the ordinary Balinese, and certainly in the observations of researchers of drama in modern-day Bali.

For example, Mead sought to apply psychoanalytical insights derived from Freudian interpretations of mother-child relations in her film, "Dance and Drama in Bali" where *rangda* is interpreted as a threatening mother image; however, Balinese performers, like I Nyoman Catra, see the *rangda* figure as the chthonic power of the demonic, which is latent in each person and merely the other face of the beneficent chthonic figure represented by the *barong*, the dragon/lion, who defeats her (personal communication, I Nyoman Catra to Kathy Foley, October 12, 2002). Mead's collection in the museum of carvings, paintings, and puppets stands as material evidence of her intellectual pursuits, silent yet visible evidence of Mead's mental inquiries until some researcher gives it voice.

While in Bali, Mead collected about 280 puppets for exhibition, some of which were partially finished to show the techniques of construction. Also, she obtained a set of tools for making puppets. Current puppet-making techniques remain consistent with practices of the 1930s. Moreover, most of the figures are readily recognized to those trained in the iconography of Balinese wayang. Parwa figures (from the *Mahābhārata*), *Rāmāyana* figures and others used for Cupak (Tjupak is a greedy villain who persecutes his refined younger brother) are present along with the witch used in the Calonarang performance and demon figures. As mentioned previously, Mead collected demons, ogres and monsters and puppets with exposed genitalia with an exuberance that may have encouraged villagers to create new exotic and erotic images to satisfy her interest. Balinese artists are quick to respond to market forces and since new demonic characters can be innovated at will, the number produced is limited only by the creativity of the maker. While dangling breasts and exposed penises are not out of the ordinary in Balinese figures and remain significant representations of the tantric aspects of the performance tradition, the average *dalang* needs only a limited number of such figures to present a performance, and the same pieces can serve for many different puppet plays. Thus, the collection probably is not representative of the pieces that might have been found in an ordinary puppet chest of the period.

In addition to the standard pieces and the exotic ones, there are a few that will be mentioned for their remarkable creativity. Two made by I Made Oka represent Balinese dance of the period. One puppet depicts

two little dancers of *legong*, the classical, palace dance performed by prepubescent girls. Here the two dancers are attached so that they move together as they would in real life. These figures are able to move their hands and bend at the waist enabling a skilled *dalang* to mimic the dance with remarkable accuracy. Another is one single figure of three girls dancing *janger*, a popular performance genre of the era.

Costume and posture of the puppets is consistent with the practice of the present. Different puppets represented

Legong dancers are among the *wayang parwa* figures collected in Bali by Margaret Mead (70.3/ 800). (Courtesy the Division of Anthropology, American Museum of Natural History.)

different stages in a character's life. For example, the figure representing the death of Abimanyu, son of the *Mahābhārata* hero, Arjuna, is represented by a puppet pierced by many arrows. This figure symbolizes the scene when this hot-blooded youth is lured to the battlefield in the absence of his father by his ruthless uncles, the Kurawas, to die at their hands. Its St. Sebastian–like depiction reflects the power of expression that Balinese artists communicated through this medium.

While most of the Balinese shadow figures lie in storage cabinets, a representative sample of this collection is on view in the recently reopened Hall of the Pacific Peoples. Mead's research area — Oceania and the Pacific — came to include insular Southeast Asia. To most Indonesians and Philippine Islanders, this anomalous grouping appears as a disjuncture with their sense of identity and inclusion in the modern-day economic and political body ASEAN, or the Association of Southeast Asian Nations.

Mead's interest in puppetry prompted her to purchase a number of Turkish *karaghöz* shadow puppets in 1955 when she was there on a visit. This increased the Turkish holdings of AMNH from a few paper-and-hide figures collected by Erlangan around 1906. Turkish puppets, representative specimens of this comic shadow puppet genre of the Islamic world, were added by Erda in 1985. Bettie Erda was a key figure in the next major addition to the puppet collection.

Exhibition and the Conscious Collector

Bettie Erda came to the Department of Anthropology in the early 1970s to help sort through artifacts in the Asian collection in preparation for the construction of a permanent exhibit.[13] Erda, a dancer by training, was attracted to the puppet collection, and, as an aside to her regular responsibilities in the department, she began to prepare a puppet exhibition. This very popular exhibit, titled Puppets: Dance and Drama of the Orient was held in the museum from 1974–1975. As an outgrowth of this exhibit Erda wrote a short article about the Chinese shadow theater and documented the story entitled "The Chaos Box," which is illustrated with beautiful color photographs of the main characters (1975). Although not a bonafide scholar like Laufer or Mead, Erda's enthusiasm and interest attracted to her the assistance of scholars (e.g.,

Awasthi in India) as she traveled in Asia in pursuit of puppet traditions. While there she purchased a number of good figures that added to the breadth of the overall collection. In addition, Erda's interest brought to the attention of museum personnel good collections that could be purchased (such as the Bekker purchase) and puppets from research areas. Erda herself donated about fifty-eight puppets: representative pieces from Turkey, Java, Thailand, and India.

How do different areas construct their figures? Which areas use figures that are opaque and which areas use transparent ones? What is the size of the puppet and the quality of the cutwork? Such general questions rather than specific ones can be answered by looking at the figures Erda acquired.

The enthusiasm for the exhibit at the AMNH led to the curation of an exhibit at the Katonah Gallery in Katonah, New York, from March 18 through May 27, 1979. In the mid–1970s, through a grant from the National Endowment for the Arts, Erda was encouraged and mentored in her work by UCLA professor Mel Helstien and other scholars who were, in the same decade, putting together an exhibit of Asian figures at the UCLA Museum of Cultural History (1976), now known as the Fowler Museum. The Katonah exhibit, with a representative sample of puppets from the AMNH collection, yielded a catalogue, which is an excellent survey of puppet traditions and a sampling of the museum's puppet collection (Erda 1979). Erda's sensitivity to the nuances of the puppet genre is evident in her dedication of the catalogue to Margaret Mead, who died shortly before the opening of the exhibit. "Margaret Mead has joined the ranks of the guardian spirits who are welcomed at every shadow performance. To her, in recognition of her generous encouragement, this catalogue is respectfully dedicated" (1979, 4).

During the time that Erda was working in the museum an exceptional group of Indian shadow puppets (*tholu bomalatta* in Andhra Pradesh and *togalugombe atta* in Karnataka) were purchased. It is unfortunate that the beautiful figures — which include multiple images of Hanuman the monkey general (big, small and even carrying his master Rama), *Mahābhārata* heroes, naked clowns, and composite figures with men and women in erotic sport — have little information to assist in the identification of figures. Many of these Indian acquisitions came from an art dealer in New York City and, as is often the case when a craft becomes a commodity, valuable information about their history is lost. However, an analogous set was assembled by Mel Helstien for the UCLA collection and the identifying information from that set might usefully be consulted to establish the iconography of the beautiful collection at the AMNH (see *Asian Puppets: Wall of the World*, the UCLA catalogue by Helstien and others, 1976). Figures as large as 60 in. are found in this set; delicate tones of rose, ochre, green and black tint the large, transparent figures. Additional Indian figures include a few examples of *thol pavakutu*, the shadow theater of Kerala in South India, and the *ravanachhaya* of Orissa.

Erda, with an exhibition to prepare for, traveled extensively in Asia, contacting major scholars of research areas with puppet traditions. She enlisted the help of Dr. Sarah Bekker to acquire Thai figures and visited Songkhla and Nakhon Si Thammarat in southern Thailand, the home of *nang talung* (the small, transparent shadow theater of southern Thailand), the source of the AMNH's modern miniskirted girls, traditional kinnari (bird women), demons and clowns.

In 1985, again with the help of Dr. Sarah Bekker, Erda was able to acquire a group of *nang yai*, the giant leather shadow figures of the court tradition of central Thailand. These figures represent a palace-temple tradition common to Thailand and Cambodia that is now seldom performed. Large (5'× 4'), opaque shadow figures are danced in front of and behind a screen to the music of a *phipat* (Thai orchestra). The story of the *Rāmāyana* is most often presented and most of the figures in the collection are recognizable as heroes, monkeys or ogres in battle stances. One can see the composite figure of Sida (Sita), the captured wife of Rama soaring over the battlefield in the flying chariot when the demon king Thosakan (Rhavana) tries to make her think her husband is dead.

Erda ordered a set of Malay *wayang siam* from Kelantan in the 1970s while visiting that country. Hamzah bin Awang Ahmad, the carver, was one of the few *dalangs* still practicing this art, which thrived in Malaysia until the last quarter of the twentieth century. Rama, Laksmana, Siti (Sita), Hanuman and the clowns are all represented.

The kind of research that Erda undertook differed from Laufer and Mead's approaches because they sought to assemble puppets as a significant feature of a culture. Laufer and Mead stayed long enough to appreciate such traditions in the context of daily life, and they wrote detailed notes in the field describing each specific piece. Erda traveled widely, contacting puppeteers and scholars in each country, some of whom were able to help her gather more puppets for exhibition. Thus, a handful of figures came to represent a whole tradition, and information acquired for the exhibit did not necessarily get carried over into the archival record.

Conclusion

Puppets in the collection over the last century have been acquired in many different ways: some well documented, many with scarcely any information.[14] The parts of the collection which have been actively collected by museum staff reflect different phases in the history of the museum as an entity. The Chinese and Balinese collections made by Laufer and Mead reflect pure, methodical research. Erda's collection efforts give breadth if not depth to the collection. There are scattered examples of many different genres but, while the image may enchant the viewer with its beauty, the figure will reveal little insight into the genre until they are better identified in the electronic entry.

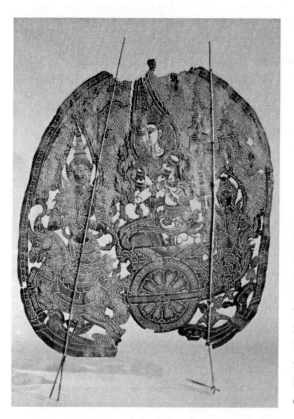

Sida (Sita) flies on a magic chariot above the battlefield of Alenka in this composite Thai *nang yai* (70.3/459). (Courtesy the Division of Anthropology, American Museum of Natural History.)

While these puppets now rest silent in their trays, they bore witness to important theater performances of Asia's past, arts that captured the imagination of those who collected them. We have chosen to tell the story of the collectors and explain why these figures caught their interest. Laufer preserved for posterity a vanishing genre; Mead psychoanalyzed a living one; and Erda put a show together. The motives that resulted in the collection are as different as the different eras within which each individual worked. They reflect the changing agenda of the museum as a whole. Though the forces that have molded the collection are varied, the end result has been the creation of a major puppet collection which awaits the researcher wishing to glean what information the collection possesses.

Notes

1. The entire Asian ethnographic collection is now available on the Internet at http://anthro.amnh.org and soon the Africa, North and South America and the Pacific collections will be available to the public.

2. Exact figures are hard to pin down. Pieces continue to be "found" as electronic processing increases the ability to cross-check data between collection areas (Africa and Asia, for example) and as terms for locations, cultures and names for puppets are identified so that each puppet is linked to more general terms and readily accessible by the searcher.

3. Northwest Coast Indian traditions are represented in the collection as part of the extensive mask collection.

4. A Maori puppet, *karetao*.

5. The oldest, a 1943 acquisition from a missionary in the Cameroons, is a double marionette figure — a male and female. There are also three from the Bambara people of Mali and two hand puppets from Senegal.

6. To cite an example, Margaret Mead in her letter of appreciation to donor George D. Pratt (November 18, 1927) says, "I am as pleased as the housewife is who wants a fur coat badly but knows the family money should be used to fill the coal bin. Had you given the money directly to the Museum, we never could have had the beautiful collection."

7. Orthography reflects the spelling used in a particular culture. Thus, Bhima in India is Bima in Indonesia.

8. Whenever possible this information has been transcribed into the note section for each puppet entry in the database. Some of the Laufer correspondence is accessible on the researcher Web database (in the Publications and Archives section) as well.

9. In the 1990s the Chinese shadow puppets were conserved. Lisa Kronthall, of the conservation department, worked diligently to separate puppets stuck together over the years without damaging the original Tung oils and color pigments. Now each figure has a separate place in a tray in cabinets in climate-controlled storage, their translucent beauty visible as if each was acquired a decade, not a century ago.

10. Wax cylinder recordings of these plays and songs from the AMNH collection are now located in the Archives of Traditional Music, Indiana University.

11. Work of this group is represented in the following publications, among others: Miguel Covarrubias, *Island of Bali* (New York: Knopf, 1937); Beryl de Zoete and Walter Spies, *Dance and Drama in Bali* (London: Faber and Faber, 1938); and Colin McPhee, *House in Bali* (New York: John Day, 1946).

12. Modern orthography for the Indonesian language has changed since Margaret Mead's time there. This paper uses the modern terms (i.e. "y" for "j" and "u" for "oe") except in the case of direct quotes.

13. Information in this section was obtained through conversations with members of the department who knew Bettie Erda: Dr. Stanley Freed, Lisa Whitall and Laila Williamson.

14. It would be useful if the identities of the characters and the locales could be researched and added to the information on the public site. A more comprehensive identification of these materials would make them a strong educational tool. In the meantime, only puppet scholars versed in the tradition concerned, can sort out the identities of those figures without their story character names.

Works Cited

Bateson, Gregory, and Margaret Mead. *Balinese Character: A Photographic Analysis*. New York: New York Academy of Sciences Special Publication, Vol. II, 1942.

Bateson, Mary Catherine. *With a Daughter's Eye*. New York: Pocket Books, 1984.

Belo, Jane, ed. *Traditional Balinese Culture*. New York: Columbia University Press, 1970.

Erda, Bettie. "Chinese Shadow Theater and The Chaos Box." *Natural History* 84 (2) (1975), 46–51.

_____. *Shadow Images of Asia: A Selection of Shadow Puppets from the American Museum of Natural History*. New York: Katonah Gallery, March 18–27, 1979.

Hirsch, Mary E. "Chinese Shadow Theater Playscripts: Two Translations." M.A thesis, University of Washington, 1998.

Humphrey, Jo. *Monkey King: A Celestial Heritage*. Jamaica, NY: St. John's University, 1980.

Laufer, Berthold. "History of the Rhinoceros," *Chinese Clay Figures: Part I*. Chicago. Field Museum of Natural History Publication 177, Anthropological Series 13, 2 (1914), 73–173.

_____. *Oriental Theatricals*. Chicago: Field Museum of Natural History, 1923.

_____. *The Prehistory of Aviation*. Chicago: Field Museum of Natural History Publication 253, Anthropological Series 18 (1928), 1.

Mead, Margaret. *Blackberry Winter: My Earlier Years*. New York: William Morrow, 1972.

Stalberg, Roberta. *China's Puppets*. San Francisco: China Books, 1984.

Walravens, Hartmut, ed. *Kleinere Schriften von Berthold Laufer: Teil 1: Publikationen aus der Zeit von 1894 bis 1910* (2 vol). Weisbaden: Franz Steiner, 1976.

_____. *Briefwechsel mit dem American Museum of Natural History: Guide to the Exhibition of the Chinese Collections, AMNH*. Berlin: C. Bell, 1991.

The Burr Tillstrom Collection and Archives at the Chicago Historical Society

BERNARD R. REILLY

The Tillstrom collection and archives at the Chicago Historical Society constitute the primary extant holdings of papers, films, artifacts, and memorabilia relating to the career of Burr Tillstrom, master puppeteer and creator of the Kuklapolitan Players and the long-running television program, "Kukla, Fran and Ollie (KFO). These materials were transferred to the Society by Burr Tillstrom through a series of gifts made during his lifetime and by bequest following his death in 1986. The materials include films and kinescopes of the early television programs and film and videocassette recordings of later KFO specials, productions, and performances; written "synopses" of programs (which were unscripted); photographs, correspondence, news clippings, and related papers; musical scores; and realia, including puppets, puppet stages, and props.

The materials are governed by restrictions placed by Mr. Tillstrom in his initial 1977 gift, reserving all copyrights and literary rights (now administered by the Burr Tillstrom Copyright Trust) and permitting reproduction or exhibition of any kinescope, film, or videotape materials only with "the prior permission of the copyright owner." The puppets, stages, and costumes were also given on the express condition that "they never be used for any performance, public or private." Study of the Tillstrom papers, photographs, and related archive materials is permitted in the Chicago Historical Society's Research Center, where a container list of the collections is available. Access to the films and television programs and to puppets and theatrical materials, is limited and must be arranged in advance.

Burr Tillstrom was born in Chicago in 1917. During his lifetime he created a multitude of puppet characters; among the most famous were Kukla (the name derives from the Russian for "puppet"), Ollie the dragon, Madame Ooglepuss, Beulah Witch, Cecil Bill, Fletcher Rabbit, and Colonel Crackie.

Tillstrom began performing as early as age five, staging puppet shows for parents and neighborhood children on Chicago's North Side. He graduated from Chicago's Senn High School and matriculated briefly at the University of Chicago, which he left to work with the Works Progress Administration in its Chicago Parks District Puppet Theater. Here Tillstrom devised and staged puppet shows in city parks and at public venues

like Cook County Hospital and the Art Institute of Chicago. It was during this period that he is said to have created Kukla, the diminutive bald-headed doll who was the first of the Kuklapolitan Players. In 1939 Tillstrom became manager of the puppet exhibits and marionette theater at the Marshall Field and Company store on Chicago's State Street and began staging Saturday morning puppets shows there, which RCA Victor broadcast over closed-circuit television from the department store.

Burr Tillstrom played an important role in the introduction of commercial television broadcasting

Burr Tillstrom with Kukla and Ollie. (Chicago Historical Society, ICHi-17044.)

Kukla and Ollie. (Chicago Historical Society, ICHi-17056.)

in the United States. RCA used Tillstrom's marionette troupe for its demonstrations promoting the new medium of television at the New York World's Fair in 1940. In 1941 Tillstrom performed on the premier telecast of Chicago's first commercially licensed television station, WBKB, which was launched by the theatrical producers Balaban and Katz. During World War II, Tillstrom staged benefit performances for the USO, bringing his unique artistry to servicemen and women in Red Cross hospitals throughout the Midwest.

In 1947 Tillstrom was asked by NBC, the parent company of RCA Victor, to produce a family-oriented, hour-long television program. Produced and broadcast over WBKB-TV in Chicago, the show, "Junior Jamboree," later "Kukla Fran and Ollie," united Tillstrom, the behind-the-scenes manipulator and voice of the puppets, with radio actress and vocalist Frances Allison. The program did not play to a studio audience, but was broadcast live. It was largely unscripted and mostly unrehearsed, the programs consisting of songs and comic banter between Allison and the various puppet characters. Of the impromptu nature of the productions, Tillstrom later said, "You don't need a script when you're talking to your friends." In line with the integration of entertainment and advertising typical in early television, the show promoted sponsor RCA Victor's television sets and services, as well as breakfast cereal, laundry detergent, and other consumer products.

In 1949, when the network's coaxial cable from Chicago to New York was opened, RCA sponsored the weekly telecast of KFO to NBC member stations. (The point of origin station was WBKB until August 1949, when the program moved to NBC affiliate WNBQ.) During its run KFO was awarded two Peabody Awards and three Emmys. In its heyday the program is said to have received 15,000 fan letters a day.

Despite a relatively strong following, the program was dropped by NBC in 1954 and was broadcast by ABC from 1954 to 1957, when it was discontinued due to poor ratings. Tillstrom later made occasional appearances on national television variety programs and specials. Notable were his appearances on a pioneering but short-lived satirical program, "That Was the Week That Was," in 1964 and 1965. Tillstrom won an Emmy for his "hand ballet" about the Berlin Wall on that program and critical praise for his puppet characterizations of Cuban premier Fidel Castro and President Lyndon Johnson's beagle.

Brief Inventory of the Collection and Archives

Typescript and handwritten synopses of "marionette plays" and puppet performances, 1930s–50s.

Printed and handwritten musical scores and arrangements developed for and/or used in KFO programs, 1940s–70s.

Correspondence regarding KFO, 1960s–70s.

Approximately 775 reels of kinescopes and films of KFO programs, 1949–1954.

Approximately 1,068 discs containing KFO audiorecordings made between 1951–1957.

55 reels of 16-mm film containing approximately 145 five-minute episodes of KFO, 1961–1970.

Approximately one hundred marionettes, hand puppets, and heads of various characters, early 1930s–70s.

Stage sets, props, accessories, and cases, 1950s–70s.

The Marionette Theatre
of Peter Arnott
at Harvard University

ANNETTE FERN

Peter D. Arnott (1931–1990) was a professor of drama who special-
ized in the theater of classical Greece. Born in Ipswich, England, he was
educated at the University of North Wales and at Oxford, earning his
Ph.D. from Wales in 1958 with a dissertation on acting in the ancient
Greek theater. He came to the United States in that same year to teach
at Iowa State University and in 1969 became professor of drama at Tufts
University in Massachusetts, where he remained until his unexpected
death from cancer at the age of fifty-nine. His many books include intro-
ductions to Greek, Roman, French, and Japanese theater, numerous
translations of classical Greek plays, a novel based on the life of Molière,
and *Plays Without People*,[1] an account of his exploration of the use of puppets for the performance of serious drama. Those puppets, together with
the archives of Arnott's academic, literary, and theatrical life, are now a
part of the Harvard Theatre Collection.[2]

Arnott's special interest was the difficulty of presenting ancient plays
to modern audiences, and the Marionette Theatre provided him with a
medium that he found superior to many others for interpreting certain
styles of drama. He described his view of the theater's mission often during the forty years of its existence; here is a typical (though untypically
stuffy) program note from 1970.

His marionette productions are not entertainment for children; in fact, he requests that children under twelve not be admitted. The purpose of the Arnott Marionette Theatre is threefold: first, to use the distinctive qualities of the medium to offer re-creation of Greek, Roman, and other types of formal drama often difficult to interpret on the live stage because of the naturalistic training and preconceptions of modern actors and directors; secondly, to offer a repertoire of plays rarely performed "live" though commonly read as set texts and so to supplement the work of university drama departments, and courses, in theatre history and classics; thirdly, to take these plays to places where they would not normally be seen, and sometimes where theatre would not be seen at all, at a fraction of the cost of importing a live company.[3]

These worthy goals, expressed frequently elsewhere in writings, lectures, and interviews, were the principles upon which the theater was founded, but they do not account for the wonderful theatricality of the performances themselves or for the magical effect they seem to have had upon those who saw them. For this we must look to the unusual synthesis of the puppet theater's special characteristics — Arnott's broad and deep scholarly knowledge of the theatrical, literary, and social milieu of the plays he chose to produce, and (not least) his own formidable abilities as a performer.

Arnott had played with puppets and toy theaters as a child, but by the time he was in secondary school it had become clear that his interest in puppets had become far more professional. By 1948 the rudiments of his production style were in place. His puppets were marionettes, and even in these early productions he often performed alone, manipulating all the puppets himself and usually providing all the voices. By the early 1950s, the Marionette Theatre had become, definitively, a solo performance.[4] During these first years of the theater's existence, Arnott offered a diverse menu of productions: a condensation of Marlowe's *Doctor Faustus*; an extract from André Obey's *Noah*, using abstract puppets with featureless wooden blocks for heads; a few scenes from Shakespearean comedies; *Peter and the Wolf* and *Rigoletto* to recorded music. He often described productions and puppets as experimental, but even at this time he had little or no interest in modern plays written explicitly for puppets, and many of the productions were decidedly not for children. Most productions toured to schools, community associations, and festivals.

The most successful of all these early experiments was *The Frogs* of

Aristophanes, in Gilbert Murray's translation. Arnott had learned both Latin and Greek at school, and he writes of having been fascinated by classical drama while still in his early teens. He chose to study classics in college, and the puppets went with him; *The Frogs* was performed for the first time in October 1950, at the University College of North Wales in Bangor. It proved a perennial favorite and remained in his repertoire in this form until 1955; by 1952 he was able to write that it had already been seen by more than 2,500 people, at meetings of various branches of the Classical Association of Great Britain.[5]

In 1952 he went to Oxford to take a second B.A., and the Oxford *Isis* noticed his arrival: "Oddest Freshman this term is Peter Arnott of Exeter, who keeps marionettes."[6] At Oxford the puppets appeared in *La Traviata*, to recorded music, and in an early version of *Les Fourberies de Scapin* of Molière (later to become one of his favorite productions), and, in January 1953, the *Agamemnon*, in Arnott's own translation. Though the first performance of *Agamemnon* was not entirely successful owing, wrote Arnott, to lack of rehearsal, by October of that year it had improved enough to receive a favorable notice in the *Times Educational Supplement*.[7] He returned to Wales for his M.A. and Ph.D., by this time clearly destined for an academic career, but the Marionette Theatre continued to occupy him; puppet opera and Shakespeare disappeared from its repertoire, to be replaced by additional Greek and Latin plays. In 1956, he presented *The Birds* of Aristophanes to the annual meeting of the Classical Association and toured the production for a year throughout the British Isles.

In 1958 he came to the United States, to teach in the classics department of Iowa State University. He found himself, as he put it in a later interview, "rather frustrated by traditional scholarly explications of the plays which always seemed to miss the point and concerned themselves with matters of grammar, matters of archeology, matters of textual studies which never seemed to be truly relevant to the play as play...."[8] He left classics for the theater department, where he finally felt at home. His reputation as a puppeteer accompanied him to America, and in addition to teaching, writing, directing, and performing, he toured extensively with the Marionette Theatre. The repertoire of Greek and Latin plays continued to expand, while from the non-classical theater Molière's *Scapin* was joined by Racine's *Phèdre*, Marlowe's *Doctor Faustus* (this time in its full length), Jonson's *Volpone*, and the medieval morality play, *Everyman*.

Performances were in English, and the translations from Greek, Latin, and French were now always his own. By 1958 he had married, and his wife Eva took on the not inconsiderable responsibilities of booking the touring productions, as well as of constructing puppet bodies and creating costumes. At his most active he gave thirty to forty performances on tour a year; his files list 332 places visited between 1958 and 1990.

Response to these productions was extraordinary. Puppet theater in Britain in the first half of the twentieth century was thought to be exclusively for children, or, at best, a cabaret entertainment displaying elaborate trick work or self-conscious pictorial effects. Despite the existence of investigations into the expressive potential of the puppet performer by such theorists as Arthur Symons and Edward Gordon Craig, to most audiences puppets were not to be taken seriously. Announcements of Arnott's productions were generally met with a sort of amused skepticism; audiences reported that they went prepared to be polite. A typical account of the actual experience is the one provided by Hubert C. Heffner in his foreword to *Plays Without People*.

> Some years ago when H. D. F. Kitto, that masterly interpreter of Greek tragedy, was visiting us at Indiana University, he told me of a remarkable experience which he had recently had in witnessing a performance of Euripides' *Medea* done with puppets. He said when he first heard that a young teacher of Greek, then serving in one of the colleges in Wales, was performing Greek tragedy in this manner, he assumed that such a representation would be ludicrous; hence when he later had an opportunity to see the *Medea*, he went out of curiosity prepared to be quietly amused. To his amazement, when the play was over, he realized that he had forgotten all about puppets and amusement and had witnessed a remarkably moving performance of Euripides' tragedy.[9]

The Australian classical scholar G. H. Gellie provides a similar report of his own experience, this time of a comedy, in his book review of Arnott's *An Introduction to the Greek Theatre*.

> In 1956 I saw a performance of the *Birds* of Aristophanes presented on a stage-set about three feet wide and two feet high. I was sitting 100 feet from the set in a large hall and before the lights went out I comforted myself with the thought that Greek drama was Greek drama and that, as a person professionally involved, I should lend

my patient support even to the sillier manifestations of it. Then the lights went out and Mr. Arnott began. Gaily-costumed puppets very quickly created a convincing world in their own dimension. The hall became the theatre of Dionysus and for an hour and a half it was 414 B.C.[10]

Though Arnott found American audiences more receptive to the idea of puppets in serious drama than the British had been, they still had to be convinced. Reporting on a production of *Medea* in 1958, his first performance in the United States, a *Daily Iowan* reporter begins, "In Peter Arnott's puppet presentation of *Medea* ... there was at first a sense of good-humored curiosity: i.e., how well would a Greek tragedy find expression through this charming medium?" In no time, however, the reporter finds himself drawn into the performance: "The hands manipulating the strings were forgotten, and the white-faced wooden Medea became a person to be feared, hated, and pitied."[11] More than twenty years later, John Engstrom, writing about a performance of the *Oresteia* at Tufts expresses similar doubts: "To a Western audience, it probably sounds like a dreadful idea. Greek tragedies performed with marionettes. Silly. Cute. Juvenile. But within the first few moments of his recent performance ... English puppet-master Peter Arnott commanded respect."[12] The archives bristle with similar narratives from student newspapers, metropolitan dailies, scholarly newsletters, and many files of personal correspondence. Audiences came expecting the worst, or not knowing what to expect, and departed conscious of having had a satisfying and often enlightening theatrical experience.

Arnott was acutely conscious of the low repute of puppets among theater practitioners of his time; his most sustained attempt to influence this perception was *Plays Without People*, and in a 1964 letter to the person responsible for publicizing the book he sets out many of his concerns.

I fancy that you will have to deal with the same factors in selling the book as I do in selling the performances on which the book is based — namely, that people who are interested in puppetry tend, on the whole, not to be interested in serious drama, and vice versa.... I have always found the best approach is to treat this thing from the standpoint of theatre, primarily, rather than from that of puppetry. Most puppeteers are avid for anything that appears in print about their art, and you should have little trouble in getting the book across to them. I am far more interested in appealing to theatre practitioners who normally dismiss puppetry as beneath their attention — and there is, in point of fact, a fair amount in the book that will interest theatre historians, whether they care for puppets or not.... I am trying to suggest that your publicity should take the line "This is an examination of a number of important problems of period play-revival, with suggestions as to how these problems may be solved by the use of non-human performers" rather than "Puppets! Puppets! Puppets! See what clever things the little dolls can do! See, Dick, see! The puppets are performing Aeschylus!" ... I have been dealing with this problem for sixteen years, and have finally, performance-wise, got it licked; I do think it would be valuable to apply the same technique to the book.[13]

Puppeteers were apparently not as avid for the book as might have been anticipated; Arnott reports having been attacked by "an *aficionado*" for using in it ideas that had been expounded by American puppeteers thirty years earlier,[14] and the publisher reported that it had not sold as well as had been hoped. There were reviews in humanities and library journals, though, and the book retains a steady readership among puppetry scholars and practitioners today.

Despite skepticism from both theater historians and classical scholars, and comparatively little interest from other puppeteers, Arnott was sure of his ground and continued to develop new productions. *Oedipus the King, The Clouds, Antigone, Electra, The Bacchae, Alcestis,* and *Hippolytus* were added, one by one, to the plays already in his repertoire. Only six or seven plays were offered for booking in a given season, and by the mid–1980s only the classical plays remained, perhaps reflecting the fact that most of the touring productions were requested by school or university classics departments or classics clubs and associations.

Arnott performed on an open stage some six feet wide by two-and-a-half feet deep, without a proscenium. The rear of the stage was masked to about waist height, leaving the upper half of the puppeteer completely visible, though generally not in light. Scenery might be minimal or elaborate, depending upon the needs of the production; the puppets themselves, about eighteen inches to two feet in height, tended to be quite simple. The bodies were stuffed and jointed cloth, for lightness and portability; the heads were of plastic wood molded on wooden dowels. Lighting came from modified desk lamps on stands; normally there was no

Peter Arnott performing *The Bacchae*. Puppets (left to right) are a Chorus woman, Dionysus, Pentheus. (Photograph from the Harvard Theatre Collection, dbMS Thr 409, Papers of Peter Arnott.)

music, and special effects were employed only sparingly. An entire production, including the stage, could be packed into two suitcases for touring.

Since Arnott manipulated all the puppets himself, as well as supplying all the voices, he found it necessary to devise a simplified control. With it, he could easily hang puppets not in use backstage, have characters at rest onstage when they were required to be in the scene but not active, and, when necessary, work a puppet with one hand. In his writing Arnott stressed the simplicity and even crudity of his materials. A self-confessed "mediocre technician," he was unmoved by performances in which extraordinary technical virtuosity was employed for what he considered to be trivial purposes, and he could be a little unkind to practitioners whose involvement with the text was not as serious as his own. Similarly, he was vociferous in insisting that his plays were not for children, not because he had any particular disdain for children themselves — he had three of his own and was evidently a devoted father — but because his plays were so very obviously for adults. That audiences responding to his advertising saw only that the performances were to be by puppets and not that the puppets were performing plays likely to be long, violent, obscene, psychologically complex, or otherwise unsuitable for the very young was a source of constant wonder and irritation to him.

Though he had no interest in creating a disjointing skeleton marionette or a troupe of realistic ballet dancers, Arnott took great pleasure in finding puppet-appropriate solutions to problems not readily solved by human actors. Puppets could fly easily or disappear; his Helen in *Doctor Faustus* had no face, so that one could imagine her to be as beautiful as possible. In *Medea*, the murder of the children could be seen in shadow through the palace wall. God in medieval plays was his own seemingly enormous hand, descending from above; the god Dionysus, at the beginning and end of *The Bacchae*, was his own face, lit from below.

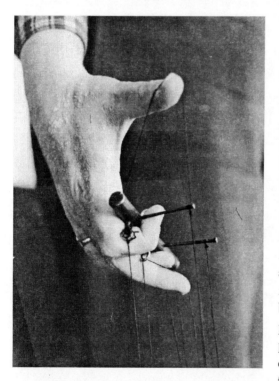

Peter Arnott demonstrating his marionette control. (Photograph from the Harvard Theatre Collection, dbMS Thr 409, Papers of Peter Arnott.)

The issue of scale was central to his notion of how and why to present Greek plays with puppets. He had been aware from his earliest performances of this repertoire that the plays worked, but did not understand quite why until he visited Greece and saw the actual theaters. "Greek theatres were huge," he wrote, and went on to explain that the choice for a modern revival striving to recreate the conditions of the original is either to perform them in a surviving classical theater, as is done in Greece, or to shrink the performance. "I use marionettes to give the sense of a performance which is taking place some distance away," he said. "Once this is done, I have found that all the conventions become meaningful again. All the verbal conventions built into the play to explain things to an audience that can't see very much become justified; and the play works again in the terms for which it was designed."[15]

The verbal conventions of Greek theater also provided a platform for Arnott's considerable powers as an actor. Since classical Greek plays employed a limited number of actors, each playing several parts, and since the structure of the dialogue in these plays was highly formalized, it required very little alteration of the texts to make them suitable for performance by a single speaker. George Speaight, writing in 1955 about the performances of John Wright, noted that Wright "...mounts longer and more elaborate plays than most puppeteers of his generation, with a welcome use of human readers, but the perfect synthesis between voice and puppet has perhaps yet to be found."[16] Arnott himself had made some early and unsatisfactory experiments using reciters or recorded texts and had come to the same conclusion. In his case, this perfect synthesis was accomplished by combining all the functions in his own person. In another sense, taking on every aspect of the performance—creating the puppets, moving them on the stage, choosing the words that they would speak and actually speaking those words himself—made him feel that he himself was inhabiting the historic theater he was striving to recreate: "The Greek drama's author was his own actor, his own choreographer, his own director, his own designer. So at least in the early period, for all practical purposes, the play was a one-man performance."[17]

All the plays that Peter Arnott chose to perform with marionettes shared characteristics that made them both appropriate for puppet performance and difficult of access for modern actors and directors. Whether classical Greek or Latin, neo-classical French, Elizabethan English, or medieval, their language, movement style, and historical and social milieu placed them effectively out of reach for most theatergoers and students of drama. Arnott saw the revival of historic plays as one form of translation, and the goal of his particular form of translation was to make these dramas both authentic and accessible. As is so often the case, he put it best himself: "I am arguing, therefore, that the acceptable formality and artificiality of the marionette offers one solution to the problem [of recreating formal acting styles]. By presenting the plays in a medium which is itself at a remove from reality, one can make the non-realistic attitudes and conventions of the plays more immediately acceptable."[18]

Throughout his career Arnott searched for methods to make historic drama more accessible. His translations, while faithful to their originals, were above all meant to be readable; his books, though scholarly and well researched, were meant for a general audience. In most of his writing about the use of puppets for the performance of serious drama, Arnott presented himself as an educator searching for the most evocative manner of reviving certain historic theatrical forms. In his productions, even dimly seen in the few grainy, nonprofessional videos that survive in the archives, it is clear that, whatever the didactic motive, by the time they reach production, the plays are powerful, immediate theatrical experiences. It seems then that he was right: that puppets, performing his translations with his voice, and informed by his knowledge of the theatrical, literary, and social milieu of the period, could make classical drama immediate to modern audiences. There is some irony in the fact that, even though so much evidence exists in archival resources to tell us what it is that Arnott thought and did, without his presence the actual experience of his performances is almost as remote to us as those he sought to recreate.

A Note About the Archive

The Peter Arnott Collection contains documentation of his entire career as a professor, actor, director, author, and puppeteer. The archive is arranged by the format of the material; with the exception of the puppets themselves, items related to the Marionette Theatre have not been segregated into a separate series. The collection includes videotapes of productions of *Antigone*, *The Bacchae*, and *Oedipus the King*, and a number of audiotapes; the videotape of *The Bacchae* includes a lecture by

Arnott at Carleton University on the subject of using marionettes to perform Greek drama. An on-line finding aid is available in the Harvard Theatre Collection; though production titles are given in the notes to the files, no distinction is made in the notes between live and puppet performances.

There are approximately eighty puppets in the archive, representing characters from the following plays: *Alcestis, Antigone, The Bacchae, The Clouds, Cyclops, Electra, Hippolytus, Medea*, and *Oedipus*. The portable puppet stage, scenery, and lighting equipment, though present in the collection, are not yet described in the finding aid. Puppets from productions no longer in the repertoire were recycled for later use, so it is likely that only a very few have survived intact. Among the items in a box of fragmentary or unidentified puppets are four heads for characters from *Les Fourberies de Scapin* and a "Charlie McCarthy" ventriloquist's dummy, identified by Eva Arnott as Peter Arnott's earliest puppet toy.

The author wishes to thank Eva Arnott, first of all, for her decision to keep the archives of Peter Arnott's academic and performing life together in a single collection, providing scholars with the opportunity to see precisely how one influenced the other; and second, for her generosity in sharing her memories of the way her husband worked within several conversations and e-mails during the writing of this chapter.

Notes

1. Peter D. Arnott, *Plays Without People: Puppetry and Serious Drama* (Bloomington: Indiana University Press, 1964).

2. Harvard Theatre Collection, dbMS Thr 409, *Papers of Peter Arnott* (cited hereafter as Arnott Papers).

3. Program, Indiana University at South Bend, "The Premiere Performance of *Agamemnon*," Saturday, October 3, 1970, in Arnott Papers.

4. In the Arnott Papers, the earliest productions of the theater are chronicled in a scrapbook, "Experimental Marionette Theatre," which Arnott maintained from 1948 to 1957. From 1958, the activities of the marionettes are documented in clippings, correspondence, articles, and other material dispersed throughout the archives.

5. Manuscript note in Arnott Papers, "Experimental Marionette Theatre."

6. Clipping, Oxford *Isis*, October 29, 1953, in Arnott Papers, "Experimental Marionette Theatre."

7. Clipping, *Times (London) Educational Supplement*, October 23, 1953, in Arnott Papers, "Experimental Marionette Theatre."

8. Interview with Porter S. Woods (ca. May 1982). Typescript in Arnott Papers.

9. Arnott, *Plays Without People*, 11.

10. G. H. Gellie, book review, "*An Introduction to the Greek Theatre*," *AUMLA: Journal of the Australasian Universities Language & Literature Association*, no. 12 (November 1959): 73.

11. Stan Hansen, "Curiosity in the Beginning — Sense of Tragedy at End: Arnott's Medea Becomes a Character," *Daily Iowan*, October 29, 1958, clipping in Arnott Papers.

12. John Engstrom, "Theatre: Pulling Strings, Classic Puppetry," *Boston Phoenix*, July 8, 1980, clipping in Arnott Papers.

13. Peter Arnott, letter (carbon copy of typescript) to Irene Sidor, Indiana University Press, March 1, 1964, in Arnott Papers.

14. Peter Arnott, "Puppets and Greek Tragedy: The Dream Landscape," *Explorations*, no. 24 (March 1969): 98.

15. Suzanne Cowan, "Peter Arnott's Marionettes and *The Bacchae*," *Theater* (Summer 1980): 50.

16. George Speaight, *The History of the English Puppet Theatre*. (London: George G. Harrap, 1955), 268.

17. Cowan, "Arnott's Marionettes," 53.

18. Arnott, *Plays Without People*, 28.

The Lou Harrison Collection: Music and Puppetry East to West

KATHY FOLEY

The puppet collection of the University of California at Santa Cruz includes examples of various Asian puppets and selected Western figures that rise from the interaction of East and West in the emerging field of Pacific Rim music-puppetry. The collection represents the interest of major American composer Lou Harrison in object theater and the puppet-music performances inspired by Asian models that are characteristic of West Coast America since the 1970s. This essay will detail the intellectual framework that gives rise to the collection, note the pieces that may be of interest, and explain the research potential of the set.

The collection was donated to the University of California by Lou Harrison in 1997, along with other material that documents the life and work of this major artist whose work has been strongly influenced by the music of East and Southeast Asia. Harrison's first major encounters with puppetry came during the Depression, in the context of the WPA in San Francisco, where he was involved as a young artist. He was exposed to the work of Ralph Chessé and other important West Coast puppet artists. In the 1970s he served as a musician for Pauline Benton, who did demonstrations of Peking-style Chinese shadow puppets. Benton had studied and collected shadow figures in China with Lee T'uo-ch'en, the major shadow player in Peking prior to World War II. Returning to the United States, she formed a company, the Red Gate Players, and performed for thirty-five years. In the 1970s, Harrison provided percussion and other musical accompaniment for her presentations. Harrison, who had studied Korean and Chinese music, found her project appropriate for his musical inclinations. The pair met through the American Society for Asian Arts, a summer program that brought top Asian artists to teach American students and eventually gave rise to the Center for World Music, an organization that, since the 1970s, has brought Asian and Asian-influenced American artists together to learn music, dance, and puppetry.

Harrison's collection was mostly acquired in the 1970s and 1980s and represents two thrusts. One aspect is Harrison's ongoing interest and research into Asian puppet forms, especially those of Indonesia and China. The other aspect is his interest in American puppetry, which fuses music and object theater. The collection contains figures by Majorie Batchelder, author of *The Puppet Theatre Handbook* and a major American puppeteer. Figures made by Batchelder's husband, Paul McPharlin, who authored *The Puppet Theatre in America: A History: 1524–1948* and founded the Puppeteers of America in 1936, are also in the collection. Also present are figures from Harrison's own puppet operas, which were inspired by his work with Benton and, later, his growing interest in Javanese music and puppetry.

In 1974 Harrison was hired to teach contemporary music at the Center for World Music in Berkeley, California. At the same time, Professor Robert Brown, with financial support from Sam and Louise Scripps, mounted an extensive program of Asian performance, with emphasis on South and Southeast Asian material. Harrison began to study Javanese gamelan under the noted Jogjakarta palace master, Pak Chakaningrat, and experienced the beauty of Javanese, Sundanese, and Balinese *wayang* (puppetry). The interaction of music and puppetry and the ease with which the composer could create music on the gamelan ensemble appealed strongly to his aesthetic sense. The way that Asian puppet genres give sound a visual form, as stately music accompanies the entrance of a refined monarch or staccato percussion "rat-a-tats" as demons fight battles, appealed to Harrison, whose strong visual aesthetic augments his rich acoustic explorations. He began collecting puppets and creating his own puppet operas from this time.

Lou Harrison, October 1993. (Photograph by Rita Bottoms.)

The Asian Collection

Perhaps the most stunning set in the collection is the *wayang kulit* figures from the 1986 World Exposition in Vancouver. A beautifully carved set with approximately thirty figures was specially created by the premier Jogjakarta puppetmaker and master, Sukasman. Harrison, who took his Javanese orchestral gamelan group to participate in a festival that was sponsored by the Indonesian government, purchased the puppets after the performance of a *Rāmāyana* story at the festival. Later, after a period as a Fulbright scholar in New Zealand, Harrison traveled to Indonesia. He acquired a set of children's toy puppets (*wayang kertas*, paper *wayang*). Over one hundred delicate, flat figures are represented. They are intricately painted in the style of the north coast Javanese city of Cirebon. These figures are documented with names and are a useful tool for understanding the iconography of Cirebon-style Javanese puppetry. Selected *Mahābhārata* figures from central Java are also to be found, including high-quality representations of Arjuna. There is also a Javanese *wayang klitik* (flat wooden puppet) of an ogre king, two Balinese *wayang parwa* shadow figures, and two *wayang golek purwa* (round wooden figures from the Sundanese tradition of western Java), including Batara Guru (S[h]iva) and a Gatotkaca, the son of Bhima, a hero of the *Mahābhārata*. Both were made by puppet carver and martial artist Herman Suwanda.

Shadow figures from India and mainland Southeast Asia are also included. The translucent shadows of Andhra Pradesh can be seen in a miniature *Rāmāyana* set of eleven puppets, which was distributed in the United States during the 1970s as an educational tool to teach the epic. A couple of large Andhra Pradesh figures are present for comparison with the small figures. Two Rajasthani *Kathaputli* string marionettes are in the collection, as are two Turkish *karaghöz* figures, representing the comic hero Karaghöz and his friend Hacivat. A single Thai *nang talung* puppet is also included.

Chinese shadow puppet figures include ten Peking-style figures from the epic story *Journey to the West,* including Monkey, Pigsy, and the monk hero who brings the Buddhist scriptures to China. A set of twenty-six papier-mâché hand puppet figures from Taiwan also includes the monkey episode puppets, as well as figures from other stories. Finally, there is a Japanese rod puppet and two Japanese string puppet toys.

The American Collection

Sixteen figures from Marjorie Batchelder's story of Navaho in the Southwest were acquired by Harrison after the death of this major American puppeteer. The figures were made sometime in the 1940s or '50s. The piece shows tourists and Indians encountering each other in Santa Fe. A string figure, Bishop of Guadalupe, also represented Batchelder's work. Shadow figures made with gels for a Paul McPharlin show are also included in the collection. The figures appear to have been inspired by Chinese shadow puppets. Unfortunately, the figures have deteriorated, and the puppets must be handled with care. A toy theater Harrison acquired at Pollock's in London is in good condition.

The remaining figures represent Harrison's own work. Two rod puppets that were created by Rob Gordon for Harrison's 1970s opera, *Young Caesar*, while fragile, continue to give a sense of this important opera. In addition to fusing music and puppetry, this piece was an early work that

Lou Harrison with *Young Caesar*'s physician, October 1993. (Photograph by Rita Bottoms.)

addressed issues of gay love. The commissioned work was presented in Pasadena by five singers, five musicians, and five puppeteers. At the time, it created an uproar because of its subject matter. The music used two contrasting modes, diatonic and Persian/Indian, representing Rome and Asia Minor, respectively. The work of Spanish composer Pedro Manuel de Falla and his *Master Peter's Play,* done as a puppet show in Paris avant-garde circles, was an initial inspiration for this work. After the first performance, a second shadow-puppet version of *Young Caesar* was done with new puppets by Bill Jones, and some of these shadow figures are also in the collection. *Young Caesar* was significant in that it was Harrison's first attempt to bring his interests in puppetry and composition together to present a Western story.

His next major puppet work was *Puss and Boots,* which had a gamelan score and was generated while Harrison was a professor of music at Mills College. While the *Puss and Boots* puppets are not in the collection, one can get a sense of the style of Mark Bulwinkle, the artist who works in wrought iron, who made the *Puss and Boots* figures. After the performance, this Oakland-based artist made a set of forty-nine figures, entitled *Lou and Bill Visit Nature* as a gift to Harrison. In the set, which is part of the UCSC collection, one sees Harrison and his partner in music and life, Bill Colvig, riding in their beat-up Volkswagen bus and canoeing. Trees, picnic condiments, lighting, rain, a smiling sun, fish, animals, and angry clouds are part of the exquisite set. Character and narrative have been welded into the lovely wrought-iron figures, which give insight into the life and love of two wonderful musicians and artists of our time. The set got its performance debut at a memorial service for Bill Colvig, who died in 2000. Kathy Foley was the puppeteer for this shadow show, *Lou and Bill Visit Nature,* with the music composed by Lou Harrison and executed by Harrison and Charles Hansen. The show was a tribute to Colvig, the young Caesar, who inspired and supported Harrison's musical endeavors. Colvig built gamelan and was a musician in many of Harrison's performances.

Significance

While the collection is relatively small, it tells a significant story. In addition to being a place where researchers can see figures from a variety of Asian forms, especially shadow puppets, this collection documents an important thrust in puppet/music theater of this generation. It shows how West Coast avant-garde artists adapted the performing traditions of the Pacific Rim in order to generate a new movement in American object theater. Asian-influenced fusion works like *Young Caesar* and *Puss and Boots* are part of a larger experimental movement that has brought together musicians, visual artists, and puppeteers. Julie Taymor, Larry Reed, and my own work, which includes a puppet opera, *Hamlet*, and *Faustus at Wittenberg*, with the score again by Lou Harrison, are examples of such work. Many — Harrison, Taymor, Reed, and I — first experienced this possibility of a *gesamtkunstwerk* in the context of the American Society for Asian Arts/Center for World Music, where Harrison studied and taught. Asian performances presented by the Center for World Music demonstrated the possibility of a new kind of puppet work through its models of Chinese, Javanese, Balinese and Sundanese puppet-music performances. While the collection bears the strong imprint of one man, Lou Harrison, it tells a story of the larger East-West encounter that has become an important root of music-puppetry in contemporary America.

The Dwiggins Marionettes at the Boston Public Library

Roberta Zonghi

Step into the Rare Books and Manuscript area of the Boston Public Library and discover a most delightful, unexpected treasure: William A. Dwiggins's collection of marionettes. Displayed in its own quarters, just to the right as you approach the department on the third floor, the collection was donated to the Boston Public Library on July 18, 1967, as part of a much larger Dwiggins Collection. The marionettes represent a distinctly different, special side of the noted advertising artist, type and book designer, and illustrator.

Born in 1880, William Addison Dwiggins grew up in Cambridge, a small Ohio town. He studied art and lettering in Chicago with Frederic Goudy at the Frank Holme School of Illustration. In 1903 he returned to Cambridge, where he set up his own print business, the Guernsey Shop, to produce finely illustrated and printed books. Three years later, when his business venture proved unsuccessful, Dwiggins joined Goudy at his Village Press in Hingham, Massachusetts. Not long after Dwiggins's arrival, Goudy moved on to New York. Dwiggins, now working with local men important in the field of printing — D. B. Updike and Bruce Rogers, among them — had at last found his home. He was receiving commissions from Houghton Mifflin and Merrymount Press, as well as advertising clients such as Direct Advertising, Strathmore Paper, and Paine Furniture.

Throughout his lifetime in art, Dwiggins was a meticulous craftsman, serious and dedicated. A perfectionist, his type designs and book layouts gave testament to his keen eye and imagination. By the 1930s he had proved himself a successful artist, illustrator, and businessman. From the mid- to late 1930s, he began to develop his famous type designs, creating Electra in 1935 and Caledonia in 1939. Dwiggins's remarkable output consisted of illustrations, design work or type design for more than 468 books, hundreds of advertising commissions, and nineteen complete type designs. It does not seem possible that he would have had any time or energy left for another project, but the collection of marionettes at the Boston Public Library proves otherwise.

Marionettes and Other Works in Wood

On the one hand, his marionettes are lighthearted and amusing; on the other, they are marvelous examples of engineering and design. The intense, dedicated designer directed the same concentration and passion for perfection to his marionettes that he gave to every other aspect of his work and creation. According to Dorothy Abbe in *The Dwiggins Marionettes,* Bill Dwiggins loved working with wood. His other loves — type design, book design, advertising design, and calligraphy — generally took precedence, but a peek into his archives at the library reveals many examples of his work in wood. He was talented in the use of his hands and mind. Presented the problem of how to complete a design project, he would create a special tool for just that task. In the Dwiggins Room, we find a variety of such unique tools. We also discover wooden furniture designed and carved by Dwiggins, including a couch upholstered with a Dwiggins-designed rug, sewn by his wife Mabel. Moving on to the Dwiggins storage room, we find a sewing table created by Bill for Mabel to make her work on his projects simpler and more efficient.

His most exciting, extensive creations in wood are in Dwiggins's theater, theater equipment, and his marionettes. Once he began a project, he had to see it through to the absolute end. In designing and carving marionettes, he also needed a vehicle in which to showcase these wondrous characters. The result was an entire theater in the garage behind his house on Irving Street in Hingham, Massachusetts. Named "Point Five Irving Street," the puppet theater could accommodate up to forty-five attendees with room for a few more "crashers" — his term for the uninvited guests who turned up whenever a performance was held. Point

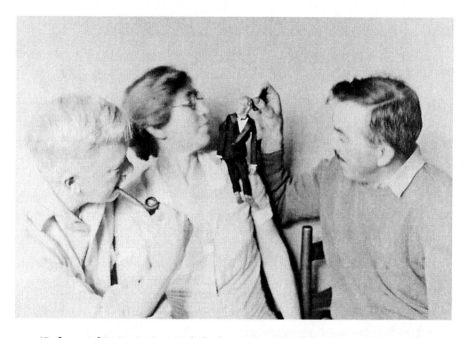

(*Left to right*): Dwiggins, Mabel, the marionette of Crosby, and Crosby him-self, probably photographed by Dorothy Abbe, from the Abbe Collection, Folder 2-F-1. (Boston Public Library/Rare Books Department. Courtesy the Trustees.)

Five Irving Street was situated among the apple trees in his backyard. Dwiggins and company proudly declared it "the only theatre that has a foyer with natural effects."

He even wrote plays to feature his wooden actors and actresses. He produced the plays, printed the tickets, and created sound-effect machines and lighting apparatuses that thrilled him as much as they thrilled his audiences. All this adventure in puppetry began in 1928. A member of the Hingham Manuscript Club, MIT Professor William Crosby read from a play that he had written for his children, *The Mystery of the Blind Beggarman, or Billy Brown's Bravery*. For William Dwiggins, "the play started the whole racket as a matter of fact—[Crosby] read it to us one night at the Manuscript Club and we saw that we had a call to build a marionette outfit and produce it."

At that time Mr. Crosby was the only one of the group who had had experience in making marionettes, since he had created a clothespin puppet to illustrate his play for his children. According to Ardra Soule Warle in "Clothespin into Püterschein" (*World Youth*, May 23, 1936), there followed two years of whittling and costuming by Mr. and Mrs. Dwiggins, Professor Crosby, and other members of the Manuscript Club. The group set about creating twenty-six characters for the play, including a dog, a rat, and a ghost. Bill Dwiggins was the master carver, and Mabel Dwiggins took on the task of sewing the costumes. Ardra reported that "the whittling parties turned into manipulation parties" as the members learned their lines and the technique of moving the parts of their puppets. They first rehearsed on a temporary stage, but Dwiggins soon rectified that with the creation of Point Five Irving Street.

Some time after the publication of Dwiggins's play, *Millennium I* (1945), a play detailing the war of machines on men, he and Dorothy Abbe produced an elegant brochure entitled *What Are the Dwiggins Marionettes?* Beginning with "Marionettes under the Püterschein Authority," the brochure provided many historical details on the beginnings of the Dwiggins marionettes. The first play, *The Mystery of the Mysterious Beggarman, or Billy Brown's Bravery* (1933), was described by Dwiggins as a "World Premier After Three Year's [*sic*] Preparation."

For at least a dozen years Dwiggins enjoyed working with his marionettes. In 1935 Paul McPharlin included an essay by W. A. Dwiggins, entitled "Counterbalanced Marionettes," in *Puppetry: An International Yearbook for 1935*. In it Dwiggins shared his theories on motion and manipulation: "If motions in general could be left to gravity on one side and string-pull on the other, the manipulator could give his main attention to fine shades of expression via stance, gesture, etc. The system shown in these diagrams allows almost automatic motion...." His diagrams for the making of marionettes are as precise and detailed as the designs he created for all his professional jobs in advertising or publishing.

About 1937 he produced a second set of marionettes according to his own "Püterschein system," based on his years of experience making and performing with marionettes. The new system resulted in marionettes with exquisite lifelike movement. Gerhard Unger, type designer, researcher, and scholar, noted that Dwiggins's marionettes had tremendously angular facial features. During his research on type design, Unger read that, once when Bill Dwiggins was sitting in the audience of a puppet play, he noticed that the faces appeared flat and unnatural, almost inhuman. Dwiggins determined to solve the problem; his designs produced not only marionettes with extremely angular features that were human and lifelike to the audience, but they also influenced the design of his typefaces. The final page of his handbook, *Marionette in Motion,* notes that "W. A. Dwiggins sets forth in this study the ways of making and working marionettes so that they will be well-balanced, manageable, and convincing in motion."

Also in 1937, Dwiggins moved his marionette theater into his new studio directly across the street from his home at 30 Leavitt Street in Hingham. With this move, he realized his dream of a fully equipped miniature theater — the theater that came eventually to the Boston Public Library. Dwiggins's colleague, longtime friend, and collaborator, Dorothy Abbe, was also the executrix of his will. She saw to it that the collection came to the Boston Public Library. She personally oversaw the design and installation of his library and workroom, called the Dwiggins Room, the Theatre, and the Marionette Room, which was officially opened to the public on June 21, 1976. The speaker at the event was Professor Basil Milovsoroff of Dartmouth College, a contemporary of Dwiggins.

Like Dwiggins, Dorothy Abbe was fascinated and thrilled by the marionettes. She shares her feelings in her book on the Dwiggins Mari-

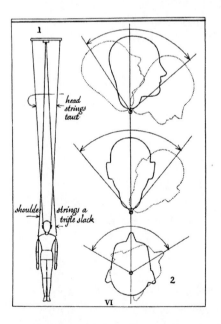

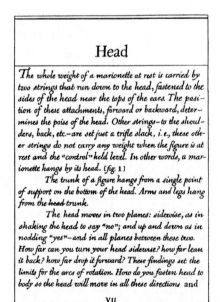

Head

The whole weight of a marionette at rest is carried by two strings that run down to the head, fastened to the sides of the head near the tops of the ears. The position of these attachments, forward or backward, determines the poise of the head. Other strings—to the shoulders, back, etc.—are set just a trifle slack, i.e., these other strings do not carry any weight when the figure is at rest and the "control" held level. In other words, a marionette hangs by its head. [fig. 1]

The trunk of a figure hangs from a single point of support on the bottom of the head. Arms and legs hang from the head-trunk.

The head moves in two planes: sidewise, as in shaking the head to say "no"; and up and down as in nodding "yes"—and in all planes between these two. How far can you turn your head sidewise? how far lean it back? how far drop it forward? These findings set the limits for the arcs of rotation. How do you fasten head to body so the head will move in all these directions and

Two-page spread from *Marionette in Motion,* by W. A. Dwiggins. (Boston Public Library/Rare Books Department. Courtesy the Trustees.)

onettes: "It is a long while since those first days when, as one of the family, I could, at will, open the 'cage' back of the miniature stage, not only to look at, but actually to handle, the delicate little creatures that hung there — the marionettes that Bill had so lovingly contrived in the 'spare time' of a dozen years or so. Even now, I cannot forget the emotion which filled me then, as I first perceived the beauty, skill, and imagination with which they were made."

Entering the Dwiggins Marionette Room, you are greeted by a self-portrait — or self-marionette — of William A. Dwiggins overseeing a collection of parts and diagrams for the making of marionettes. To your left and right are groupings of the figures arranged by play. Beginning on the left, you will meet characters from *Prelude to Eden*: Azrael, an archangel; Dijul, a kindly antediluvian; Lilith, a young woman; and Draco, the District Warden who became the Serpent (note that the descriptions are

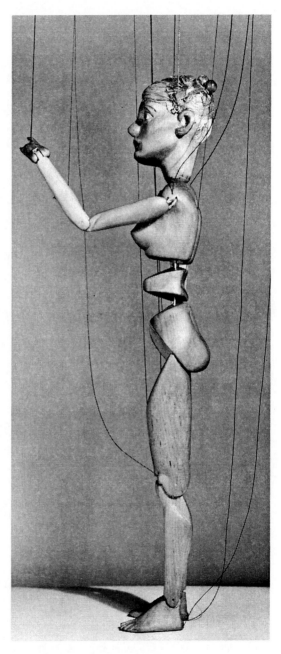

Dorothy Abbe's photograph of the marionette Lilith. (Boston Public Library/Rare Books Department. Courtesy the Trustees.)

in Dwiggins's own words). Next we view Brother Jeromy, a mendicant friar; Dame Greenmantle, a fifteenth-century housewife; and Dame Holland, a neighbor (seated) from the play *Brother Jeromy*. The last and largest grouping on display is from *The Princess Primrose* and includes the Bird; the Master of Ceremonies; the Rabbit, who conversed with the Bird; the Princess Primrose; Baba, her Afghan hound; Uncle Nurrhedin, the magician who created magic episodes; the Monkey, who climbed down the magic rope; the Metal Demon, who rose from the earth; the Ice Demon, who came down from the sky ... and many more imaginative and intriguing characters.

While you are at the library, plan to dig into the Dwiggins and Abbe archives. The following list provides a guide to the marionettes in the collection as well as works on puppetry, many of which probably influenced Dwiggins in his marionette projects.

Puppetry Books in the Dwiggins, Abbe, and Püterschein Collections at the Boston Public Library

Histories

Abbe, Dorothy. *The Dwiggins Marionettes: A Complete Experimental Theater in Miniature.* New York: Harry N. Abrams, 1970. (Abbe 2000.27 PF)

Ackley, Edith Flack. *Marionettes—Easy to Make! Fun to Use!* New York: Frederick A. Stokes Co., 1929. 1 vol.; front, ill.; 26 cm. (Abbe 2000. 27. 4)

Boehm, Max von. *Dolls and Puppets.* Philadelphia: David McKay Co., 1935? (Abbe 2000.27. 7)

Cruikshank, George. *Punch and Judy*, with twenty-eight illustrations. NY: Rimington & Hooper, 1929. 1 vol.; ill.; 21 cm. (Abbe 2000.27.10)

First American Puppetry Conference & Festival. Detroit, 8–11 July 1936. (Abbe 2000.27.15)

Fisher, Douglas. *Wooden Stars.* London, New York: T.V. Boardman, 1947. 1 vol.; ill.; 24.5 cm. (Abbe 2000.27.14)

Fletcher, J. Kyrle. Catalogue 54, spring 1936. *Theatre including books, manuscripts, playbills ... & marionettes.* London: Fletcher, 1936. 1 vol.; ill.; 21.5 cm. (Abbe 2000.27.11)

Green, Dana Saintsbury. *Masks & Puppets.* ("How to do it" series number 32). London & New York: The Studio Publications, 1942, 83, [1] p., ill.; 25.5 cm. (Abbe 2000.27.3)

Inverarity, R. B. *A Manual of Puppetry.* Portland, Oregon: Binfords & Mort, 1938. 1 vol.; ill.; 20.5 cm. (Abbe 2000.27.8)

Kaus, Gottfried. *The Salzburg Marionette Theatre.* Salzburg: Residenz Verlag, 1966. 1 vol.; ill.; 18 cm. (Abbe 2000.27.6)

McPharlin, Paul. *The Puppet Theatre in America: A History 1524–1948.* With a supplement:

Puppets in America Since 1948, by Marjorie Batchelder McPharlin. Boston: Plays Inc., 1969. 1 vol.; ill.; 24 cm. (Abbe 2000.27.2 — other copies in Rare Book Department on SCT.95.171 and WAD 469)

Puppetry Bulletin, 1937–1938. Paul McPharlin, editor. Birmingham, MI, pp. [65]–88. (Abbe 2000.27.17.5)

Puppetry 1931 [–1935]: A Yearbook of Puppets & Marionettes. [Volume 2–6]. Paul McPharlin, editor. Detroit. Puppetry and the Puppetry Imprints, 1931–5. 5 vols. ill.; 16 × 23.5 cm. *Note: issue for 1933 is extra illustrated copy number 14. (Abbe 2000.19 nos. 12–16)

Puppetry 1936–7: An International Yearbook of Puppets and Marionettes. Volume 8. Paul McPharlin, editor. Birmingham, MI: Puppetry Imprints, 1937. 2 vols.: ill.; 16 × 23.5 cm. (WAD 470, Abbe 2000.27.17)

Puppetry 1938: An International Yearbook of Puppets and Marionettes. Volume 9. Paul McPharlin, editor. Birmingham, MI: Puppetry Imprints, 1938. 1 vol.; ill.; 16 × 23.5 cm. (Abbe 2000.27.18)

Rossbach, C. Edmund. *Making Marionettes.* New York: Harcourt Brace, 1938. [12], 196 p.; illus.; 23.5 cm. (Abbe 200.27.1)

Schumann, Peter. *Puppen und Masken: Bread & Puppet Theater.* Frankfurt Am Main: Fischer Taschenbuch, 1973. 1 vol.; ill.; 19 cm. (Abbe 2000.27.9)

Puppetry Handbooks

Dwiggins, William Addison. *Marionette in Motion: The Püterschein System.* Handbook XII. Detroit, MI: Puppetry Imprints, 1939. [2]. XV, [3] p.; ill.; 20.5 cm. (Abbe 2000.27.5) — inscribed to DA from WAD on front flyleaf.

McPharlin, Paul. *Animal Marionettes.* Puppetry Handbook X. Birmingham, MI: Puppetry Imprints, 1934. 7, [1] p.; ill.; 24.5 cm. (Abbe 2000.27.12)

_____. *Marionette Control.* Puppetry Handbook VII. Birmingham, MI: Puppetry Imprints, 1934. 7, [1]; ill.; 23 cm. (Abbe 2000.27.16)

Nelson, Nicholas, and Hayes, J. J. *Trick Marionettes.* Puppetry Handbook VI. Birmingham, MI: Puppetry Imprints, 1935. 32 p.; ill.; 24.5 cm. (Abbe 2000.27.13)

Marionettes

In the Dwiggins archives, the following entries can be found under "Marionettes" (for call numbers, please refer to WAD Box #).

Machine Characters for Millennium I: Display, Theatre Room: pg. 108; Item #123.
Marionette Construction: pg. 107; Boxes 105pb–107pb; Display, Marionette Room.
Marionettes for Billy Brown. Display, Marionette Room.
Marionettes under the Püterschein Authority. Display, Marionette Room.
Miscellaneous Material: pg. 107; Box #109.
Photographs: p. 75; Box #88; #88pb.
Stand for holding marionettes: pg.108; Item #124 — see also Plays.

Plays

Brother Jeromy (pg. 73, Box #83 & 83pb)
Marina (pg. 73, Box #84; 84pb)

Millennium I (pg. 72, Box #82 & 82pb)
The Mystery of the Blind Beggarman, or Billy Brown's Bravery (pg. 75; Box #87 & 87)
Prelude to Eden (pg. 74; Box #85 & 85pb)
Princess Primrose (pg. 74; Box #86 & pb)

The Puppet Collection of the National Museum of American History

ELLEN RONEY HUGHES *and*
DWIGHT BLOCKER BOWERS

The Smithsonian's National Museum of American History (NMAH) stands proudly as the guardian of such national icons as the Star Spangled Banner, the ENIAC computer, and the lap desk upon which Thomas Jefferson drafted the Declaration of Independence. Along with these treasures is an array of artifacts within the museum's entertainment collections that uniquely represents how Americans have experienced puppetry. Marionettes, rod and hand puppets, and ventriloquist figures in the collection span over 150 years of American popular entertainment.

In the words of Bil Baird, a puppet is "an inanimate figure that is made to move by human effort before an audience." Rich in art, drama, and comedy, puppetry is one of the oldest and most beloved forms of theater in America. It draws on many sources to create its own expression and continually innovates and adapts in a changing world. And as a medium of expression, puppetry has its own aesthetic principles, techniques, and ways of conveying ideas. As a group of artifacts, puppets dramatically reflect the many facets of American culture.

In the years that followed its opening in 1964, the National Museum of American History centered its attentions on documenting material culture of military and technological achievements. Since the late 1970s, however, there has been a focal shift in exploring topics and artifacts representing social and cultural history, with a significant emphasis on American popular culture. The puppet collection is a direct result of that initiative and it has steadily grown in scope through generous donations by leading puppeteers and their families into an exhibition of excellent quality. Today, it continues to be an important element of the museum's overall portrait of American identity.

The National Museum of American History's puppet collection consists of a number of subsets, grouped by the creators of the artifacts. What follows are sketches of these groupings that make up the museum's puppet collection, arranged largely in chronological order of date of acquisition.

Hazelle and J. Woodson Rollins Collection

Hazelle Hedges Rollins (1910–1990) founded Hazelle, Inc., a company that, in 1975 when she retired, was the world's largest exclusive manufacturer of marionettes and hand and finger puppets. Before opening her own company, the Kansas City, Missouri–born puppeteer studied with Tony Sarg. She designed over three hundred puppets, and she held four patents in the puppetry field, including the airplane control marionette designed for ease of manipulation.

During her fifty-year career in puppetry she and her husband, J. Woodson Rollins, assembled an extensive collection of puppets, many of them old and fine quality American examples, which they offered as a gift to the Smithsonian in 1977. Among the nearly one hundred puppets accepted for the collections were two Civil War–era hand puppets; toys, marionettes and hand puppets used in early television commercials; a gnome marionette from the 1939 World's Fair; artifacts from the Yale Puppeteers and Turnabout Theatre; and a dramatic nineteenth-century minstrelsy set.

The minstrel show collection includes a top-hatted Mr. Tambo, the end man who provided music and comic repartee; Mr. Bones, a disassembling skeleton; a horse skeleton; and the only white character, a policeman. Mr. Tambo is a marionette of painted wood with strings and an attached holder. Such marionettes were said to have been used in a traveling show based on a Mississippi River boat between 1850 and 1870.

Among the Yale Puppeteers' artifacts donated by Rollins and her family was a papier-mâché Dancing Girl, resembling Josephine Baker, used by the Yale Puppeteers from 1943 to 1960. The Hollywood-based Yale Puppeteers, formed in the 1920s by Harry Burnett, Forman Brown, and Eli Richard Branden, was one of the few American puppeteer groups that had its own playhouse from the 1930s to the 1960s. Playbills from their unique Turnabout Theatre were also donated. The theater had a puppet stage for marionette shows at one end and live performances were presented after intermission at the other end. The audience would turn their seats around to view the rest of the show.

An Evil Gnome marionette used at the 1939 World's Fair by the Tatterman Marionettes in the General Electric pavilion production came with the Rollins collection. The play, *Mrs. Cinderella,* picks up the classic story after Cinderella and the Prince marry. The couple moves into their drafty castle, inhabited by evil gnomes who do everything the old-fashioned difficult way without electricity. The fairy godmother admonishes the beleaguered star to call General Electric, and a GE repairman arrives with new electrical appliances. *Mrs. Cinderella* was one of thousands of performances given all over the country by the Tatterman Marionettes, led by William Duncan and Edward Mavley. The puppet remains in its original costume with an overlay of paint from later productions, a common fate of theatrical puppets. These puppets were donated by Hazelle and her husband, J. Woodson Rollins, and their daughter and son-in-law, Nancy R. and Gene Krupa.

Bil Baird's Slugger Ryan

Bil Baird's (1904–1987) puppetry career spanned more than seventy years, beginning when he was only seven years old. His talent, intellect, and energy combined to build one of the greatest reputations in the history of puppetry. Baird's collection of over two thousand rod and string puppets have performed in vaudeville acts, nightclubs, television shows, films, and theaters, both in America and abroad. After working for five years with the great puppeteer Tony Sarg, he formed Bil Baird's Marionettes in 1934 and soon after built puppets and trained puppeteers for the Federal Theatre Project. While performing, Baird became a cultural ambassador of puppetry for the State Department by touring India,

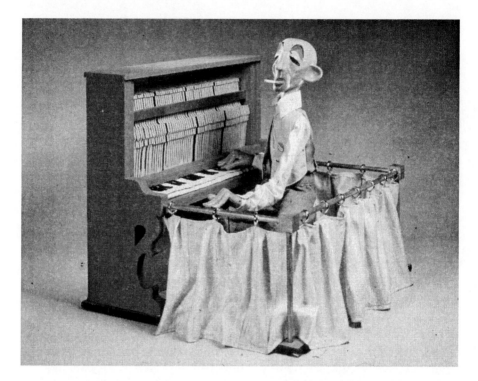

Bil Baird's Slugger Ryan hosted the first Baird television show. Donated by Bil Baird. (Smithsonian Institution)

Russia, Afghanistan, and Nepal in the 1950s, and he wrote *The Art of the Puppet*, in which he shared his knowledge and love of puppetry. Baird's wife Cora, also a puppeteer, was his working partner for most of his career until her death in 1967. That same year, Baird opened his own theater and studio in New York City.

Slugger Ryan captures Baird's hallmarks of caricature and satire. The plastic and wood rod puppet was a 1970s re-make of a cigarette-smoking, honky-tonk piano-playing puppet that Baird first used in the late 1930s at Radio City Music Hall. Slugger Ryan was modeled after Hoagy Carmichael, a popular composer, pianist, and vocalist of that time. The puppet later hosted the first Baird television show. Bil Baird donated Slugger Ryan in 1980.

Suzanne, the Dancing Doll

Suzanne is a life-size dancing doll that was used by Tommy Wonder and Don Dellair, an internationally known duo who sang and danced in nightclubs from Puerto Rico to Paris. This doll played a special role in the life of Tommy Wonder. As a child, Wonder developed a physical condition that prevented him from walking. In order to assist him, his mother stuffed some old clothes together and supported them with a broomstick. This makeshift doll, which Wonder named Suzanne, helped him to learn to dance and walk.

The current Suzanne was made in 1940 by the Westmore Brothers, of the famous family of makeup artists who determined the look for a number of Hollywood leading ladies during the 1930s, '40s, and '50s. The rubber face is modeled on that of the Oomph Girl, Ann Sheridan, the Warner Brothers' screen siren who starred in such 1940s films as *Kings Row*, *Nora Prentiss*, and *Shine On, Harvest Moon*. The puppet has shoulder-length auburn human hair, glass eyes, and a padded, rather voluptuous body. It is currently dressed in a black gown; however, its donor also included a second gown of white chiffon and satin, designed by Parisian couturier Hubert Givenchy. Completing the costume are two pairs of patent shoes: one set for Suzanne and the second pair for Suzanne's puppeteer-dancing partner. Inside the puppet is the original broomstick that formed the basis for the therapeutic puppet created by Tommy Wonder's mother.

Along with Suzanne, Wonder and Dellair also donated elements of their own costumes worn in their act. The jackets are black velvet decorated with glass beading. Also included is a prop cane used by Wonder.

Howdy Doody

The introduction of television to American homes in the late 1940s opened up a new and enormous national audience for puppetry. From 1947 to 1960, "The Howdy Doody Show," starring the freckled, grinning cowboy marionette Howdy Doody, reigned supreme as the leading children's variety program on network TV. Howdy's fellow cast members were a mixture of live actors and other marionettes. The former group included Buffalo Bob Smith, a cowboy master of ceremonies, and Judy Tyler, as the Indian Princess SummerFall WinterSpring.

While the initial Howdy Doody marionette was made by others, from 1952 to 1960 the puppets on the show were made and manipulated by Margo and Rufus Rose of New York City. The Howdy Doody puppet in the NMAH collections is one of at least three actually used on the Howdy Doody show during its marathon 2,300-episode run on NBC-TV. It was designed by Milt Neil and created by Rufus and Margo Rose, using parts from an earlier puppet made by Velma Dawson. Rufus did the construction and animation, while Margo did the modeling, painting, and costuming. Howdy Doody has a wooden head and body. The puppet wears a western-themed costume with a red handkerchief tied around his neck, a bright plaid shirt, denim jeans, and cowboy boots with a pattern embossing on the top. The puppet continues to be one of the most popular items in the collection with multiple generations of visitors. Howdy Doody was donated to the museum in 1980 by Margo Rose.

Manteo Family's Agricane de Taria

Agricane de Taria, a dashing knight of Charlemagne, thrilled and enraged audiences in an Italian puppet drama. *Orlando Furioso* was based on an Italian version of the epic poem *Song of Roland*. It evolved over centuries into a traditional Sicilian episodic puppet play featuring hundreds of marionettes acting out bloody battles, heroic deeds and romantic love scenes. As many as fifty of the puppets might be on stage at once. Among the most famous performers of this tradition in America was the Manteo family, who thus provided a venue for immigrants and their offspring to

Agricane de Taria, five-foot rod puppet from *Orlando Furioso*, New York City. Donated by Miguel Maneto. (Smithsonian Institution)

remain connected to their heritage. The Manteo version of *Orlando Furioso* had nearly four hundred episodes and took thirteen months to enact. Originally the dialogue was in Sicilian dialect, then in Italian, and later in mixed Italian and English.

Agrippino Manteo, himself the son of a Sicilian puppeteer, came to America from Argentina, bringing with him his family, puppets and entertainment genius. Opening his first theater in New York's Lower East Side in 1923, he and his children gave nightly performances to mainly Italian-American audiences until 1937, when their theater closed. Second and third generations continued under the direction of Miguel Manteo, giving occasional performances at venues such as the Smithsonian's American Folklife Festival.

The Manteos' armor-sheathed puppets stood between four and five feet high, depending on their importance and weighed up to one hundred pounds apiece. Rod puppets were hung on a rail and manipulated from above via two steel rods. The knight Agricane de Taria in the museum's collection had been purchased in Italy for the Manteo production and was donated by Miguel Manteo.

Donald Cordry Puppets

Donald Cordry (1907–1978), an enormously talented carver and puppeteer, opened a company with Rupert and Margo Rose in 1931 called Donald Cordry's Marionette Co. The company's first productions were hand-puppet versions of popular plays of the time. In 1934 Cordry began a partnership with Tony Sarg in New York, in which he designed and produced Sarg's shows and taught in Sarg's summer school. Between 1933 and 1934, Cordry's company performed *The Three Wishes*. It was Cordry's final production; to preserve his declining health he retired to Mexico with his wife. His fantastically carved puppets and sets were shipped in crates to Mexico and remained there for almost fifty years. After the puppeteer's death, his puppets from *The Three Wishes* and two tattered Dolly Sisters puppets were donated by Dorothy Mann Cordry, his widow.

Edgar Bergen's Charlie McCarthy

The ventriloquist figure Charlie McCarthy and his creator, Edgar Bergen, won international fame in stage, radio, television, and cinema

Donald Cordry's carved figures for *The Three Wishes*. Donated by Dorothy Mann Cordry. (Photograph by Kim Nielson, Smithsonian Institution.)

from the 1930s through the 1960s. The Chicago-born Bergen discovered early in life that he had a skill for both ventriloquism and comedy. In 1922 Bergen had carvers Charles and Theodore Mack create a puppet figure for him, which he named Charlie McCarthy. Bergen had McCarthy modeled after an Irish newsboy he had observed hawking newspapers on a city street.

Bergen and McCarthy first became a popular duo as a result of their performances on Chautauqua and vaudeville circuits, both in the United States and abroad. However, it was their frequent broadcasts on network radio that established them as stars. Charlie McCarthy's popularity was phenomenal, remaining in the top percentile of ratings throughout the twenty-two-year run of their radio show. The pair also made personal appearances, appeared in fourteen motion pictures, and starred in their own television series. In Bergen's many performances, he became well known for his showmanship, irreverent wit and charm, and exceptional humor. Bergen and McCarthy had a far-reaching influence on ventriloquism and the comic art of puppetry. As a result, Bergen became the model for virtually every ventriloquist who followed him.

The Charlie McCarthy ventriloquist doll in the Smithsonian collections was used by Bergen between 1936 and 1945. He has a movable mouth, and his wooden head, hands, and feet are painted. His eyes are glass. He is nattily dressed in his trademark cotton and satin tuxedo with a small rosebud on the lapel. Charlie McCarthy was a gift of the Bergen Foundation in 1981.

Paul Winchell's Jerry Mahoney and Knucklehead Smiff

In 1936, Paul Winchell, a young ventriloquist, won first prize on the *Major Bowes's Original Amateur Hour,* a popular radio show in the 1930s. Turning this early success into a career, Winchell and his wooden partner, Jerry Mahoney, became popular performers on American radio and television, in films, and in theater. In 1951, Winchell added a new character to his act, Knucklehead Smiff. Jerry Mahoney and Knucklehead Smiff's comic repartee became his most popular puppet act until Winchell, Mahoney and Smiff retired in 1981. In addition to being an accomplished puppeteer, Dr. Paul Winchell has also been a practicing dentist and an inventor; he holds a patent for an artificial heart.

The Jerry Mahoney puppet in this collection was made of wood and plastic wood by Frank Marshall in 1936. Both Mahoney and Smiff have detachable heads; holes in the backs allow for hand access to controls for the movable eyes and mouths. The gifts of Paul Winchell, Jerry Mahoney was donated in 1981 and Knucklehead Smiff in 1983.

Punch and Judy

Traveling the Eastern seaboard, the Reverend W. E. Hitchcock of Brimfield, Massachusetts, an itinerant preacher and showman, performed a Punch and Judy show around the end of the nineteenth century. His collection consists of one rag-doll puppet and six wood puppets carved between 1880 and 1895. The selection of puppets suggests that the Reverend Hitchcock added a moral twist to his shows, perhaps performing them as animated sermons. Accompanying the puppets, in addition to draperies and backdrops, was a panoramic painting of twelve scenes called The Great Pictorial Museum, which Hitchcock also used to further enlighten and entertain his audiences.

The Punch and Judy show collection includes seven hand puppets: Punch, Judy, Devil, Ghost, Darkie, Magician, and Preacher. Traditionally, the Punch and Judy show has evoked sympathy and laughter from American audiences since the early 1800s, when traveling punchmen, also known as professors, brought this farce from England. Punch had come to England as a marionette from Italy, where he had been a minor character in the *commedia dell'arte* tradition.

Punch has universal appeal as the common man at odds with his surroundings. His uncommon responses have often provoked laughter: tossing the crying baby out of the window, tossing his wife out of the window, and hanging the policeman, while getting away with it all. However, these antics may have ensured the demise of this raucous puppet show in an America increasingly concerned with public morality; even the introduction of a crocodile to make Punch pay for his crimes could not save the show.

The Federal Theatre Project

The Federal Theatre Project (FTP) was created in 1935 as a way to employ jobless theater professionals and make the performing arts available to vast numbers of citizens. Although it was the most popular cultural project of President Roosevelt's New Deal, it was also the most controversial of government-funded programs in the era and was disbanded in 1939. During its brief life, the FTP used puppets as an integral part of its presentations; the marionette units alone presented an average of one hundred shows per week in twenty-two states.

The NMAH Federal Theatre Project Puppet Collection is centered on two subgroups of objects. The first is the work of Molka Reich, who joined the Miami, Florida, FTP in 1935. Although she began as an actress, she soon became a puppeteer, working with marionettes as a way to encourage and entertain children in her geographic area. Reich traveled all over the state, giving puppet performances of such familiar stories as *Treasure Island* and *Jack and the Beanstalk*. Reich not only made the marionettes, but she also built the stages and wrote and adapted scripts.

In 1982, she donated to the NMAH collections the puppets from *Jack and the Beanstalk*, along with such props as the beanstalk and the golden goose. The Jack puppet is an eleven-stringed marionette with a control bar and has wooden arms and legs, and papier-mâché hands. He is dressed in a vest, hat, plaid wool socks with ladybug buttons, a blue shirt, and beige pants. The Giant is a ten-stringed marionette with a control bar. His legs and shoulders are made of wood, and his arms and hands are made of cloth. He has a plastic head and wool hair. The character's costume consists of a red plaid shirt, a black neck bow, a black belt, brown pants, and black boots. The Golden Goose is made of cloth and is painted gold and copper. In addition to the *Jack and the Beanstalk* materials, Reich also donated a marionette cat puppet in 1985. The puppet was used in a Baba Yaga play in the 1930s. This marionette, made of canvas, is operated by a wood airplane control and seven strings. It has a movable mouth and is very flexible.

The second artifactual representation of the Federal Theatre Project stems from a high school puppet production presented at the Washington, DC, Marionette Festival, which was jointly sponsored in 1937 by the FTP and the Department of Playgrounds of the District of Columbia. The purpose of this festival was to entertain and to teach about the marionette theater and to demonstrate to Depression-era children and parents how inexpensive such an undertaking could be. From the festival, the Smithsonian collections contain a dwarf marionette, from a production of *Snow White and the Seven Dwarfs*, created by Washington, DC, teacher William N. Buckner. Buckner sought to use puppetry as a way to introduce his students to classic stories and fables. The dwarf marionette was first used at the Armstrong High School in Washington, DC. Buckner donated the object to NMAH collections in 1980. It has hand-carved (by Buckner) limbs and head and is dressed in a green hat, black vest, and white shirt.

Jim Henson's Kermit the Frog and Oscar the Grouch

Kermit the Frog and Oscar the Grouch, two felt and plush creatures from the fertile mind of Jim Henson, are perhaps the most wildly
popular and widely recognized puppets in the national collections. It is
particularly appropriate that they now reside at the Smithsonian, since
Jim Henson spent most of his formative years in Washington, DC, and
got his professional start there in the early 1950s as a puppeteer on local
television variety shows. Both Kermit and Oscar are vibrant representatives of Henson's eclectic mix of fanciful beings that he called Muppets,
a term combining the words marionette and puppet.

The Muppets were among the first puppets to be created specifically
for television, and Henson developed imaginative techniques of construction and performance tailored specifically for the medium. Henson's
Muppets run the full range of puppetry styles, from string to rod to life-
size body-suit puppets, offering near-limitless possibilities for the use of
puppets in a variety of programmatic formats and media.

In addition to his remarkable contributions to the world of puppetry, Jim Henson endeavored, during his all-too-brief career, to raise
the intellectual, moral, and artistic standards of American entertainment
through his work in family and adult television programs ("Sam and
Friends," "The Muppet Show," "Storyteller"), educational children's television ("Sesame Street," "Fraggle Rock"), and feature films (*The Muppet
Movie, The Dark Crystal, Labyrinth*). His work was the result of his own
genius, coupled with that of his many talented collaborators, including
his wife and co-founder of the Muppets, Jane Nebel Henson and pup-
peteers/writers/factota Frank Oz, Don Sahlin, and Jerry Juhl, to name
just a few of the many.

Kermit the Frog is easily Henson's most celebrated and iconic Muppet. Since his creation in the mid–1950s, Kermit has undergone a considerable transformation. Henson constructed the first Kermit in 1955
for the madcap, five-minute television show "Sam and Friends," which
aired on the Washington, DC, NBC affiliate, WRC-TV. He built the
character using his mother's discarded green spring coat for the body and
a halved ping-pong ball for the distinctive eyes. Then, as now, Kermit's
body is hollow with small rods attached to the arms, to allow for hand
movements, and the legs are stuffed and hang loosely. The mouth is open

and lined with red felt with a pink felt tongue. (The first Kermit still resides in the collections at the Jim Henson Company in New York City.) Over the next decade, Kermit evolved from being a green lizard-like character to a vivid lime-hued frog, replete with crenellated collar and flippers. The version of Kermit in the national collections was created for "Sesame Street" around 1969. Kermit has been at the Smithsonian since the early 1980s and has been part of the permanent collections since 1994.

Irascible and scowling, but eminently lovable, Oscar the Grouch was acquired by the Smithsonian in 1989 for an exhibition commemorating the twentieth anniversary of "Sesame Street." Nestled in his metal trashcan lair, Oscar is made up of green, shaggy plush for the body, red and black felt for the mouth, and white and black plastic for the eyes. He is currently on display on the museum's first floor, in a case devoted to artifacts representative of children's television programming. Along with Kermit and Oscar, the collection also includes archival videotapes of various television and film appearances of Muppet characters. The videotapes were donated by the Jim Henson Company.

George Pal Puppets

George Pal pioneered an innovative use of stop-frame puppet animation, a painstaking process achieved by moving each puppet figure and shooting each change on a single frame of motion picture film in a series of progressive steps. At each frame shot, the head, arms, and legs of a character are changed according to the motions or actions needed. This creates the illusion of fluid motion when the film is viewed at normal speed. Pal was also the first producer-director to film narrative interaction between stop-frame animated puppets with human actors.

Pal launched his American career in 1940 when he joined the staff at Paramount Studios in Hollywood. His initial charge was to produce a series of short-subject puppet films that he had created in Europe called Puppetoons. The Puppetoons gained worldwide popularity, not only because of Pal's amazing technique, but also because the stories and musical scoring were of superlative quality, which appealed to children and adults alike. The Puppetoons addressed a wide variety of subject matters, such as fairy tales and jazz themes. George Pal was also popular for his work in feature films; during his long career he accumulated eight Academy Awards.

A number of George Pal's puppet creations have been donated to the National Museum of American History. The Yawning Man, an elf puppet with twenty-seven different, interchangeable faces, was used in the motion pictures *Tom Thumb* (MGM, 1958) and *The Wonderful World of the Brothers Grimm* (MGM, 1962), both of which won Pal Academy Awards. The Yawning Man illustrates the complexity of stop-frame animation. Pal originally created his puppets out of wood, which required nearly ten thousand individually carved figures for eight minutes of film footage. To save time and expense, Pal made the body and limbs of The Yawning Man out of latex, with a wire core that makes it pliable. Each face, carved of wax, expresses part of the yawn. If each of the twenty-seven faces were used for one frame of film, the entire sequence would occupy no more than one second in the completed motion picture. The Yawning Man is costumed in a hooded tunic of orange and brown suede. His feet, hands, and ears are foam rubber covered with vinyl. A wooden box contains the twenty-seven interchangeable waxy faces. Also, from the film *The Wonderful World of the Brothers Grimm* is a similar puppet, dressed in a red and brown costume, with an accompanying wooden box containing sixteen different faces, two eyes, one pair of hands, and an extra face for the Yawning Man.

The puppets used in the animated film *Tubby the Tuba* in the collection include the leading character of Tubby the Tuba — a miniature tuba made of gold-painted plaster bearing a childlike face. At the base of its wooden platform is a green plastic frog; three violins of varying sizes, equipped with four strings apiece and a wooden bow; and a platform puppet, with a miniature guitar, violin, and large drum attached to its base. Platforms and sticks are present where other instruments used to be attached. The detached pieces are a cymbal, a small drum with four wooden bells alongside it, and two drums with an attached wooden rack holding two cowbells. Pal received an Academy Award nomination for his work on *Tubby the Tuba*.

A Date with Duke (Paramount, 1947) is a humorous short film featuring Duke Ellington, who performs jazz music and has conversations about jazz style with a number of Puppetoon characters. Puppets from the film include a grand piano, two glass perfume bottles, four puppet fragments, and four Dancing Devils. The piano is black and has no keyboard, and its lid is hinged. One perfume bottle is made of clear fluted glass with blue stripes and is adorned with a decorative metal neckpiece that is carved with flowers and embellished with sequins. The collar of the bottle is circled by two rings of metal beads. The other glass perfume bottle is cut in an octagonal shape. A ring around the middle is carved in rectangular shapes, and it is decorated with sequins. The metal top is an actual vial from a perfume container. Three of the puppet fragments are heads; each has felt hair and a trumpet flowerlike figure extending out of the mouth. Two of the three puppets have plastic headpieces that are decorated with sequins. The fourth fragment is a metal top for a perfume bottle. It is made of glass, is decorated with sequins, and has a metal round on top. The four black Dancing Devils are mounted on a wooden platform and have yellow horns and red noses. These Devils were also used in several of Pal's earlier animated films.

From *Tulips Shall Grow,* an early Pal short film made at Paramount in 1942, are the puppets of Jan, and the Nuts and Bolts Screwball soldier. Jan is a wooden Dutch boy with a detachable head, and his features are painted black, white, red, yellow, blue, brown, and silver. The Nuts and Bolts Screwball soldier consists of a metal prop attached to a wooden base that is holding a figure, carved and painted to look like metal nuts, bolts, and screws in the shape of a soldier.

In addition to the puppets and props, the collections also include two videotapes of the short subjects *Tubby the Tuba* and *A Date with Duke.* The George Pal materials were donated to the museum in 1988 by Mrs. George Pal, with the special assistance of Walter Lantz.

The Brewery Troupe Collection

In 1998, the National Museum of American History's Jerome T. Lemelson Center for Invention and Innovation commissioned Brad Brewer, of the Brewery Troupe of Freeport, New York, to create a puppet play about the life of Lewis Latimer, the noted African-American inventor and scientist. Founded in 1973, the Brewery Troupe's goal is to interpret African-American literature, music, and humor through the art of puppet theater. Brewer received his training while working with Henson Productions in the 1980s. The puppet play *Lewis Latimer: Renaissance Man* was performed at NMAH in December 1998 for school and family audiences and was later broadcast on the Fairfax Network in March 1999.

The puppets created for this production include representations of Frederick Douglass, Thomas Edison, and Lewis Latimer. They are made primarily of felt. Following the end of the various stage presentations in which they were used throughout the 1999 season, the Lewis Latimer puppets were donated by the Lemelson Center to the museum collections.

"Jump-Jump of Holiday House" Collection

Broadcast between 1950 and 1954 on the Los Angeles NBC-TV affiliate, the children's puppet program, "Jump-Jump of Holiday House," was created by actors Mary and Harry Hickox. Similar in milieu, if not in execution, to Jim Henson's early TV efforts, the puppets in the NMAH collection include the principal characters Jump-Jump, Sleepy Slim, Achi Paggli, and Sir Rhyme-A-Lot. Jump-Jump is an elf string puppet with movable eyes, mouth, and hands. It has red hair and wears a red cap, red jumpsuit, a red-and-white striped shirt with a white felt collar, and green felt shoes. Sleepy Slim is a lion hand puppet that has a brown wood face and leather hands and wears a red polka-dot flannel nightshirt. Achi Paggli is a clown hand puppet with a white face, a blue felt hat and red hair and is costumed in a green coat. Sir Rhyme-A-Lot, a medieval knight, is a hand puppet, with a wooden face, silver helmet with a blue plume, and a silver and red cloth body.

Captain Kangaroo

"Captain Kangaroo" premiered on CBS in 1955. Bob Keeshan (1927–2004), the creator of this long-running children's television show, got his start in television on "The Howdy Doody Show," where he created the character Clarabell the Clown. On "Captain Kangaroo" Keeshan played the title role, while Hugh Brannum played his pal, Mr. Green Jeans. Puppetry and animated cartoons rounded out the show. Puppets Bunny Rabbit and Mr. Moose engaged in conversations that helped illustrate moral precepts. After CBS canceled the show in 1984, it was picked up by PBS, where it aired until 1992. Robert Keeshan donated the Mr. Moose puppets, Bunny Rabbit, Captain Kangaroo's costume, and Grandfather Clock.

Various examples of the NMAH puppet collection have been used in a number of Smithsonian exhibitions and have also been lent to various exhibitions at other museums throughout the country. However, in 1980, the National Museum of American History had the opportunity to showcase the collections at length in an exhibition called Puppets and Things on Strings, which focused on 150 years of puppets across a wide spectrum of American popular entertainment. The collections will be featured again in America Plays, a new exhibition of sports and entertainment being planned for a 2004 opening at the National Museum of American History.

III

Puppetry in Action

"Bringing Together Man and Nature"[1]: The Theater of Julie Taymor

ALAN WOODS

Julie Taymor won two Tony Awards in 1998, as best director of a musical and for best costumes. That she was one of the first women to be honored as best director was widely noted.[2] That she was also the first puppeteer — regardless of gender — to win a directorial Tony was generally unnoticed in the enormous public success of the stage version of Disney's *The Lion King*. She arrived at that point after a lifelong journey of exploring puppets, theatrical myth, and cross-cultural experimentation.

Julie Taymor rejects the label of puppeteer, however. In an interview during the summer of 2000, she exploded vehemently when she discovered, among the interviewer's papers, a copy of James M. Brandon's "Julie Taymor as Puppet Artist." "Christ! Why have you given her this to read? Oh God, this is exactly what I'm not!" was her response. Later, Taymor apologized: "I'm sorry for over-reacting, but I can't bear it when people see me only as being about puppets, when I feel that my work is so much more than that" (Cavendish).

Labels do limit, as Taymor understood all too well. Indeed the enormous success of *The Lion King* both aided and hindered her second production to reach Broadway, *The Green Bird*, in the spring of 2000. A chatty column in New York's *Daily News* noted just before the opening, "Her stunning, Tony Award–winning New York Stage debut" set a high

225

level for *The Green Bird*; "anticipation is sky-high. Will it be her second blockbuster?" (O'Haire).

The Green Bird was not a second blockbuster — at least, in part, because much of the public perceived it as a second *Lion King*, and the "bawdy, decidedly adult affair ... — with enough vulgarity and sexual and scatological humor to make a Howard Stern fan blush" (Gardner) both disappointed and horrified those expecting a new variation on the Disney spectacle.

Taymor has in fact spent much of her career avoiding the label "puppeteer." "I really don't consider myself a puppeteer," she told an interviewer as far back as 1983. "I am a theatre maker, a mixed media artist. I just use puppets as one medium, even though I use them a lot" (Jenner 112). And in 1992 Mel Gussow wrote in *The New York Times Magazine* that "she designs puppets just as she designs and sculpts masks, but she is not a puppeteer — the dread P word that the director keeps trying to avoid but that adheres to her like superglue" (50).

Yet puppetry is central to Taymor's career, both literally and figuratively. The ways in which she has explored the potential of the puppet make her part of a puppet renaissance, while simultaneously she was shattering the notion of traditional puppetry. She draws from a wide range of diverse traditions, juxtaposes elements derived from those traditions, creating often startling (and always fascinating) syntheses of the visual with the aural. While labels are confining, they can also be useful in identifying aspects of an artist's work, as long as their limitations are recognized. And although she has said, "I don't use puppets if I don't need to. The Taymor style is to adapt the style according to the piece" (Snyder), all the major Taymor productions include some form of puppetry, with the possible exception of the version of *Salome* she staged in the 1990s.

Taymor certainly benefited from the modern revitalization of an ancient puppetry tradition that the present volume celebrates. Taymor's innovative work as a creator of puppets and as a designer garnered her first commissions in the off-off–Broadway and regional theaters; her imaginative work as a director capable of combining elements and images from a dazzling range of sources brought increasingly wide attention, propelling her from a leading figure of experimental theater to an internationally recognized cultural icon, directing opera, film, and stage productions–and even, in that clear sign of acceptance, her own American

Express commercial. The use of puppets is central, according to many observers, to *The Lion King*'s enormous impact; as Benedict Nightingale commented, "to see Julie Taymor's reinvention of The Lion King [*sic*], with its masks, simple props and gorgeously inventive puppets, is ... to be reassured that the theatre is one medium able to keep the imagination alive and alert in a mind-numbing era."

Taymor's early life and influences have been exhaustively explored with the media focus created by the enormous success of *The Lion King* in 1998, followed shortly thereafter in 2000 with *Titus*, her debut as a feature film director. A major exhibition of her work, Julie Taymor: Playing with Fire opened in 1999, also focusing major attention on her career and effectively placing *The Lion King* within the context of her quarter-century of theatrical experimentation.[3] That exhibit occasioned a new edition of the major publication, *Julie Taymor: Playing with Fire*, the richest source of information about her career to date.

Raised in a middle-class suburb of Boston by creative and politically active parents, she performed at the Children's Theatre of Boston from the age of nine or ten or eleven or twelve,[4] then she studied during her high school years in India, Sri Lanka, and at L'École de Mime Jacques Lecoq in Paris. Taymor's formal education culminated at Oberlin College, where she learned from experimental theater elder Herbert Blau and acted in *The Seeds of Atreus* and *The Donner Party: Its Crossing*, presented by Blau's performance ensemble, Kraken.[5] She also apprenticed with the Bread & Puppet Theater; these early influences are now well known to those following the director's career. Taymor repeatedly acknowledges Blau's influence, particularly his concept of the "ideograph," a concrete emblem of character or thought, which is central to her own work. She recently defined the concept succinctly: "An ideograph is an essence, an abstraction. It's boiling it right down to the most essential two, three brush strokes" (Schechner 38; see also, for example, the discussions in Blumenthal and Taymor 12, and Jenner 115).

Importantly, Taymor's early experiences included significant exposure to nonrealistic forms. At a very young age, she has said, "I was given a marionette stage. I animated things and made them come alive. I had puppets very young" ("Bravo"). Her early exposure to Asian work as a teenager and to Lecoq's mime techniques, particularly his major emphasis on working with masks, was also highly influential. It was at L'École Lecoq that she was introduced to a sophisticated use of objects as puppets:

"Madame [Renée] Citron animated objects, so it was really about mime, about understanding shape, form, and substance ... what is animation? It's that you can really put life into inanimate objects. And that's the magic of puppetry" (Schechner 36).

Equally well known is the influence of Taymor's experience studying traditional Asian theatrical forms, first in Seattle and then in Indonesia, on Watson and Ford fellowships for four years. The rich mixture of performance with everyday life in Indonesia became a catalyst for Taymor; as she later commented, "There's no word for artist in Bali. It's just what you do. What we would call putting on a play, dancing, playing music, that's not your profession: that's part of your act as a human being" (Solman).

Taymor produced her first original work, *Way of Snow*, in Java and Bali in 1974. In its use of ritual elements, masks, puppetry, projections, and reliance on movement and other nonverbal forms of communication, *Way of Snow* signaled the direction Taymor's artistic development was to take. While her career's trajectory has been steady, many of the hallmarks of her later work are present in *Way of Snow*, even if only in embryonic form.

Way of Snow is a trilogy of short pieces, each of which explores "the struggle for both physical and spiritual survival in three different worlds" (an Eskimo region, Indonesia, and a nonspecific urban metropolis, respectively; Blumenthal and Taymor 55). Taymor sculpted masks and headdresses and made shadow puppets for use in the three sections. Her imaginative use of physical properties — white chicken feathers at the opening were transformed into representations of Arctic snow, shadow puppets meticulously made of both leather and plexiglass, impressively expressive oversized character masks transformed human actors into giant puppet figures — combined techniques, materials and styles from a wide variety of sources and traditions, both Asian and European. This eclectic transformation of disparate elements into a stylistic form made coherent by Taymor's own aesthetic became the major sign of the director's mature style.

Puppets, both shadow and rod, are present in *Way of Snow*, as are the gigantic figures inspired by Taymor's early work with Peter Schumann's Bread & Puppet Theater, together with an awareness of the potential of masks fostered by her training with Lecoq. Again, however, Taymor transcends her sources, combining Schumann's notion of giant figures with the deeply expressive facial features of Lecoq's character masks to produce figures that are both abstract and emotional: exemplifications of the ideograph concept learned from Blau.

Way of Snow presents many of Taymor's later artistic concepts as well. Notably, it is an idea-driven piece. Taymor lists the themes: "insanity, depravation, [*sic*] shamanism, progress" (Blumenthal and Taymor 55). Taymor's entire output is marked by a strongly intellectual take on the material. Her richly inventive design work for other directors in the first decade of her career always interprets the material, shaping and providing possibilities for director and performers alike. Her mask and puppet-like sculpted figures for the Center Stage (Baltimore) production of Christopher Hampton's *Savages* (1982) create the ritualized world of Brazilian natives destroyed by European invaders, while the magical masks, giant shadow puppets, and *bunraku*-inspired doll puppets created for André Serban's *The King Stag* at American Repertory Theatre in Cambridge (1984), so shaped the acting style that Taymor not only designed the costumes and visual elements, but also choreographed the actors' movement patterns.[6]

The pieces Taymor created in Indonesia, *Way of Snow* and *Tirai*, were both reworked for performances in New York, in 1980 and 1981 respectively. She did not create another theatrical work of her own until 1984, spending the intervening years collaborating as a designer with other directors. After co-adapting and directing Thomas Mann's *The Transposed Heads* for the Ark Theatre in 1984, and designing the puppetry and masks as well,[7] Taymor turned to a commission from the American Place Theatre. Drawn from eighteenth-century sources, *Liberty's Taken* was the first full-length musical theater work on which Taymor collaborated with composer Eliot Goldenthal, her artistic and eventually personal partner.

Produced for two weeks in the summer of 1985 by the Castle Hill Festival in Ipswich, Massachusetts, *Liberty's Taken* delivers a wildly satiric take on the American Revolution. The musical was adapted from two major sources: an anonymous eighteenth-century satiric novel, *Adventures of Jonathan Corncob, Loyal American Refugee,* and the biography of Deborah Sampson Gannett, an indentured servant who disguised herself as a man in order to fight the British. Taymor and David Suehsdorf, her collaborator on the book, added a third major character, Jonathan's abandoned (and pregnant) hometown girl friend. Taymor said the team "made no attempt to give a history lesson but rather to tell a story that had not

Installation view of *Liberty's Taken*, Julie Taymor: Playing with Fire exhibition. (Photograph by Richard K. Loesch. Published by permission of Richard K. Loesch and Julie Taymor.)

been heard. No George Washingtons, John Adamses, or midnight rides of Paul Revere. No famous battles, no tea, no Declarations, and no winners. Rather, a collage of aspirations and awful truths during a war for freedom" (Blumenthal and Taymor 95). The visual style Taymor devised, along with set designer G. W. Mercier and costume designer Carol Oditz, placed *Liberty's Taken* firmly in the realm of the ideograph, further developing Taymor's range in puppetry and masks, which she designed.

Full-head masks and dummies were used to expand the cast of about twenty live actors to 150. Actors playing soldiers, for example, had dummies strapped to their sides, so that each actor became, in effect, a full squad. Exaggerated character masks and mechanical devices pointed to central character elements: Jonathan's avaricious Uncle Winter sported a giant mechanical hand, each finger of which could be operated as he grabbed for more things; the self-satisfied Donewells, a Tory family, wore fleshy, smug full-head masks. A Punch and Judy stage wandered the streets of Boston, an apparatus hiding a single performer who operated the hand puppets with their comments on the actions of the Boston

Committee of Safety, itself an assemblage of heads mounted on a rolling cart.

Taymor created stage pictures that both furthered and commented on the action. A sea battle was performed by shadow puppets of the opposing ships against an upstage screen, while the ships' figureheads, mounted on seesaws, rolled back and forth, the respective ship captains balanced at the far ends of each seesaw. As Blumenthal notes, "The effect was a screen-in-screen, wide-angle shot and close-up at once" (30). And for scenes set in and around a New York brothel, Taymor created a twenty-foot-high figure of a madam, with a British flag over her face. Beds popped out between her legs, with miniature copulating couples visible behind the skirt.

Liberty's Taken proved too expensive to be produced by the American Place; its theatrical life was limited to the two weeks in Massachusetts. "It remains the Taymor classic that practically no one saw," according to Blumenthal (31). In its seamless integration of live actors, puppets, masks, and doll figures, *Liberty's Taken* demonstrated a new maturity and cohesiveness in Taymor's artistic vision.

Taymor's next production was Shakespearean: she directed *The Tempest* for Theatre for a New Audience in New York, opening in 1986, creating the puppets and masks, with sets and costumes by Mercier and incidental music by Goldenthal. Revived for the Shakespeare Festival in Stratford, Connecticut, in 1987, the production was eventually taped and scenes broadcast on the PBS series, "Behind the Scenes," in 1993–1994.[8]

Again, Taymor used shadow-puppet techniques to change perspective and view. The opening tempest was conveyed, with appropriate lighting and sound, by a large sail carried onstage, behind which a metal shadow image of the ship was manipulated. The scene on board was performed in front of the sail, with the effect similar to the sea battle in *Liberty's Taken*: close-up scene juxtaposed with the long-shot behind it. For the sinking of the ship, the sail collapsed and the miniature sails on the shadow ship burst into flames, ignited by Ariel.

Taymor drew upon Asian theater techniques again in *The Tempest*. In a convention borrowed from the Kabuki, black-clad figures moved over the raked black sand that was the performance area, manipulating objects and characters to accomplish Prospero's magic. Ariel was performed by an actor dressed and hooded entirely in black, with her right hand manipulating a face mask attached to a diaphanous scarf, her left hand gloved in white. The mask danced in the air, while the performer spoke Ariel's lines, echoing the relationship of performer to puppet in the Japanese *bunraku*. This approach allowed for a stunning *coup de théâtre* at the end: Prospero freed Ariel by removing her hood, uncovering the actor's face. With her face visible for the first time, she left the magic performance space by exiting through the audience — literally freed from Prospero's control.

If Ariel's realization was borrowed from Japanese forms, for Caliban Taymor turned to the Mud Men of New Guinea for inspiration. Caliban's full-head mask resembled a stone head, with crude openings for eyes and mouth; the actor, clad only in a loincloth, his nearly nude body covered with whitish clay, first appeared rising up through the black sand of the set. This Caliban was as literally a creature of the earth as Ariel was of the air. And like Ariel, Caliban was freed by being unmasked: Caliban cracks open the rock head, hitting it with one of the logs Prospero forces him to carry as punishment for rebellion.

Taymor made an aesthetic breakthrough with *Liberty's Taken*, without much public notice. Her artistic growth was recognized with *Juan Darién: A Carnival Mass*, the musical piece she created with Goldenthal. Lyn Austin of the Music-Theatre Group, Inc., commissioned the work and pushed it forward by giving Taymor and Goldenthal an opening date before anything was written (Austin). *Juan Darién* remained in performance for almost a decade. First performed in 1988 as part of Music-Theatre Group's New York season, it was revived in 1990 (winning two Obies), then toured to festivals in Canada and Europe. A major revival at Lincoln Center in 1996, coproduced with Music-Theatre Group, led to five Tony Award nominations,[9] and brought Taymor's work to the attention of the Disney Corporation, then seeking someone to create a theatrical version of their animated film, *The Lion King*. *Juan Darién*'s first productions led to Taymor's receiving the first Dorothy Chandler Performing Arts Award in Theatre in 1989 and was a significant factor in her receiving a MacArthur Foundation Fellowship in 1991.

Juan Darién was indeed stunning. Adapted from a short story by Uruguayan writer Horacio Quiroga, the piece examined the very nature of humanity itself, through the metaphor of a jaguar cub transformed by the power of love into a human boy — then transformed back into a wild beast by the inhumanity visited on him by a callous society. Taymor and Goldenthal told the story through visual elements; Goldenthal set the

Latin Mass, adding a Lullaby with his own lyrics, and a "Trance" song for Juan, using Quiroga's text (7).[10]

Taymor contrasted puppets, masked figures, and human faces extensively in *Juan Darién*. The figure of Juan himself, she noted, was transformed five times: "as a jaguar cub (rod-and-string puppet); next he becomes an infant (hand-manipulated doll); at age ten he changes into a four-foot-tall bunraku puppet with realistic features; and upon the death of his mother he becomes a flesh-and-blood boy." His final transformation is back into a jaguar: "this time the child's face can be seen through the open mouth of the animal mask...." Juan retains "his humanness although his exterior is that of a ferocious beast" (Blumenthal and Taymor 136). The double vision (Juan as jaguar with the human Juan visible inside the jaguar mask) reinforced the central theme of *Juan Darién*; that same double vision would surface in later Taymor productions: her version of Stravinsky's *Oedipus Rex* in Japan (1992), the first version of *The Green Bird* in 1996, and *The Lion King*.

Other oversized figures appeared in *Juan Darién* as well: a ninefoot-tall schoolmaster, with the flapping pages of a book for his head and a long pointing finger; the schoolroom was a walking stage with three puppeteers manipulating the stage and the rod-puppet students. Both are reminiscent of devices employed earlier in *Liberty's Taken*. Taymor also employed carved figures, manipulated by black-clad and hooded human figures. As Taymor points out, once he is transformed into a flesh-and-blood boy, Juan is the only human actor visible on stage. At the point of his metamorphosis back into the jaguar, the puppeteers remove their hoods; Juan's final persecution is at the hands of a manifestly human group (Blumenthal and Taymor 136). Taymor manipulated masks and carved figures for emotional and dramatic effect: the bodies of plague victims and the crowd of jaguars were carved, while the death of Juan's human mother became apparent when he removed her mask and washed it. Taymor later reported that a ten-year-old, watching her videotape, said "Oh, he's washing her soul"; she added, "He got it exactly, quicker than some adults who are extremely literal-minded" (Gussow 78).

For Mr. Bones, an evocation of Latin American All Souls' Day figures, Taymor created a dancing skeleton, attached at the feet and, by rods, to the hands and head of his human manipulator. Mr. Bones, a macabre master of ceremonies, was termed "both trickster and a god" by

Taymor (Blumenthal and Taymor 132); the technology used to create this figure would also reappear a decade later in *The Lion King*.

Juan Darién's success also attracted the attention of the producers of the PBS series, "American Playhouse," who commissioned Taymor to create a piece. The result was *Fool's Fire*, adapted from Edgar Allan Poe's short story, "Hop Frog," which was broadcast over PBS in March 1992.[11] For the film, Taymor created full-body costumes and heads, sculpted from latex. Mel Gussow describes the effect: "The pompous king has cheeks like sides of mutton and narrow evil eyes. Around him are his grotesque courtiers, with obscene folds of flesh and distorted features.... They are bizarre and bulbous puppets, gargoyles molded out of latex..." (48).

Fool's Fire used a sharply raked setting for the banquet scene, capturing in three dimensions the look of Italian Renaissance forced perspective on two-dimensional painted canvases. By having only the central figures — Hop-Frog, the dwarf court jester, and Trippetta, a dwarf brought in to amuse the court with whom Hop-Frog falls in love — played by unmasked actors, Taymor emphasized their humanity, juxtaposed with the brutishness of the court. Trippetta and Hop-Frog became the sympathetic human figures, while the full-body costumes and full-head masks make the inhumanity of the king and court concrete.

The final image of *Fool's Fire* is Hop-Frog, manipulating marionette versions of himself and Trippetta, flying away from the burning castle. Hop-Frog is poised over a miniature castle setting, looming enormously above the narrow world from which he's escaped, both literally and metaphorically, visually gigantic in ironic counterpoint to his diminutive status among the grotesque giants of the court.

In 1992, Taymor staged her first opera, Stravinsky's *Oedipus Rex*, for which she also did the masks and sculptures, performed at the Saiko Kinen Festival in Japan.[12] Drawing on studies of both the Haniwa sculpture of early Japan and Cycladic sculpture from the second millennium B.C.E., Taymor devised majestic headdresses for Oedipus, Jocasta, and Creon; impassive faces in the Cycladic style sat on top of the singers' heads, extending the figures. Giant hands and flowing costumes completed the hieratic volume; the double view of the three major figures reached its climax when a red silk cord was looped around Jocasta's headdress. Her Cycladic head flew upward at the moment of Jocasta's suicide by hanging, as the singer sank down. Similarly, Oedipus plunged spike-like

Installation view of *Fool's Fire*, Julie Taymor: Playing with Fire exhibition. (Photograph by Richard K. Loesch. Published by permission of Richard K. Loesch and Julie Taymor.)

pins from Jocasta's headdress into the eyes of his mask-crown for the blinding sequence. *Oedipus Rex* also featured a setting of wooden slats suspended over water, the symbol of purity, used at the end of the opera to wash away the pollution Oedipus had brought upon Thebes. Taymor used a vividly graphic and gigantic sphinx, manipulated on rods by the chorus, and created clay-covered bodies for the plague victims.

After *Oedipus Rex*, Taymor staged several operas,[13] and revisited Shakespeare for Theatre for a New Audience, with her production of *Titus Andronicus* in 1994. It was to be the basis for her feature film debut in 2000 entitled *Titus*.

With *The Green Bird*, produced in 1996 for Theatre for a New Audience in New York and at the La Jolla Playhouse in California,[14] Taymor returned to the fantastic and refined her use of puppet conventions. As with earlier productions, *The Green Bird* employed puppets, half-masks, full-head masks, and carved figures, many manipulated by visible puppeteers in the manner of the *bunraku*. But for the first time, Taymor called attention to one of those puppeteers: the titular Green Bird himself, a bewitched prince. "I didn't put a mask on his face. I didn't want to hide his facial expression ... he is the shadow of the bird. So the personality, the yearning to be a prince again, was always there. I explored the dialectic between the puppet and the human character" (Schechner 43–44).

The "double event"—seeing both the puppet and the puppeteer simultaneously so one is conscious of both—works most famously in *The Lion King*. Many commentators have noted that the opening number, "The Circle of Life," elicits tears from audience members. Taymor claims that's the result of seeing humans inside the animal figures, visibly manipulating the puppets: "Isn't that the power of it? Isn't that the beauty? So I think people cry because first of all it is surrounding you, which is something that film and TV again do not do. They're two-dimensional mediums. So you get this incredible sense of the space. And a theater becomes a sacred space" (Solman).

The visible manipulation of the elements, revealing the effort needed to create the illusion of movement, is the hallmark of Taymor's later work with puppets. She makes no effort to hide the mechanics, unlike traditional Western forms. Nor, unlike many of the Asian forms from which she takes inspiration, does she routinely utilize conventions of perceiving the visible puppeteer as invisible. Instead, her most recent work insists on keeping the source of the magic apparent. For Taymor, this is what involves the audience: "I'm using your imagination to combine with my imagination. I don't need to give you the literal reality, otherwise you can't see it with new eyes" ("National Press Club Luncheon" 7).

Julie Taymor may not be a puppeteer in a literal, narrow sense of that word and may have good reason for rejecting the label. It cannot be denied, however, that she has expanded the meaning of that label by employing puppets in magical, innovative, original, and highly exciting ways. Puppets are a major element in her mature works, equal to the other creative components, part of a carefully crafted artistic and intellectual whole. Thus it is certainly appropriate that she is currently exploring, with the Disney Corporation, a possible new Broadway musical based on the classic tale of a puppet striving for humanity, Carlo Collodi's *Pinocchio* (Freudenheim).

Notes

1. The title phrase is taken from Julie Taymor, "Artist's Talk," Wexner Center for the Arts, Ohio State University, 17 Sept. 1999.

2. Irish director Garry Hynes was named Best Director for a play for *The Beauty Queen of Leenane*; Hynes's award was announced seven minutes before Taymor's, making Hynes literally the first woman to receive a Tony for directing. Taymor also won the Outer Critics' Circle, Drama Desk, and Drama League Awards for her direction.

3. Julie Taymor: Playing with Fire, Wexner Center for the Arts, Ohio State University, Columbus, Ohio, opened on September 18, 1999, and closed March 19, 2000, after having been extended. It was curated by Sherri Geldin and Chuck Helms. The exhibit opened at the National Museum of Women in the Arts, Washington, DC, on November 16, 2000, and closed February 4, 2001. It then traveled to the Field Museum, Chicago, opening on June 12, 2001, and was scheduled through November 4, 2001. Objects in the exhibit were from the personal collections of Julie Taymor, with materials from *The Lion King*, courtesy of Disney Theatrical Productions. Eileen Blumenthal and Julie Taymor's *Julie Taymor: Playing with Fire* was revised and expanded, and the 1999 edition served as a catalogue of the exhibition. At the present writing, the future of the exhibit and the eventual disposition of the objects forming it remain unknown.

4. Sources differ on Taymor's first performance work; Sylviane Gold says she was nine in "The Possession of Julie Taymor," *American Theatre* Sept. 1998: 22; ten is the age given in Blumenthal and Taymor, 10, and elsewhere. Taymor gives her age as eleven in Robert Brustein and Julie Taymor, "Recapturing the Fantasy in Our Lives," *The New York Times* 16 Apr. 2000: 2, 5, while she was quoted a week later as saying twelve (Jim Slotek, "Queen of the Jungle: Julie Taymor," *The Toronto Sun* 23 Apr. 2000: S6).

5. See Blau's account of the latter in Herbert Blau, "The Donner Party, Its Crossing," *Theatre Journal* 32 (1980): 141–56.

6. *The King Stag* remained in the ART repertory for several years, touring to festivals; it was revived for a national tour in 2000–2001.

7. Taymor further reworked *The Transposed Heads* into a musical in 1986, performed at the American Musical Theatre Festival in Philadelphia and at Lincoln Center. Eliot Goldenthal composed the score.

8. *Behind the Scenes with Julie Taymor*, co-production of Learning Designs and Thirteen/WNET-TV. New York: First Run Features, 1998.

9. It was nominated for best musical, Taymor for best director of a musical, Goldenthal for best music and lyrics, Taymor and Mercier for best scene design, and Donald Holder for best lighting design.

10. In scenes VII and VIII, Juan also sings the multiplication tables in Spanish.

11. The film was premiered at the Sundance Film Festival in Utah before being broadcast. Taymor's by-then familiar group of artists collaborated with her: Goldenthal composed the music, while G. W. Mercier designed the sets; Michael Curry, a skilled technician, joined the team to solve technical problems; Taymor designed the costumes and the characters.

12. A film of the opera premiered at the Sundance Film Festival in 1993 and was aired on PBS.

13. *The Magic Flute* in Florence and Turin in 1993 and 1994 respectively; *Salomé* for the Kirov Opera in Germany and Russia, 1995, Finland in 1996, Israel in 1999; *The Flying Dutchman* for the Los Angeles Opera, 1995, and the Houston Grand Opera, 1998.

14. The commercially unsuccessful Broadway production of *The Green Bird*, discussed above, was expanded and revised from the 1996 version.

Works Cited

Austin, Lyn. Personal interview, 9 January 1998.

Blumenthal, Eileen, and Julie Taymor. *Julie Taymor: Playing with Fire,* updated and expanded ed. New York: Harry N. Abrams, 1999.

Brandon, James M. "Julie Taymor as Puppet Artist." *The Puppetry Page.* www.sagecraft. com/puppetry/papers/Taymor.html. 1995.

"Bravo Profile: Julie Taymor." Bravo Cable Programming, 19 May 2000.

Cavendish, Lucy. "Review: The Arts," *Sunday Telegraph* [London] (16 July 2000), 11.

Freudenheim, Susan. "In Development: Taymor and Disney Are Working on a New 'Pinocchio.'" *Los Angeles Times* (8 Oct. 2000), Calendar: 80.

Gardner, Elysa. "Bawdy 'Bird' flies high with puppet spectacle." *USA Today* (19 Apr. 2000), 5D.

Goldenthal, Elliot. "Notes." *Juan Darién: A Carnival Mass.* New York: Sony Music Entertainment, 1996.

Gussow, Mel. "The Looking Glass World of Julie Taymor." *The New York Times Magazine* (22 March 1992), 42–53, 78.

Jenner, C. Lee. "Working with Puppets." *Performing Arts Journal,* 7:1 (1983), 103–116.

"National Press Club Luncheon with Julie Taymor." Federal News Service transcript, 15 Nov. 2000.

Nightingale, Benedict. "Benedict Arnold's Five Best West End Productions." *The Times* [London] (16 Dec. 2000), n.p.

O'Haire, Patricia. " 'Bird' A Feather in Her Cap," *Daily News* [New York] (17 Apr. 2000), New York Now, 42.

Schechner, Richard. "Julie Taymor: From Jacques Lecoq to *The Lion King.*" *TDR* 43:3 (1999): 36–55.

Snyder, Joel. "Sharing the Story Within: An Interview with Julie Taymor," *National Endowment for the Arts Explore.* www.arts.gov/explore/ taymor.html. 1997.

Solman, Paul. "Lion King's Queen." "The News Hour with Jim Lehrer." www.pbs.org/ newshour/bb/entertainment/jan-june98/taymor_6-5.html. 5 June 1998.

Exhibitions and Collections of the Jim Henson Company

LESLEE ASCH

The Jim Henson Company has been creating puppets for over forty years. Over that period thousands of beloved characters have been created. While these puppets and related set pieces and props do not constitute a true "collection" in the traditional museum sense, the importance of these figures has been widely recognized, both nationally and internationally. While the Jim Henson Company does have an extensive archive of articles, print materials, sketches and photographs, the large majority of the puppets remain in regular use in the various productions. As of this writing, it is estimated that there are roughly four thousand five hundred puppets in existence in the New York inventory alone. Only a limited number of puppets from the overall collection has been designated as a historical collection, which contains puppets no longer able to be used in production. These are now for display purposes only, and this collection remains family-owned. This collection, which is the portion that will be archivally preserved for future use, contains approximately three hundred fifty puppets, two hundred props and related posters and original framed photographs and artwork. It contains all of the original Sam and Friends puppets, including the original Kermit, created in 1955 by Jim Henson from his mother's green spring coat. It also includes the puppets used on the first season of "Saturday Night Live," a few "Sesame Street" characters, classic "Muppet Show" characters and extensive holdings from the films *The Dark Crystal* and *Labyrinth*. In March 2001, the end of the Jim Henson Company's exhibition program came, exactly one year after the sale of the company. The collection and its future uses are now being reevaluated by the family and The Jim Henson Legacy.

To understand the scope of the collection, it is important to understand Jim and the company's work. In 1954, a young high school student set out to make his entrance into the world of television. He learned that the local television station was auditioning puppeteers for a new show, so he sat down and made a puppet. Needless to say, Jim got the part and the rest, as they say, is history. Jim Henson went on to expand and redefine the scope and possibilities of the form on television and in film. What differentiated his work from those who had blazed the path before him was that Jim's work was designed for television from the start. He was not taking a style developed for live theatrical performances and adapting it to television; rather, television was his stage. Jim continued to do work on local Washington, DC, television stations, which expanded to include numerous commercials and an Emmy Award–winning series entitled "Sam and Friends," created with his partner and wife-to-be, Jane Nebel. "Sam and Friends" ran for six years right before the popular "Huntley-Brinkley" show and Steve Allen's "Tonight Show." This was a sophisticated adult audience, and Jim and Jane's style of outrageous and hip fun caught on.

The Jim Henson Company has created exhibitions of its characters since 1979. The first exhibition was held at the Amsterdam Avenue Gallery of the New York Public Library of the Performing Arts at Lincoln Center. This was originally conceived as an opportunity to display the actual puppets simultaneously with the screening of the first *Muppet Movie* held at the adjacent Bruno Walter Auditorium. There was initially considerable concern and much discussion as to the techniques that could be employed to guard against the puppets appearing lifeless in an exhibition. As these characters had already become quite beloved and believable, great care was taken through positioning and lighting to convey the impression that the characters were merely stopped temporarily, frozen in action, in order to be able to meet their audience friends directly. A style of floor-to-ceiling glass case was chosen to allow full access and visibility for audiences of all ages, and theatrical lighting was an integral part of the presentation. Kids who were found repeatedly hugging the whole cases seemed to confirm the success of the efforts. By the time of the first exhibition, the puppets in the Henson inventory were from the earliest "Sam and Friends" to the then-hit show, "The Muppet Show." The exhibition also included characters from "Saturday Night Live," "Sesame Street," *Emmet Otter's Jugband Christmas* and a series of *Muppet-land* specials.

The success of this initial foray into the world of museums and exhibitions proved so successful that, at the invitation of Steve Brezzo, director of the San Diego Museum of Art from 1979 to 1999, a national tour was begun. This exhibit, entitled The Art of the Muppets, chronicled the history and process of the creation of the Muppets. It toured to nineteen cities from 1980 to 1986. The exhibition consistently broke attendance records and significantly increased museum membership everywhere it toured. It was seen by over two and one half million people during its tour.

Following the success of The Art of the Muppets tour, a new exhibition, The World of Jim Henson: Muppets, Monsters & Magic was created. Unlike The Art of the Muppets, this exhibition was designed to be an international touring show because, by 1987, when it was created, the Muppets had achieved worldwide recognition. At its height, "The Muppet Show" was seen in over one hundred countries and was viewed in fifteen languages. This exhibit expanded to include characters from newer Henson productions, including "Fraggle Rock," the Muppet movies, and *The Dark Crystal.* But as with The Art of the Muppets, the exhibition strove to do more than just chronicle production history. Through interactive displays and video footage, it attempted to illustrate a glimpse of the creative process and the development of a body of work. Muppets, Monsters & Magic was honored as the first temporary exhibition of The Museum of the Moving Image in London and opened at that museum with a special ceremony officiated by H.R.H. Prince Charles. Concurrent with this tour there were two smaller gallery exhibitions entitled The Vision of Jim Henson. One toured internationally until 1998, and the other continues to tour in the United States in an updated version incorporating many of the company's newest productions.

In addition, several special exhibitions were created. In 1983, for the release of *The Dark Crystal,* exhibitions were held in New York, Los Angeles, Japan and Australia. In creating the film, every aspect of this imagined civilization was considered and developed. It was, therefore, intriguing to display items such as the cups, bowls and cutlery, not as props from a ·film, but rather as uncovered archaeological artifacts from a lost culture.

For the release of *Labyrinth,* six simultaneous exhibitions were created. A wonderful touring exhibition was also created featuring Miss Piggy's Art Treasures or the Treasures of the Kermitage, a series of Muppet parodies of great art masterpieces. In addition, special exhibitions were created to document specific time periods in Jim Henson's creative development. These included exhibitions for his alma mater, the University of Maryland, and for the Greenwich Library, documenting the time period in which he resided in Greenwich, Connecticut. The department has also participated in exhibitions and collections nationally and internationally, with long-term loans to many of the other collections covered in this book, as well as The Pittsburgh Children's Museum, The Museum of the Moving Image in London, and a number of international puppet museums.

Although the focus of this chapter is the puppets of the Jim Henson Company, I know that there is often confusion regarding the differences between the company and the Jim Henson Foundation. The Jim Henson Company is the owner and creator of all the Henson television and film endeavors. Until March 2000, Jim Henson's family owned the company. At that time it was sold to the German marketing and television company, EM T.V. In September 2000, the separation was completed between which puppets belonged to EM T.V. and which would be retained by the family. The latter are the items we have been discussing as the collection.

The Jim Henson Foundation was created in 1982 by Jim Henson to expand the scope and understanding of the field of puppetry. To this end, the Foundation gives grants to artists to develop new works of contemporary puppet theater. In 1992, these efforts were expanded to include the first International Festival of Puppet Theater. It is not overstating the truth to say that these festivals have had a profound effect on defining and expanding the understanding and the borders of the art form. As executive director of the Jim Henson Foundation and producing director of the Henson International Festival of Puppet Theater, I produced exhibitions in conjunction with the five festivals held biennially between 1992 and 2000. While few of the materials displayed in these exhibitions remain part of the Henson collection, their documentation and research does. (Future uses of the Henson collection will be determined by the Jim Henson Legacy.) I list these exhibitions below.

1992: Breaking Boundaries was created by The Center for Puppetry Arts in Atlanta and curated by Nancy L. Staub. This exhibition focused on eleven contemporary artists of the 1980s and their contributions to the field. It included Eric Bass, Janie Geiser, Jim Henson, Ralph Lee, Jon Ludwig, Roman Paska, Peter Schumann, Theodora Skipitares, Julie Taymor, Hanne Tierney, and Paul Zaloom. For the New York presentation, as it was held at the enormous Main Gallery of the New York Public Library for the Performing Arts at Lincoln Center, I selected additional pieces by the represented artists that could further illustrate the scope of their work.

1994: Revealing Roots was conceived by Kerry McCarthy, former director of the museum at The Center for Puppetry Arts. It was co-curated by McCarthy, Barbara Stratyner, curator of exhibitions for the New York Public Library, and me. I designed the exhibition with Don Vlack, the library's head designer. This exhibition sought to examine the cultural roots of contemporary puppet theater. The underlying principle was that contemporary artists did not take something relegated to children's theater and try to recreate it as an adult form, but rather they found inspiration in cultures in which puppetry's power and wholeness was always evident. Work was featured with its influences from Africa, Japan, Indonesia, Native American cultures, Mexican Day of the Dead celebrations, and European church antecedents.

1996: Puppets and Performing Objects of the 20th Century was co-curated by Barbara Stratyner, John Bell and me. I conceived of this exhibition as an exploration of all of the varied and inspired artists who had experimented with the object in performance. The exhibition began with Alfred Jarry's *Ubu Roi*, which was particularly fitting as it marked the hundredth-year anniversary of the creation of the play. The exhibit was mounted in cooperation with The Munich Stadtmuseum, which houses one of the largest international collections of puppetry.

1998: Puppet Inspirations was a smaller gallery-style exhibition held at the Newhouse Museum of the Snug Harbor Cultural Center on Staten Island. It featured puppeteers who are also painters and painters who were inspired by puppetry. The initial inspiration for this show was the discovery that noted Dutch puppeteer Neville Tranter had created an extensive collection of strikingly beautiful paintings while on tour with his performances.

2000: Forms in Motion was held at the Cooper Union for the Advancement of Arts and Sciences, in collaboration with the New York Public Library for the Performing Arts at Lincoln Center. It was comprised of two parts. Part One, "Collaborative Forms," featured the puppets and sets from a historic collaboration between Federico García Lorca, playwright, and designer Hermenegilda Lanz, and composer Manuel de Falla. On January 6, 1923, the play *La Nina que riega la albahaca y el principe pregunton (The Little Girl Who Waters Basil and the Nosy Prince)* was performed by Lorca in his living room, using puppets created by Lanz; Manuel de Falla accompanied them on piano. I had heard this story four years earlier while assembling the 1996 exhibition and knew that it would be a must to display these puppets and sets. This exhibit marked the first time these figures were seen outside of Spain. Part Two, "Sculptural Forms," featured the work of six U.S. artists whose work addresses the kinetic power of the sculptural form.

In conclusion, while the exhibition work goes beyond the scope of discussion of the collection, I believe it has established a strong basis for scholarship and understanding in the field and has exemplified the broad ranging extensions possible through this expansive art form.

Howdy Doody in the Courtroom: A Puppet Custody Case

PHYLLIS T. DIRCKS

Howdy Doody, the ingenuous, grinning, freckle-faced puppet who befriended millions of American children during the forties and fifties, recently found himself again in the forefront of the American public consciousness, but this time his appearance had a distinctly contemporary flavor to it. Howdy Doody was the subject of an involved custody case in United States District Court in Hartford, Connecticut, to determine a permanent home for the beloved puppet. The disputants were the family of the late puppeteer, Rufus Rose, and the Detroit Institute of Arts. The Detroit institution, which houses one of the three largest puppet collections in the country, claimed that Rose had promised to give the puppet to the museum, whereas the Rose family maintained that Rose had only thought of doing so, but that Rufus had not made a "completed gift" and that there was not a sufficient contract of agreement for him to do so. The Rose family further claimed that this puppet was not even the true original Howdy Doody. The awarding of Howdy Doody to the Detroit Institute of Arts by Judge Christopher F. Droney on January 23, 2001, concluded a historic case in American puppet history.

Howdy Doody has a unique place in American cultural history because the twenty-four-inch puppet became the star of television's first genuine hit show. From 1948 to 1960, when "The Howdy Doody Show" was televised five days a week, Monday through Friday, from 5:30 P.M.

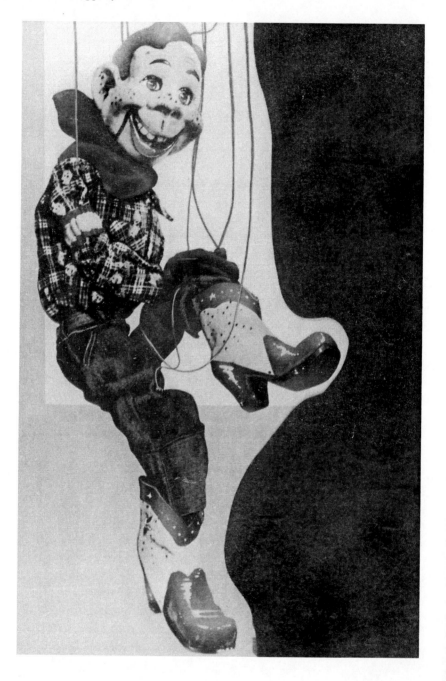

Howdy Doody. (Courtesy the National Broadcasting Company, Inc.)

until 6:00 P.M., watching Howdy became a pre-dinnertime ritual in thousands of American homes. In the days when test patterns dominated the screens during daytime hours, "The Howdy Doody Show" claimed a number of firsts: it was the first network weekday children's show, the first show to broadcast more than one thousand continuous episodes, and, later, the first show in color on television. On June 23, 1949, "The Howdy Doody Show" used split-screen capabilities, linking Howdy in Chicago with the show's host, Buffalo Bob Smith, in New York. This was one of the first instances of a cross-country connection, a technique that figured prominently in the Kennedy-Nixon debates of 1960.

But Howdy Doody appealed to the imagination of children in ways that far exceeded the novelty of the new electronic medium. Except for the first four months of his existence, Howdy Doody was recognized by his red hair and freckled face: a country boy wearing blue jeans, a checked shirt, a bright bandanna, and a cowboy hat. Howdy, the image of wholesome unpolished honesty, carried on a running conversation with Buffalo Bob Smith and with the other cast members, who were both marionettes and humans. Much of the success of the show was due to the natural charm of Buffalo Bob, who treated the marionettes as if they were people; the children of America soon followed (Williams 803). Parents, too, responded to the bright-faced marionette who taught the children valuable practical lessons, such as how to cross the street. In story and song, Howdy was a good influence, urging his viewers to use his own name, "Howdy Doody," whenever they met people. In short, Howdy Doody became the "ultimate role model of a good little kid" (Smith and McCrohan xiii).

But the original Howdy Doody was actually an émigré from Bob Smith's days as an radio entertainer when, by means of his voice alone, he created the character of an appealing country bumpkin who said "Howdy Doody" repeatedly, presumably for lack of any social or conversational skills. The original Howdy Doody was only a voice — with no physical body. But when Smith was invited to appear on television on NBC's "Puppet Playhouse" on December 27, 1947, the demand for a flesh-and-blood Howdy Doody to satisfy the visual appetites of viewers grew. Since "Puppet Playhouse" featured Frank Paris's puppet act, "The Toby Tyler Circus," the show's producers turned to Paris to create a tangible Howdy Doody.

Paris, a resourceful veteran puppeteer, responded by crafting a new head that he planned to attach to the body of one of his circus puppets, but he couldn't complete the makeover by show time (5:00 P.M. on Saturday night). This was unsettling news for Buffalo Bob: New York was coping with a twenty-five-inch snowfall, which had closed all theaters, movie houses and other public entertainment meccas. Snowbound New Yorkers were closeted at home, all free to watch the new show. Eddie Kean, the show's lyricist, came up with the ingenious idea of pretending that the physical Howdy Doody was present, but the country boy was too shy to go on camera. Desperate, Buffalo Bob agreed to the scheme and pretended to his audience he had brought along his friend, Howdy Doody, but Howdy insisted on remaining in Smith's desk drawer.[1] The cameraman showed a tight shot of the drawer while Buffalo Bob carried on a conversation with his own voice. The next day, *Variety* was enthusiastic, and the ratings were excellent (Ritchie 212).

The problem was solved, but not to everyone's satisfaction because, when completed by Paris, Howdy incarnate looked dark and forbidding, totally lacking the charm and ingenuousness that Smith's warm, friendly voice had attached to Radio Howdy. Nevertheless, ominous-looking Howdy appeared on the television show for four months during 1948. Despite the fact that Paris's puppet was "ugly to the point of being grotesque" (Davis 42), the warmth of Smith's voice prevailed, and the character was well received. In fact, he was so well received that the kiddy audience responded wildly to the gambit that Howdy would run as President of the Kids in the 1948 presidential election. Though his opponents were formidable — Harry Truman, Thomas Dewey, and Henry Wallace — Howdy felt his prospects were good. He would campaign as "the only candidate *completely* made of wood" (Bianculli 140). His platform: two Christmases and one schoolday a year, more pictures in history books, double sodas for a dime, and plenty of movies (Stark 14).

When Buffalo Bob offered a free "Howdy Doody for President" button to any child who wrote in for one, NBC was besieged with sixty thousand requests, a phenomenon that has been described as "a marketing landslide of historic proportions" (Davis 48). NBC rejoiced in its success and quickly capitalized on its marketability, obtaining commercial sponsorship from the Colgate Corporation. Soon the Continental Baking Company (the makers of Wonder Bread), and Ovaltine and Mars candy joined the team. Within a month, "The Howdy Doody Show" could boast two sponsors per day and was sold out for years ahead (Davis 48).

But Howdy's high visibility also brought its share of calamity. When toy buyers and distributors, including Macy's, which had received hundreds of requests for a Howdy Doody doll, approached Paris, a quarrel erupted among Paris, who had created the puppet; NBC, which owned Paris's puppet, and Bob Smith, who owned the rights to the Howdy Doody character. Paris, who had actualized Howdy, felt that he was being cheated and stormed out of the studio one afternoon, taking the Howdy Doody puppet with him. "It was one P.M., and we had a show to do at five that night," recalled Eddie Kean (Davis 49). Again, no puppet for the show!

This need to explain Howdy's absence from the show, for the second time, prompted Kean to devise an elaborate scenario in which Howdy was said to be on the campaign trail during this election year. A large United States map in the studio allowed Smith to track Howdy's campaign travels for his television audience. In the meantime, NBC took advantage of Howdy's absence to hire Velma Dawson, a well-known puppet maker from California, to create a Howdy whose good looks would match his endearing personality. The television audience was told that Howdy had seen one of the presidential candidates and was worried about his own physical appearance. Thus he would consult a plastic surgeon and have his entire face changed so that he would be the best-looking candidate. In mid–June, the newly visaged Howdy Doody arrived, red haired and freckle-faced, with prominent ears; he wore jeans, a bandanna over a checked flannel shirt, and a cowboy hat. His mouth moved and his eyes rolled. This was the puppet that came to be known as the true original Howdy or Howdy One, a concept that had vast ramifications in the recent court case. The earlier Howdy crafted by Paris, described by Smith as "the ugliest puppet imaginable" (Smith and McCrohan 32), was dubbed "Ugly Howdy."

The appealing new Howdy dominated television screens across the country from Monday to Friday; at 5:30 every evening, Buffalo Bob opened the show with the question, "What time is it, kids?" The forty young members of the studio audience, who came to be known as the Peanut Gallery, squealed, "It's Howdy Doody time!" before launching into the show's theme song, to the tune of "Ta-ra-ra-boom-de-ay." This was perhaps television's first foray into interactive programming, as the audience members played an active part in the shows. Young viewers vied for tickets and a chance to sit in the Peanut Gallery; it was quipped that expectant mothers were requesting tickets for their unborn children (Stark 16). The Peanut Gallery drew soon-to-be luminaries Sigourney Weaver, John Ritter, Joe Namath, and future baseball star Johnny Bench.

Howdy's popularity soared as he was joined in Doodyville by a cast of characters that included the uncommunicative Clarabell the Clown, who never spoke but reacted by squirting seltzer and honking a horn; Chief Thunderthud, the dynastic chief of the Ooragnak tribe, who introduced the nonsense word, "Kawabunga" into the language as an exclamation of surprise; the beautiful Princess Summerfall Winterspring; John J. Fadoozle, the police inspector; and grumpy Mayor Phineas T. Bluster.

The combination of charm, slapstick, and elementary singable instruction attracted audience and performers alike. *Life* magazine, the arbiter of American culture of the fifties, warmly endorsed the fact that "youngsters like to identify themselves with [Howdy's] jaunty, invincible, personality."[2] Bob Keeshan, who later became Captain Kangaroo, was the original Clarabell the Clown. A Canadian version of the show was created, with the young actor Robert Goulet as host under the name of Timber Tom. Reporter Carl Bernstein, later of Watergate fame, won a Howdy Doody lookalike contest in his youth. And Howdy dolls, inflatable toys, games, nightlights and posters flooded the market as the puppet and his friends became a familiar part of the everyday experience of children across the country.

Philip Huber, a ranking contemporary marionette artist, dates his interest in puppetry to his fifth birthday, when his mother gave him a Howdy puppet. He tells of watching "The Howdy Doody Show" and then reading books from the public library to learn how to build and manipulate puppets (Jackson 1). And Howdy continues to hold our interest: in Herb Gardner's *A Thousand Clowns,* in which the nonconformist Murray Bums and his nephew live in a cluttered Manhattan walkup, a Howdy Doody puppet is a prominent part of the décor. Howdy Doody is so deeply embedded in our national psyche that a Howdy Doody puppet occupies a place of honor in the Smithsonian Institution, having been donated by Margo Rose in 1980 to the National Museum of American History.[3]

"The Howdy Doody Show" was unquestionably a major triumph of early television. Besides its lovable star and its very singable theme song, which was engraved on the minds of youngsters all over the nation, the show foreshadowed the later success of interactive television, preceding

Phil Donahue, Jerry Springer, and others. It also demonstrated the lucrative market value of advertising directed specifically to children, and it paved the way for other live children's shows, such as "Kukla, Fran and Ollie," "Rootie Kazootie," and "Ding Dong School." But despite its popular and commercial success, it eventually succumbed to a rival children's show, "The Mickey Mouse Club." Significantly, the rival signaled the beginning of a new generation of children's television shows. "The Mickey Mouse Club," introduced in 1955, was televised at 5:00 P.M., a full thirty minutes before "The Howdy Doody Show." It was filmed in Hollywood with child performers and no studio audience; "The Howdy Doody Show" was produced live from New York with a live studio audience and adult performers. "The Mickey Mouse Club" was clearly cheaper to produce and easy to repeat. As Stephen D. Stark remarked, "The future belonged to the mouse" (19). In June 1956, "The Howdy Doody Show" was relegated to a Saturday morning slot, known to insiders as "Saturday-morning kids' ghetto" (Davis 192), and in September 1960, its popularity waning, "The Howdy Doody Show" came to an end.

During Howdy's heyday, he was meticulously cared for by Rufus and Margo Rose, two renowned puppeteers who had been hired by NBC in 1952. The Roses kept the puppets in optimal working order, repairing and replacing parts as necessary. They created new characters, such as the old sea captain, Windy Scuttlebutt, and they replicated others, including a pair of Howdy Doody puppets for the Canadian version of the show. Velma Dawson, creator of the original Howdy Doody, believes they made a Photo Doody, a lookalike stringless Howdy Doody that was used expressly for publicity purposes.[4] In 1978 Margo wrote to a friend, a staff member at the Detroit Institute of Arts who had expressed an interest in acquiring some of her material: "Are you interested in pictures + clippings in scrapbooks? Or just puppets. I have duplicates of many things."[5]

After the show's finale in 1960, the disposition of the puppets was left to Rufus Rose and Roger Muir, the show's producer; they decided that Rose should keep the puppets in his studio in Waterford, Connecticut. However, a fire in the Rose studio in 1961 destroyed or damaged many of his puppets, including some from the Howdy Doody entourage. NBC sued Rufus Rose and his insurance company for neglect; Rose countersued NBC (Davis 209). In the settlement that followed those suits, NBC awarded Rose "ownership of all the Howdy Doody marionettes," contingent upon two stipulations: first, that Rose not use the puppets commercially as characters from "The Howdy Doody Show," and, secondly, that Howdy Doody eventually be placed in the care of the Detroit Institute of Arts.

How then does a carefully preserved cultural icon of the magnitude of Howdy Doody become a prominent figure in a U.S. District Court case? The fate of Howdy Doody, always intertwined with that of Buffalo Bob Smith, became complicated when Smith wrote to Rufus Rose in 1970, asking if he could borrow the Howdy Doody puppet in order to set up a tour of various college campuses and military bases. Smith saw this as an opportunity to generate income. Rose accommodated Smith, telling him, "I am sending to you via parcel post the one and only original HOWDY," but he pointedly reminded him of the stipulation from the lawsuit, "that Howdy himself eventually be placed in care of The Detroit Institute of Arts which maintains and displays the foremost national collection of puppets. Therefore I hand HOWDY on to you with this mutual understanding and responsibility."

In 1993, eighteen years after the death of Rufus Rose, Buffalo Bob, still in possession of the puppet, had his attorney, Edward Burns, write to Margo Rose to inform her of Smith's wish to sell Howdy Doody; Margo's son, Christopher, wrote back, reminding Smith of the NBC stipulation that the puppet be placed in the Detroit Institute of Arts. In April 1998, after the death of Margo Rose and as a preliminary step to settling her estate, Christopher Rose journeyed to North Carolina to reclaim the original Howdy Doody. Instead, he and Bob Smith drew up an agreement to sell Howdy Doody, stating that this was "the original Howdy Doody puppet that was used on over 2,300 Howdy Doody TV shows on NBC from approximately 1948 to September 30, 1960." A Photo Doody, the stringless Howdy Doody that was crafted for photo sessions and subsequently owned by the show's producer, Roger Muir, had been auctioned for $113,000 in October 1997, a fact that may have influenced Smith, who had lost $700,000 in an insurance fraud in Florida. However, Bob Smith died in July 1998 at the age of eighty, and that agreement was never consummated. In February 1999, the Detroit Institute of Arts sued the Rose estate, the three sons of Rufus and Margo Rose, and Mildred Smith, widow of Buffalo Bob Smith, asserting its claim to ownership of the Howdy Doody puppet.

The unprecedented popularity of the puppet meant that numerous

Howdy Doody puppets had been created: "millions," according to Velma Dawson, the creator of the original Howdy. Joe Lang, who has studied the issue carefully, concludes that "today, among the living, there's no consensus about how many Howdy Doody puppets were made or what became of them." In the early days of the show, producer Roger Muir had a backup puppet crafted by Scotty Brinker; this puppet came to be known as Double Doody, and Double Doody himself was replicated many times. There were also many Photo Doodys. "The genesis of Howdy puppets is almost biblically tangled," according to Lang (7).

At issue in the court case was the identity of the puppet Rufus Rose had called "the one and only original HOWDY." In May 2000, attorneys for both the Rose family and the Detroit Institute of Arts appeared before Judge Christopher F. Droney in United States District Court in Hartford to argue competing motions for summary judgment, the lawyers for each side maintaining that their case was so strong that no trial was needed. Mark Block, attorney for the Roses, maintained that Rufus Rose's plan to give Howdy Doody to the Detroit Institute of Arts was only a plan, subject to change. He also questioned the definition of "original." "Mr. Rose could have been talking about the body of the puppet when he said 'original' in his letter to Bob Smith," he stated, alluding to the fact that the Detroit Institute of Arts had defined 'original' as a puppet with the head made by Velma Dawson. The Roses by this time had placed the Howdy puppet that Christopher Rose had recovered from Bob Smith in a bank vault in Rhode Island for safekeeping.

Stuart Rosen, attorney for the Detroit Institute of Arts, insisted, "There's no question the original puppet is what they have in their possession. They know it. We know it." Nevertheless, in December 1999, Mark Block had Howdy exhumed from the bank vault and invited Velma Dawson to his Groton, Connecticut, office to determine if the Howdy Doody in the possession of the Roses was Howdy One. Alan Semok, a puppet restorer, opened the back of the puppet's head for the crucial test. Ms. Dawson scrutinized the contents on December 14, 1999, and announced that the work was not hers; thus the Roses' puppet was not, in fact, Howdy One. "It didn't look the same," she told me in an exclusive interview.[6] But in February 2000, Ms. Dawson, on further examination of numerous puppets at NBC, recognized the puppet she had examined in Connecticut as her work, indeed. Ms. Dawson said she was not concerned with the puppet's body since she was sure the body parts were necessarily changed many times, but that she recognized the head of Howdy One from certain markings on the skull and by the way it had been sanded. Quite simply, she told me, "It looked like what I had made." She submitted an affidavit acknowledging her recognition of the Roses' puppet as Howdy One.[7] Velma Dawson's testimony on the identity of Howdy One was crucial. Originally a dancer with the Denishawn Company, Velma Dawson had turned to puppetry as a hobby after her marriage and, by 1948, had developed a reputation for her work, causing NBC to recruit her for the then puppetless "Howdy Doody Show." She was told what costume the new Howdy was to wear and was asked to create a ten-year-old cowboy. She modeled the head in plasticene, made a mold, and then cast the head in plastic wood, hand-shaping the base of the neck; the body was made of wood. Two weeks later, when the appealing, freckle-faced puppet was completed, she was paid four hundred dollars.[8] The original mold for the head of Howdy Doody remains in her Palm Desert, California, home today.

Judge Droney considered Ms. Dawson's testimony, as well as the testimony that conflicted with it. Christopher Rose testified that no single surviving Howdy puppet can be called the original and that perhaps Velma Dawson's puppet was destroyed in the 1961 fire. Rhoda Mann Winkler, the show's head puppeteer for the five years between the demise of Frank Paris and the arrival of Rufus and Margo Rose, examined the Rose puppet and declared that it was not the original. "Feeling him, touching him, playing with him — I knew Howdy intimately for five years, every day on the air, and that was not him. I don't think there is an original Howdy anymore." Asked what she thought happened to Velma Dawson's original puppet, Ms. Winkler answered, "I think he's dead. I think he was messed up in that fire [at the Rose studio]. I think he fell apart and could not be put together in the same way." Her feeling is not far from that of Roger Muir, the show's first producer. "[...] if you say this is the original Howdy, well, it wasn't the original Howdy. There's no one original.... It's a composite Howdy."

Supporting Muir's opinion was the anecdote he related about the return flight Bob Smith made from Washington, DC, one afternoon after he had appeared on the Capitol steps with Howdy as part of an "I am an American Day" celebration. Muir thought that perhaps Howdy flew in the pilot's cabin; what he was sure of was that somehow Howdy's head was bashed in on that flight, and Smith arrived at the studio two or three hours before showtime with an unusable puppet. "Well, there was a mad scramble to get a puppet. Now whether Double Doody's head was switched or what not," Muir continued, "there were a lot of crazy times down through the years." Muir's anecdote underscores the fact that performing puppets are innately fragile and that there is a continuing need to re-fashion puppets and replace body parts. This consideration further blurred the search for the original Howdy Doody.

Two other factors might have complicated Judge Droney's cogitation; both were contained on the audiovisual tape of a four-hour interview with Margo Rose. The first factor was the changing fortunes of the Detroit Institute of Arts, and the second was Margo Rose's own remarks about the Howdy Doody puppet. Gary Busk, audiovisual archivist for the Puppeteers of America, the most influential American puppetry organization, taped a four-hour interview with Margo at a puppetry conference in the early 1980s. During that interview, she mentions that, because of the retrenchment the Detroit Institute of Arts had undergone during the seventies and the consequent lessening of funds for the puppetry collection, she might look for another home for her puppets. This supports Christopher Rose's contention that there was no firm plan to give the puppet to Detroit. Curiously, during that interview, she mentions the Howdy Doody puppet her husband had given Bob Smith as Velma Dawson's puppet. However, Busk himself has reservations: "In reality it's like a museum saying it's got George Washington's ax. The head has been replaced two times and the handle has been changed five times, but it's still the same ax. Now it's almost at that point with Howdy."

On January 23, 2001, Judge Droney, in a forty-page decision, awarded ownership of the Howdy Doody puppet held by the Rose family to the Detroit Institute of Arts.[9] The Court ruled that "the DIA has shown that it is the owner of the Howdy Doody puppet as a matter of law." Judge Droney stated that a letter written by Rufus Rose to NBC in 1967 promising to donate the Howdy Doody puppet to the Detroit Institute of Arts was "a clear contractual agreement." He continued: "The clear intent of Rufus Rose and NBC, as expressed in that contract, was that the puppet be placed in the museum. Although there may be a question as to whether this Howdy Doody puppet was exactly the same in 1960—after the wear and tear of over two thousand shows—as it was when first created in 1948, there is no question that the puppet now in the Rhode Island bank and subject to this case is the same that existed at the end of the show and the same that was the subject of the agreement between Rufus Rose and NBC in 1967."

Burt Dubrow, a television producer who was a longtime friend of Bob Smith, mused on the case: "Once again Howdy's an innocent bystander. It's keeping right in character; he had nothing to do with it, he did nothing wrong. It's almost as if he's saying, 'I'll stay in here until all this is over and everything works out, like it always does'" (Kilgannon 42). The court case is now history, and Howdy Doody has traveled from his casketlike bank vault to the Detroit Institute of Arts. Museum Director Graham Beal has promised that "along with our many historic puppets, Howdy Doody will be cared for under the highest standards of museum conservation and will be exhibited for the enjoyment of the public."[10]

The publicity surrounding the Howdy Doody custody case and its resolution, which places the puppet in a public setting, have recalled vivid and sweet memories for many current baby boomers. Stories of forty- and fifty-somethings who journeyed miles to meet Buffalo Bob and have their pictures taken with him, as he toured shopping malls with Howdy during the eighties and nineties, are rampant. As one boomer summed it up, "What Howdy and Bob brought to life in us were our very first thoughts and hopes and dreams" (Smith and McCrohan ix). Doodyville was indeed a children's paradise of the forties and fifties, and for many of today's baby boomers, it will never be lost.

Notes

1. Stephen Davis details the events of December 27, 1947, in *Say Kids! What Time Is It?* 35–38. See also Michael Ritchie's *Please Stand By*, 207–212.

2. Cited in Stark, 17.

3. See Hughes and Bowers, "The Puppet Collection of the National Museum of American History," in this volume.

4. Telephone interview, February 22, 2001.

5. Many of the details relevant to the involvement of Rufus and Margo Rose in the DIA v. Rose case are drawn from Joe Lang, "Strings Attached," *Hartford Courant Northeast,* 21 May 2000, 7–9.

6. See note 4.

7. *Detroit Inst. of Arts Founders Soc'y v. Rose,* 127 F. Supp. 2d 117, 122 (D. Conn. 2001).

8. Velma Dawson notes the existence of several inaccurate printed accounts of her dealings with NBC.

9. *Detroit Inst. of Arts Founders Soc'y v. Rose,* 127 F. Supp. 2d 117 (D. Conn. 2001).

10. Associated Press, 2001.

Works Cited

Associated Press. "Judge Rules Howdy Doody Puppet Belongs with Detroit Museum." 25 January 2001.

Bianculli, David. *Dictionary of Teleliteracy.* New York: Continuum, 1996.

Davis, Stephen. *Say Kids! What Time Is It?* Boston: Little, Brown, 1987.

Dawson, Velma. Telephone interview. 22 February 2001.

Detroit Institute of Arts v. Christopher S. Rose, James P. Rose, Rufus R. Rose, and Mildred Smith. Civil Action No. 3:99CV00221 (CFD). United States District Court for the District of Connecticut.

Jackson, Cari. "Pulling Strings." http://www.hubermarionettes.com/News/Attache.htm. 23 January 2002.

Kilgannon, Corey. "Say, Kids, What Time Is It? Howdy Doody *Custody* Time!" *New York Times* 27 February 2000.

Lang, Joe. "Strings Attached." *Hartford Courant Northeast* (21 May 2000), 7–9.

Ritchie, Michael. *Please Stand By: A Prehistory of Television.* Woodstock, NY: Overlook Press, 1994.

Smith, Buffalo Bob, and Donna McCrohan. *Howdy and Me: Buffalo Bob's Own Story.* New York: Plume, 1990.

Stark, Steven D. *Glued to the Set.* New York: The Free Press, 1997.

Williams, Suzanne Hurst. "The Howdy Doody Show." *Encyclopedia of Television.* Ed. Horace Newcomb. Chicago: Fitzroy Dearborn Publishers, 1997.

The Fundamentals of Marionette Care

MINA GREGORY, MAUREEN RUSSELL,
and CARA VARNELL

Perhaps the greatest challenge to maintaining a puppet collection is the need to balance the conflicting requirements of caring for that collection and the mandate to exhibit the puppets or use them for performances. Whether it is a public or private collection, the primary function of collection care should emphasize the stabilization of the physical condition of the art and artifacts. With many puppet collections, the challenge comes in meeting the conflicting responsibilities of performance and preservation. Exhibition and performance are essential if the collection is to be shared with the public but should be considered the secondary function since the handling of artifacts can cause permanent damage. With puppets, the exhibition and use involves the stresses not only of handling, but movement as well; add to that the challenges of safe transport, and the possibilities of rapid deterioration and permanent damage increase.

After a brief overview of fundamental preservation principles, this chapter sets guidelines for safe storage and display of collections and offers recommendations for those collections that are still used for performance. Though the discussion focuses on marionettes, the information can be applied to any type of puppet collection.

The Museum Environment

The principles that govern the preservation of all art and artifacts are rooted in the dynamic between the environment and organic or inorganic materials. Considering the basic environmental issues of light, relative humidity, airborne contaminants and pest infestations, the art conservation community established strict standards for the care and maintenance of archive and museum collections. For more than twenty-five years these standards have governed museum-quality collections. During the past decade, institutions such as the Getty Conservation Institute, the Smithsonian and the Canadian Conservation Institute have challenged many of the accepted preservation theories, resulting in the redefining and broadening of some guidelines and a honing of others. The information that is offered here reflects the current philosophy of standards and practices for the storage and display of cultural material.

Nature's dynamic — that is, the interaction of materials with the environment — is in constant motion and is responsible for aging art and artifacts. Unless artifacts are sealed in an oxygen-free environment, they will always be susceptible to the effects of the environment around them. Like the living things they come from, organic materials have a limited life span. But it is their unique composition, whether paper, textile, leather, wood or plastic, and the conditions under which they are kept that determine their extent of life. Inorganics, on the other hand, by their nature, are somewhat more stable, but the wrong conditions can catalyze their natural tendencies to revert to their pure component parts. Metals, ceramics or glass do not deteriorate like the molecular disintegration of organic materials, but rather their deterioration is an effort to separate out into their basic compositional materials. In either case, preservation efforts are designed to try to abate these natural interactive and detrimental processes. Sometimes they can be slowed to a millenium crawl, and in other cases the battle is lost before it begins due to the inherent instability of the materials, such as the synthetic foam products often used for some contemporary puppets.

Complex composite objects such as puppets and marionettes require consideration of both categories of materials. Satisfactorily meeting the needs of disparate elements such as wood or paper, for example, in combination with metal, glass or paint, can be challenging. A clear, basic knowledge of environmental factors is the key to setting management policies appropriate to these unique collections.

Light

Light is potentially the most damaging environmental element, and all light damage is cumulative. It irreversibly fades dyes in textiles and some paint pigments and accelerates the degradation processes of all organic materials, from plastic to paper. Controlling light levels, the amount of exposure, and the quality of the light are vital to the preservation process.

Ultraviolet, visible (light seen by the human eye), and infrared light are all part of the electromagnetic scale and move along as little packets of energy called photons. Some of these photons have the potential to strike with enough force to actually break the molecular bonds of the materials that they hit. Others are weaker and at best can agitate the molecules or transfer heat. The strongest and most harmful rays are those in the ultraviolet range, which carry a force potentially equal to or greater than the molecular bonds in some organic materials.

When a photon strikes a surface, the energy it carries is transferred to that surface. If the energy transmitted is greater than the energy holding together the molecules that make up that surface, which can be the case with UV radiation, a photochemical reaction occurs that changes the molecular structure. In time the consequent alteration translates into irreversible light damage. Photochemical reactions take time to become visible to the human eye, and by the time they are recognized the artifact may be seriously compromised or essentially destroyed. Organic materials such as the paper and textiles, pigments and dyes used in marionettes and puppets are by far the most vulnerable to photochemical changes, and permanent, long-term displays are unadvisable, even under controlled light levels.

Infrared light, though weaker, also has the potential to adversely affect the material it strikes. In this case the energy is transmitted in the form of heat, which causes the inherent water molecules to vaporize, ultimately drying out materials. This lowering of the natural moisture content can cause disfiguring, cracking, yellowing or other irreversible damage to an artifact. These changes are often evidenced by discolored and dried glues, cracked wood and paint, inflexible leather or yellowed paper.

Natural daylight is extremely high in all three components: ultra-violet, visible light and infrared. Because of the wide range and amount of this radiation, sunlight can be difficult to control in archival and museum settings. If galleries, display or work areas must be lit with natural light, it is essential that all windows have UV filters. Even the best of these filters, however, do not remove all of the damaging UV rays. In the case of storage rooms, galleries and display areas, the best option is always artificial light.

Choosing the best artificial light from the myriad of options offered by the lighting manufacturers can present a significant challenge. There are advantages and disadvantages to each class of lamp to be considered before final decisions are made. Though highly cost-effective to use, fluorescent lights by design are high in ultraviolet radiation. Because of these emissions, they are inappropriate for use in an archive or museum setting without special UV filters. Those lamps designed for low UV emission have an interior coating added to help filter out harmful rays. But neither of these filtering methods lasts forever, and, if fluorescent bulbs are used, they need to be periodically checked for UV emissions.

On the other end of the scale are found tungsten or halogen incandescent lamps. These are very low in UV, but high in infrared, especially halogen lamps. Keeping the lights at a significant distance from the artifact can mitigate most of the potentially harmful effect caused by these lights. If they must be used inside a case, then the case must be ventilated and provided with enough air circulation to force the heat to escape, minimizing heat accumulation on the artifact.

A third option often used inside enclosed cases is fiber optic lighting. With this choice, the light source is kept well away from the visible area of the display case in an enclosed case or box of its own. All of the harmful heat or UV is removed from the light as it travels along the cables to its destination point, where it illuminates the artifact. This type of lighting is highly versatile, but can be prohibitively expensive to install.

When it comes to art or artifacts made from organic materials, they must be considered to have a limited exhibition life. Given that light damage is cumulative, each object has only a certain amount of time before the effects of light exposure become evident. The length of that exposure time depends largely on the light levels found in the gallery, or, in the case of performing puppets, on the puppet stage. The rule of thumb followed by some textile conservators is that an object is allowed one year of exposure time, at normal museum hours and under low light levels of five to eight foot-candles, for every ten years. In other words, an artifact can be on display under five to eight foot-candles for one year and then not again for another nine, or it could be exhibited for four months every three years or one month every year, and so on. Tracking the exhibition time of every artifact is important, but especially so when dealing with vulnerable materials like textiles, leather and other organic materials.

Relative Humidity

Relative humidity standards have been highly contested over the past ten years within the art conservation community. After many studies and extensive research, the old standard of maintaining 50 percent +/-, RH was declared not only impractical in many cases, but also not necessary. The acceptable range for RH is now much wider, and any constant reading between 30 percent and 60 percent is acceptable. The real issue is extreme, rapidly fluctuating relative humidity that happens consistently over a long period and how materials react to those changes. Studies have shown that damage can occur from constant, rapid changes in the moisture content of the ambient air, combined with the natural tendency for materials to reach equilibrium with the air. In effect, organic materials will absorb and desorb water vapor as the RH changes, in effect causing mechanical wear and tear of the material's structure.

These new standards do not mean that attention to the relative humidity in storage, display or work areas should slacken. Excessively dry environments, while good for preventing corrosion on metals, can potentially cause brittleness, shrinkage and cracks in materials such as textiles, wood, paper and certain glues used in composition objects. The worst damage is seen in painted wood and in cases where materials are constrained under tension, such as with a costume glued onto a wooden puppet body.

With high relative humidity comes the increased probability of microbiological and insect activity. Above 65 percent RH, mold will develop on textiles and paper or starch-based materials, causing irreversible staining and deterioration. Insects, seeking moisture for survival, are more likely to make a home in a collection with a slightly too damp environment than one that is slightly too dry. RH control is an important aspect of a program for integrated pest management.

There are many types of monitoring equipment available for use in storage and display areas. Whether it is a simple hygrometer that requires staff time to read and record at least twice a day, a recording hygrothermograph that will record onto paper charts the RH activity for the week, or a data logger that works with a PC, every collection should have some system for tracking and recording the changes in RH within storage rooms, galleries and even display cases.

Integrated Pest Management

Pest management requires diligence and resourcefulness in order to protect the collection from the ravages of an infestation. The most effective approach is with a comprehensive pest management program, otherwise known as integrated pest management (IPM). The first step is to establish a system to monitor insect, rodent or even microbiological activity. Left unchecked, an infestation of any kind can occur and, in a matter of weeks, cause irreparable damage to an irreplaceable collection. The following section outlines the basic steps of an IPM program. Further information can be found in conservation resources both on- and off-line. (Please refer to the Suggested Readings list at the end of this chapter).

STEPS FOR AN IPM PROGRAM

1. Understand the life cycle and feeding habits of potential pests. Most pests prefer dark, damp and dirty areas that are undisturbed for long periods of time (like many storage areas).

2. Instigate a monitoring system in collections areas. Unscented sticky traps are best for catching a realistic cross-section of the insect population. Pheromone traps are better for trapping, once a given species is isolated as problematic.

3. Routinely quarantine or fumigate any new objects that will be introduced into the collection. This may be done with a separate holding room, or by isolating the object in sealed polyethylene sheeting or a bag. Most infestations occur from objects new to a collection, and new objects should be closely monitored for several weeks.

4. If a pest is found, try to keep the body intact enough to allow for identification. Isolate the affected artifact, seal it in plastic and remove it from storage, if possible. Treat the artifact, either by freezing, anoxia or another method of eradication. Using a low-suction vacuum (cover

the nozzle with fine nylon net or cotton cheesecloth to prevent damage to the artifact) to remove any residual eggs, casings, webbing, etc. Thoroughly vacuum the area in and around the storage or the display case. Immediately dispose of the vacuum cleaner bag *outside* of the building. Insect eggs are extremely difficult to kill, and, depending on the extent of the problem, may require professional treatment.

Controlling future infestations requires collaboration between the museum or archives staff and a professional pest management company.

Airborne Pollutants

Another significant threat to archival or museum collections is found in airborne contaminants. Sulfur dioxide, hydrogen sulfide, hydrogen cyanide, carbon monoxide, ozone and formaldehyde are just a few of the components found in the air of a typical urban environment. Add to those the sticky, minute, carbon-based airborne pollutants that come from the burning of fossil fuels, as well as other airborne soils, and the need for an effective air filtration system in a museum or archive becomes evident. If the facility does not have an HVAC system, ventilating gallery and storage areas becomes a bigger challenge, and windows and poorly maintained ventilation systems can be sources of serious problems. Keeping windows closed and adding filters to suspicious out-flow vents (a cheap filter solution can be made from layers of cheesecloth) helps to keep the indoor environment clean.

All buildings have dust, and the composition of that dust depends somewhat on the location, age of the building, and the number of visitors. In addition to human skin cells, there may be textile fibers, fungal spores, pollen, carbon soot or other minute crystals. Dust also can contain metallic particulates that can corrode in high humidity, staining and deteriorating adjacent materials. When allowed to collect on artifacts, dust becomes a potential attractant for insects, a home for microbiological growth or a possible catalyst for other types of damage. Regular cleaning of floors, shelves and artifacts on display is essential to any collections management program.

Storage and Handling

The museum environment may also be broadened to include all materials, from storage locations to wooden shelving, in contact with collections. Human beings are also part of this environment, and a high proportion of damage occurs through mishandling. In this section, guidelines and tips are provided for safe storage and handling methods for a marionette collection and are intended to be used in conjunction with the environmental information already discussed. Marionettes are complex composite objects, and the following guidelines can be applied to any type of puppet collection. (Please refer to the Suggested Readings list at the end of this chapter for additional information.)

Storage

More often than not, collections reside in storage far longer than they are exhibited, handled or used in a performance. Proper storage is the most important responsibility of museums and serious collectors. Effective storage facilities and practices prevent incidental damage and endeavor to minimize the inherently deleterious effects of time and the environment as outlined earlier.

STORAGE FACILITIES

The basic factors involved in preparing adequate storage, notes on quality materials, maximizing the potentials of a given space, and tips on storing complex objects are listed below.

Choose a suitable location to store your objects. Ideally, your storage facility will have temperature and relative humidity control. If this is not possible, choose the coolest and driest area in the facility for collection storage. Often subterranean rooms have the most stable climate, assuming that dampness and mold growth are not issues in the geographical region. Make sure objects are not stored under pipes or near steam heaters, both of which can cause water damage and mold growth. Steam heaters can create a microclimate of high humidity and rapid and extreme fluctuations in the relative humidity, imposing great stress on objects. In the case of marionettes, severe climatic fluctuations cause substrates (possibly wood, composition or papier-mâché) to shrink and expand, resulting in cracks and flaking painted surfaces.

Make sure that a failure in building maintenance will not damage the stored collection. Air conditioners, pipes, HVAC systems on roofs, and air ducts can drip, leak, or dump adverse pollutants on stored collections when systems fail. Compact shelving can minimize damage from ceilings, but plastic (polyethylene) sheeting spread over the tops of shelves is also helpful. The top shelf is the most susceptible to damage, and collections managers should avoid placing objects there, if possible.

As stated earlier, light levels should be kept at a minimum. Lights in storerooms should always be turned off when no one is in the room. Similarly, keep all artifacts out of direct sunlight. If there are windows in the storeroom, install curtains, shades, blinds or UV-inhibiting screens over windows. If fluorescent lighting is used, the lamps must have filters or be otherwise treated to minimize the inherent UV light. If the current light levels are in question, UV monitors and lux meters are available in various conservation catalogues.

Plain concrete floors are preferred in storage facilities. Wool carpet should *never* be installed, since wool is always in grave danger of becoming infested with carpet beetles or other proteinaceous-eating insects. Even synthetic carpet is not desirable, since carpet inherently holds dust and is a safe, dark haven for many adverse pests. If linoleum or a sealer is placed on the floor, make sure there is time for the adhesive or sealer to off-gas completely (timing may vary, but at least a month should be allowed) before moving collections into the room. There are numerous substances that contain acidic or toxic components that off-gas when curing, all of which can seriously damage collections (see below). A professional conservator should be consulted when any major installation or refurbishing plan is instigated.

Quality materials are defined as those that do not off-gas any detrimental components as they age. Many adhesives, paints and plastics (acetate and PVC) produce acetic acid or chlorides, formaldehyde, sulfides and other undesirable components upon aging. These chemicals can, in turn, corrode metals and weaken and discolor many organic materials. Wool, some silks and many dyes and sizes in textiles are harmful to many materials. Similarly, wood and many papers and tissues contain lignin and other added acidic components, inherently and from processing, that also damage collections. Safe materials that can be in direct contact with objects are glass; enameled or powder-coated metal shelving; acid-free boards and tissues; MDF (a wood composite board that can be used in place of plywood); washed, unbleached cotton; muslin; or products made solely of polyethylene, polyester or polypropylene.

Shelving should ideally be made of enameled or powder-coated metal. Recently constructed plywood or other wood shelving can endanger collections. Similarly, painted shelves should have at least three weeks to air out prior to placing collections on them. If wooden shelves are the only option, seal all newly constructed shelves with Camger or another preferred sealant. Older wooden shelves are preferable, since most of the acidic components have already off-gassed. Even then, a barrier layer should be placed between the wood and the object, such as Ethafoam" or Volara (polyethylene foam), polyester (Mylar®) or acid-free tissue or board. Padding shelves with Ethafoam® is ideal; in case something drops or falls, damage will be minimized.

Most puppets contain porous materials, such as textiles and foam, which attract dust. In addition to being a potential danger to objects, dust also creates more work and handling of objects, since they will need to be cleaned prior to performing or exhibiting. Objects can be protected from dust in compact storage units, storage shelves with doors, or unbleached cotton muslin "curtains" attached to the shelving with Velcro. Alternatively, enclosed storage boxes, drawers or sheets of acid-free tissue placed over items on shelves may also be used.

Keep collections areas clean at all times. Make sure a maintenance system and IPM program are in place for cleaning storerooms and monitoring insect activity. Numerous museum pests survive on dust alone, and a dirty floor is a threat to collections. The first shelf on shelving units should be sufficiently high to allow for a broom or mop to clean the floor underneath. Sticky traps should be placed near doorways, under shelving units (if possible) and on shelves near objects with proteinaceous materials.

STORING OBJECTS

Marionettes are complex, inherently fragile objects. Storing them is difficult. Ideally, a marionette should be suspended from its controller, with the body of the puppet supported so as not to stress the strings. In this manner, the clothes do not wrinkle or crease and the strings never get tangled. Similarly, a marionette is more accessible to researchers/visitors in an upright position and less handling is necessary. Individual mounts may have to be made for this arrangement, which may become costly. However, it may be worth the money in the long run. Simple unbleached cotton twill tape could easily be used as the support for the body, with sections of twill tape tied in simple bows to the controller itself.

If individual mounts are not feasible, puppeteers may store the

Left: Twisting strings for storage. *Above:* For storage, wrap the twisted strings around the body of the marionette. If this crushes the costume, then wrap the twisted strings around the controller and place the controller next to the puppet.

marionettes in the following manner: Hold the marionette by the controller with one hand. Twist the marionette in one direction until the strings are no longer loose, but not so tight that any joints or strings are straining. Then, wind the twisted strings around the body of the marionette, and rest the marionette on its side in a cushioned box. (See Figs. 51, 52)

If a storage mount or box is enclosed

or lidded, a see-through window on the lid made from Mylar® would be desirable. If storage is too tight, then a picture or a copy of an image of the marionette inside a given box should be placed on the exterior, visible to the visitor. This identification method, or windows in the lids, greatly minimizes unnecessary handling.

Handling

Poor storage can degrade objects over time, by either weakening the overall structural matrix or surface, or by preferentially stressing a joint, for instance, ultimately resulting in its failure. Any damage incurred necessarily involves more handling, as strings need to be untangled, clothes cleaned and joints repaired. Even assuming that storage conditions are adequate for long-term preservation, improper handling and carelessness may rapidly and often irreparably damage marionettes. Proper handling procedures pertain whenever the object is touched, be it for research, photography, use in a performance, during installation/deinstallation, packing, or any movement within an institution.

To handle any object properly, it is important that these guidelines be followed:

1. Insure that any person handling collections is properly trained in the handling of works of art. Every new staff member in contact with collections should attend an object-handling workshop.

2. Be aware of the condition of an object prior to moving it. Check for weak spots and fragile areas, such as flaking paint, cracks, weak joints and seams, brittle foams and unstable strings. With marionettes, the strings are often stressed and can break easily, incurring further damage to the already fragile object. Similarly, their joints are often made from leather, which can become brittle and easily tear.

3. Always have a space cleared to set an object down on before it is picked up, and, if a marionette must be set down, make sure the table or cart is clean and padded with polyethylene foam or acid-free tissue.

4. Hands must be clean or gloves must be worn when handling artifacts.

5. Do not have food or drink near the marionette at any time. Water/liquid stains can be permanent on materials such as on fine suede or metals.

6. Always use two hands when moving an object. If a puppet is awkwardly sized, has multiple moving parts or is heavy, always ask for assistance and never attempt to move it alone.

7. When moving a marionette, cradle the puppet in one hand, supporting and distributing the weight as evenly as possible, and hold the controller in the other hand. If strings are weak, no damage will occur at this point. If moved on a cart, the object should be amply padded (not wrapped, but padded between objects and the container) with acid-free tissue or polyethylene foam during transportation.

8. Never place a marionette in direct sunlight or heat, no matter how temporary the movement.

9. If the marionettes will be out of storage for any length of time, dust should be prevented from settling on the surfaces. Instead of wrapping marionettes in tissue to prevent dust accumulation, which can stress appendages and joints, merely place a sheet of acid-free tissue over the object and/or container.

10. During a performance, and even just in regular museum handling, puppeteers should be extremely careful of banging appendages and marionettes against one another.

11. For temporary storage during practice or performance (if applicable), the marionettes should be hung by their controllers, with plenty of room between them. If no stands or mounts are available, the marionettes should be placed on a clean, padded table with ample space between each object, without tangling the strings.

Performance and Exhibition

These handling guidelines also pertain, should the collection be used in performances. Even if properly handled and stored, however, continued use of original objects will result in increasingly high maintenance and conservation costs and, ultimately, irreversible deterioration of the marionettes. The owner or responsible institution must make a conscious decision to accept the wear incurred over the long term, if performed. If the subsequent deterioration is unacceptable, the owner should consider retiring the object or fabricating a replica to use in its place. Creating replicas can be expensive; however, the destruction of a unique marionette or even breaking a tradition is priceless.

The Museum of New Mexico in Santa Fe has begun such a program. The sixty-five marionettes made by Gustave Baumann in the 1930s and '40s are too fragile to continue to be used in the annual Christmas performances, and replicas are gradually being made. The compromise is an excellent solution: the annual performance can continue, and the original marionettes are on display in a case near the auditorium for public appreciation.

Exhibiting Puppet Collections

For exhibiting puppets, all of the guidelines and tips mentioned earlier still apply. The light levels and exhibit time recommended earlier should strictly be followed. Temperatures in or outside of cases should never exceed 72° Fahrenheit, to avoid accelerating any natural aging processes or discoloration and weakening of materials.

All case materials should undergo Oddy Testing, which checks for the presence of acidic and sulfuric components that discolor, tarnish and weaken the numerous elements of the objects. Materials to be tested include fabrics used to cover the materials in the display floor or build-ups, or any adhesive or caulking that may exist in the object's closed environment. Plywood used to construct cases and build-ups should be sealed for these same reasons or else substituted with MDF board. Similarly, paint in display areas should be left to cure for a minimum of three weeks.

Plexiglas offers a number of advantages over open display areas. Plexiglas vitrines prevent dust accumulation and vandalism and help buffer temperature and environmental fluctuations in the gallery. Temperatures can easily soar inside cases, however, if gallery lighting is not adequately designed. Make sure temperatures inside the case do not exceed the recommended temperatures. High temperatures, in addition to accelerating deterioration mechanisms, lower the relative humidity in the case, causing potential damage to complex or organic objects when uncontrolled.

Conclusion

Adhering to the recommendations provided will help insure the long life of any puppet collection. However, even with this special care, there may be a point when a puppet will need the attention of a trained conservator. Structural damage or signs of developing deterioration should alert the collection caretakers to the need to consult an expert conservator. If one is not available in the area, contact the main office of The American Institute for the Conservation of Historic and Artistic Works (AIC) at 1717 K Street, N.W., Suite 200, Washington, DC 20006. They can also be found on-line at www.aic.org. AIC offers a free referral service for the general public, recommending only conservators with professional standing.

Suggested Readings

Environmental Control

Brommelle, N. S. "Air Conditioning and Lighting from the Point of View of Conservation." *Museum Journal* 63.1, 2 (June–Sept. 1963), 32–36, 40.

Cassar, May. *Environmental Management*. London: Routledge, 1995.

_____. "Proposals for a Typology of Display Case Construction Designs and Museum Climate Control Systems." *ICOM 7th Triennial Meeting Preprints, Copenhagen*. Paris: ICOM Committee for Conservation, 1984. 11–15.

_____, and William O. Clarke. "A Pragmatic Approach to Environmental Improvements in the Courtauld Institute Galleries in Somerset House." *Preprints, 10th Triennial Meeting, Washington, DC, USA, 22–27 August 1993*. Paris: ICOM Committee for Conservation, 1993. 595–600.

Erhardt, David, and Marion Mecklenburg. "Relative Humidity Re-Examined." *Preventive Conservation: Practice, Theory and Research. Preprints of the Contributions to the Ottawa Congress*. London: The International Institute for the Conservation of Historic and Artistic Works (IIC), 1994. 32–38.

MacCormac, Richard, and Michael Popper. "The Ruskin Library: Architecture and Environment for the Storage, Display and Study of a Collection." *Preventive Conservation: Practice, Theory and Research. Preprints of the Contributions to the Ottawa Congress*. London: The International Institute for the Conservation of Historic and Artistic Works (IIC), 1994. 139–143.

Michalski, Stefan. "Relative Humidity: A Discussion of Correct/Incorrect Values." *Preprints, 10th Triennial Meeting, Washington, DC, USA, 22–27 August 1993*. Paris: ICOM Committee for Conservation, 1993. 614–619.

Padfield, Tim. "Climate Control in Libraries and Archives." *Australian Institute for the Conservation of Cultural Material Bulletin* 14.1 & 2 (June 1988), 49–68.

Paine, Shelley Reisman. "Basic Principles for Controlling Environmental Conditions in Historical Agencies and Museums." *American Association for State and Local History Technical Report* 3 (1985).

Roy, Ashok, and Perry Smith, eds. *Preventive Conservation: Practice, Theory and Research. Preprints of the Contributions to the Ottawa Congress*. London: The International Institute for the Conservation of Historic and Artistic Works (IIC), 1994.

Staniforth, Sarah. "Environmental Conservation." *Manual of Curatorship*. Ed. John M. A. Thompson. London: Butterworths and Co., Ltd., 1984, 192–202.

_____, Bob Hayes, and Linda Bullock. "Appropriate Technologies for Relative Humidity Control for Museum Collections Housed in Historic Buildings." *Preventive Conservation: Practice, Theory and Research. Preprints of the Contributions to the Ottawa Congress.* London: The International Institute for the Conservation of Historic and Artistic Works (IIC), 1994, 123–128.

Thompson, Garry. *The Museum Environment.* Stoneworth, MA: Butterworths and Co., Ltd., 1986.

Williams, Scott. "Amines in Steam Humidification Systems." On-line posting. http://palimsest.stanford.edu/byform/mailing-lists/scl2001/0190.html. 07 Feb 2001.

Pest Management

Florian, Mary Lou. "Integrated System Approach to Insect Pest Control: An Alternative to Fumigation." *Proceedings of Conservation in Archives: International Symposium, Ottawa, Canada, May 10–12 1988.* Paris: National Archives of Canada and International Council on Archives, 1989. 253–262.

Gilberg, M. "The Effects of Low Oxygen Atmospheres on Museum Pests." *Studies in Conservation* 36.2 (1991).

_____, and A. Roach. "The Use of a Commercial Pheromone Trap for Monitoring *Lasioderma serricorne* (F). Infestations in Museum Collections." *Studies in Conservation* 36.4 (1991), 243–247.

Harmon, James D. *Integrated Pest Management in Museum, Library and Archival Facilities: A Step-by-Step Approach for the Design, Development, Implementation and Maintenance of an Integrated Pest Management Program.* Indianapolis, IN: Harmon Preservation Pest Management, 1993.

Kronkright, Dale Paul. *Pest Management and Control for Museums.* Santa Fe, NM: New Mexico Association of Museums, 1998.

Mallis, A. *Handbook of Pest Control: The Behavior, Life History, and Control of Household Pests.* Cleveland, OH: Franzak & Foster, 1990.

Pinniger, D. B. *Insect Pests in Museums.* London: Archetype Books, 1994.

SOLINET. "Pest Control Bibliography." Atlanta, GA: Solinet Preservation Program, 1994. http://palimpsest.stanford.edu/solinet/pestbib/htm.

Story, Keith O. *Approaches to Pest Management in Museums.* Washington, DC: Smithsonian Institution, 1985.

Strang, T. J. K., and J. E. Dawson. "Controlling Museum Fungal Problems." Ottawa: Department of Communications, Canadian Conservation Institute. *Technical Bulletin* 12 (1991).

Zycherman, Lynda, and J. R. Schrock, eds. *A Guide to Museum Pest Control.* Foundation of the American Institute for the Conservation of Historic and Artistic Works and the Association of Systematics Collections, 1988.

Storage and Exhibition

Blackshaw, S. M., and V. D. Daniels. "Selecting Safe Materials for Use in the Display and Storage of Antiques." *Preprints of the International Council of Museums' Committee for Conservation: Triennial Meeting, Zagreb, Yugoslavia, 1978.* n.p., 1978.

Croddock, Ann Brooke. "Construction Materials for Storage and Exhibition." *Conservation Concerns: A Guide for Collectors and Curators.* Ed. Constanze Bachmann. Washington, DC: Smithsonian Institution, 1992, 23–28.

Grattan, David W., ed. *Saving the Twentieth Century: The Conservation of Modern*

Materials, Proceedings of a Conference Symposium 91. Ottawa: Communication Canada, 1991.

Hatchfield, Pamela. *Conservation Update: Materials for Use in Proximity to Museum Objects.* Unpublished paper. New England Museum Association, October 28, 1999.

_____, and Jane Carpenter. "Formaldehyde: How Great Is the Danger to Collections?" Available from the Strauss Center for Conservation and Technical Studies, Fogg Museum, Harvard University. 1987.

Institute of Museum Services. *Collections Management, Maintenance and Conservation: A Summary of the Study.* 1985.

Miles, Catherine E. "Wood Coatings for Display and Storage Cases." *Studies in Conservation* 31 (1986), 114–124.

Motylewski, Daren. *What an Institution Can Do to Survey Its Own Preservation Needs.* Technical leaflet. Andover, MA: Northeast Document Conservation Center, August 1991.

Padfield, Tim. "The Control of Relative Humidity and Air Pollution in Show-Cases and Picture Frames." *Studies in Conservation* 2 (1966), 8–30.

Randolph, Pamela Y. "Museum Housekeeping: Developing a Collections Maintenance Program." *Virginia Association of Museums Technical Information.* Winter/Spring 1987.

Raphael, T. *Conservation Guidelines: Design and Fabrication of Exhibits.* Harper's Ferry Center: National Park Service. 1986, revised 1991.

Rose, Carolyn L., and Amparo R. de Torres, eds. *Storage of Natural History Collections: Ideas and Practical Solutions.* Pittsburgh, PA: Society for the Preservation of Natural History Collections, 1992.

Solley, Thomas, et al. *Planning for Emergencies: A Guide for Museums.* Association of Art Museum Directors, 1987.

Stolow, Nathan. "Fundamental Case Design for Humidity Sensitive Collections." *Museum News* (Technical Supplement II) 44 (1966), 45–52.

_____. *Conservation and Exhibitions: Packing, Transport, Storage and Environmental Considerations.* Stoneworth, MA: Butterworths, 1986.

Tetreault, Jean. "Display Material: The Good, The Bad and the Ugly." *Exhibitions and Conservation. Preprints of the Conference Held at the Royal College of Physicians, Edinburgh.* Ed. J Sarge. Edinburgh: The Scottish Society for Conservation & Restoration (SSCR), 1994.

Yoon, Young Jun, and Peter Brimblecombe. "Contribution of Dust at Floor Level to Particle Deposit within the Sainsbury Centre for Visual Arts." *Studies in Conservation* 45.2 (2000), 127–137.

Web Sites

Conservation Online (CoOL) is an excellent resource for other Websites, free information about conservation, and links to many national and international conservation organizations. There are numerous bibliographies, checklists and how-to's devoted to the caring for collections, pest management, and many other collections-related topics. There are also links to suppliers for any material listed in this article. http://palimpsest.stanford.edu.

National Park Service Conserv-O-Grams are excellent sources of detailed information about basic collections care issues from lighting to pest management. http://www.cr.nps.gov/csd/publications/conservo gram.

Canadian Conservation Institute also has many on-line publications available for free. You can search by subject for documents at www.cci-icc.gc.ca/frameset_e.shtml.

Sources of Materials

Many of the materials mentioned in this chapter can be purchased from stores through a catalogue, telephone, or over the Internet. This list is not inclusive nor an endorsement for the stores nor does the list include larger hardware such as shelves, HVAC systems, etc. Check with the CoOL Web site at http://palimpsest.stanford.edu/misc/commercial. html for more vendors and advice.

Conservator's Emporium
100 Standing Rock Circle
Reno, NV 89511
775-852-0404
Fax: 775-852-3737

Conservation Resources International, Ltd. (US & UK)
8000-H Forbes Place
Springfield, VA 22151
800-634-6932
Fax: 703-321-0629
www.conservationresources.com
E-mail: criusa@conservationre sources.com

Conservation Support Systems
P.O. Box 91746
Santa Barbara, CA 93190-1746
800-482-6299
Fax: 805-682-9843
www.silcom.com/~css

Gaylord Bros.
P.O. Box 490
Syracuse, NY 13221-4901
800-448-6160
Fax: 800-272-3412
www.gaylord.com/archival

Light Impressions
P.O. Box 22708
Rochester, NY 14692-2708
800-828-6216
Fax: 800-828-5539
www.lightimpressionsdirect.com

Talas
568 Broadway
New York, NY 10012-9989
212-219-0770
Fax: 212-219-0735
www.talas-nyc.com
E-mail: talas@sprynet.com

University Products/Archival
517 Main Street, P.O. Box 101
Holyoke, MA 01041-0101
800-628-1912

Fax: 800-532-3372
www.universityproducts.com
E-mail: info@universityproducts.
  com

Puppetry in Cyberspace: Developing Virtual Performance Spaces

Mary Flanagan

On-line environments — especially those that allow "avatars," visual representations of the user, to navigate and operate — are very much like large puppet theaters. If we view controlling avatars in virtual spaces as an exercise in electronic puppeteering, then reviewing puppet history can offer us insight into virtual theater practices. Puppet theater has existed throughout the world for centuries and has appealed to a wide range of audiences, often presented as a kind of folk theater in which traditional plays or stories are performed to a local audience.

Whether in real space or in virtual space, designing an agent for a specific role helps make a good performance possible. Robert Smythe, artistic director of Mum Puppet Theater in Philadelphia, notes that "puppeteers must remember that it is they, not the puppets, who provide the magic for the audience." On-line performance, closely related to puppetry as a medium, can combine a compelling narrative, human acting, graphical environments, audio, and programmatic behaviors into immersive digital worlds to generate a truly unique kind of performance. Technology is allowing us to orchestrate the level of audience participation and a particular kind of "ecology" of the on-line experience more than ever before.

Cyberspace evokes challenging questions about the fundamental nature of performance. Typically, any kind of performance employs some degree of technology, from sets, makeup, and costumes to controlled lighting and projection screens. The task of creating a successful on-line performance piece is complicated in more ways than simply the introduction of a technological interface, however; an on-line environment allows users to take on a variety of roles and for the computer to also contribute roles, as well as environmental attributes. The current merging of performance and on-line interaction is creating a genre where performers interact with other people and with computers to create a style of theatrical performance that moves far beyond realism. For example, actors may or may not follow set scripts; improvisation and audience participation must be integrated into the plan for the performance. In addition, the actors must find a way to bring unique personalities to their on-screen representations, whether through actions, graphics, sounds, or other behavioral modifications that can be performed in the context of the performance piece.

In addition to live actors, intelligent software agents, through specific or self-reflexive actions, become participants in on-line performances. The combined effect of these elements can bring artists and scientists together to use virtual space as a site for expression. To what degree will the agent be "intelligent?" Which characters should become autonomous agents? How will "real" actors and participants interact and recognize (or not recognize) other participants or the audience? The decision to use character-based autonomous agents in a piece must be determined from the content of the work; integrating agents in a project is difficult and radically questions notions of acting, identity, and participation in traditional theater.

On-line performances have been created using standalone and Web-based 2D and 3D worlds. "The Palace," a 2D graphic world created primarily for live chats, has been home to both organized performance pieces: e.g., *Waiting for Godot*, performed inside The Palace and "live" at various venues, including the Digital Storytelling Festival, in 1997 and "word streaming," the "street theater" of the internet. 3D worlds that utilize VRML (Virtual Reality Modeling Language), such as Community Place, also host live performance events. Perhaps the main challenge in staging these events is to gather multiple users with compatible technology to shared spaces on the Internet.

Artists face a threefold challenge when designing on-line performance pieces. First, one must design the interactive work to have narrative, "dramatic," or structural movement within the performance. The idea of a "finished" work has to be replaced with the idea of a work in progress, an event-driven site for art that relies on time, space, and human/technological interaction. That idea also must apply to the character-agents; new uses will be discovered for them, and technological advances will make their role in performance an ever-evolving one. Second is the challenge of attaining the desired look, feel, and context for meaningful interaction. The simple polygonal world leaves much to be explored in terms of innovation use of simplicity, but also leaves much to be desired in comparison to other digital media projects in the age of advanced streaming technologies. Detailed 3D models cannot run in a VRML world; the use of sound is limited at best. Java-based spaces (along with other supported programming environments and languages) are vital and are replacing limited "packaged" systems that relied on dot-com financing models. Third, there is the issue of logistics. On-line performance is dependent on and driven by technology. Getting users on-line and having their systems work is only part of the very real technical challenge of on-line performance. Servers get bogged down with a certain number of users; textures on polygons slow the processing of images down to a sluggish pace. Can an environment be then designed to take advantage of these severe technological limitations? What is an optimal number of users for a given system/project? In addition, this is not a populist movement. While virtual theater is indeed accessible, it usually necessitates high-end computers for viewing and participation (which implies just as much economic discrimination as does traditional theater). However, virtual performance technology is valuable due to the participatory nature that on-line performance offers. Aesthetically, virtual sets allow for a type of expressiveness that has never been imagined before.

We know that space is an essential element to many kinds of exhibitions and performances. Theater has the stage and seats, acoustics; a film relies on the play of light across the theatrical space. How does virtual space as a site for performance affect the nature of performance?

Spatial relations have been challenged historically by genres of performance art and the wide variety of participatory art. With the Happenings in the late 1950s and onward, art space was considered an "environment" and attendees were used as material for the whole piece. The audiences were seldom unprepared; in fact, scripts were often present at participatory events. So, while the Happenings were interactive, they often had fixed goals that were ultimately extensions of the creator's goals for the event. Soke Dinkla notes that these participatory events were replaced with reactive kinetic art, which replaced the instruction set given to an audience with computer-coded instruction sets for the installation pieces (Dinkla 283). In other words, the spaces of participatory art were scripted environments that allowed for some type of interactivity.

Any kind of "navigable" computer experience is relying on some kind of conception of space in order to function. Does the idea of on-line participation require that the experience be in some sort of navigable space in order to show characters, spatial relations, and the feeling of "being there"?

Traditionally, puppet theater has relied on some sort of audience participation. David Currell suggests that the puppeteer invites the audience to "supply with the imagination those other dimensions that puppets cannot achieve" (279). Theater has also relied heavily on language throughout its history — through spoken word in the West to spoken word and opera in Asia. What does this reliance on language mean in an on-line world that is limited in the use of language?

In the current VRML-generated multi-user worlds, especially those created for virtual performances, language is the primary communication medium. "Chat" scripts such as those used in performances in 2D chat-based worlds are completely text-dependent; the world "OnLive Traveler" is designed for live speech. In any event they rely heavily on language to convey meaning, although, because of its graphic nature, new technology allows artists to play with images and thus foreground graphics as a predominant factor in productions.

Virtual theater is an art form that is malleable, supple, and issues new and promising developments. The very lengthy history of theater, and especially puppet theater, has shown us that it is capable of many forms, presentation styles, ideologies, and techniques. On-line creators can choose many paths to this art form by dissecting traditional ideas of performance and recreating them in a unique way that reflects our current cultural concerns. One example of a hybrid of the virtual and the physical is the SmartlabCentre coproduction with the CAT lab at NYU, the BBC, and Mindgames, Europe, of the *Flutterfugue*, a performance in 2002 that used animated and robotic puppets in the show.

Lizbeth Goodman and her colleagues in the performance and new

The movements of dancer Lizbeth Goodman are mirrored in a virtual Java environment by a flutterfly puppet in order to enable those with physical challenges to "dance" in virtual environments.

media communities developed this experiential interface so that it might contribute to the empowerment of dancers and other creative people and bring the experience of dance to those who could, for whatever reason, not move their bodies as freely as they might wish in time with the music they love. The dancer's movements are controlled by the audience, who respond both to the music (the *Flutterfugue* score), to a collaborating dancer, a butterfly, which sometimes takes the form of a physical, mechanical puppet and sometimes takes the form of a computer-animated image. This brings a radical change in puppet theater, for now the audience has some control over puppets, thus blurring the line between audience and puppeteer.

Around the world, styles of puppet theater share some common features. Perhaps one of the significant differences is that some theater is performed through the puppets (players perform dialogue as if the puppets were speaking). The puppet theater styles of Taiwan, Java, and some European cultures use this approach. These plays mix dialogue in different character "voices" and occasionally provide some story narration. Other

An actor controls a virtual puppet behind him with finger extensions.

theatrical practices instead feature a nondiegetic human narrator to explain the story (the voice clearly is not coming from the puppets). In Elizabethan England, this person was referred to as an "interpreter." Japanese *bunraku* theater and French shadow theater likewise featured an offstage storyteller.

Chinese puppet theater, one of the oldest of these traditions, comes in three major forms: the marionette theater, the hand-puppet theater, and the shadow theater. As early as the Sung dynasty in the tenth century A.D., when other forms of Chinese theater had yet to mature, the performance techniques of both marionette theater and shadow theater were already highly developed (TECO 1996). Gods and goddesses thought to live in temples in Taiwan are traditionally believed to enjoy all kinds of theatrical performances. Live action and puppet theater are performed in front of temples several times a year, especially at the beginning and end of Ghost Month. One of the most popular puppet plays is the Matsu play.

The following briefly describes the development of the Matsu virtual performance environment, an on-line navigable puppet world based on the legend of the Chinese goddess Matsu. We chose the Matsu legend because it is a wonderfully challenging story to translate to a VR world (it occurs underwater) and because we have firsthand experience with the puppet play in a traditional Taiwanese setting. According to legend, Matsu was born in A.D. 960. Young Matsu saved her brother and father from drowning after their ship sank on a stormy night at sea through actions she performed in a dream. Matsu's miracles continued to occur, and she was called "Goddess of the Sea and Empress of Heaven." The story of Matsu is performed in women's plays and puppet theater at temples dedicated to her. While not nearly as popular in the West, puppet shows and shadow plays are a common part of Taiwanese culture.

Thus, controlling "avatars" in virtual spaces is a kind of electronic puppeteering. Is it possible to create effective *virtual* spaces for religious or ritual plays? On-line theater can be a kind of a ritual performance based on beliefs or cultural systems of meaning. Particularly in the case of imitative rituals in which the myth or part of the myth is collectively repeated (performed) either by or in the presence of a large group, on-line worlds can address this need for community that is satisfied and formalized through the imitative ritual. A feeling of shared experience, grounded in a traditional belief system, is still an important feature of contemporary Taiwan. The Matsu environment investigates the feeling of shared experience by creating a shared virtual performance space online.

The implementation of the project was similar to any implementation for a multimedia piece. First, the world was programmed and the character models were created; some characters were assigned as "autonomous" (controlled by the computer) and some as "performed" by human users. Designs for the "sets," "costumes," and "actors" were based on traditional iconography of skin puppets, or *pi ying xi*. One participant acts as the young Matsu and performs from the temporal and spatial position of her dream state. Meanwhile, Matsu, her family agents, and other members of the community are underwater, in the middle of a dream. As in the legend, Matsu must save her father and older brother from drowning; their ship has capsized and they are floundering near it. By swimming and interacting with the space, the avatars interact physically with object/agents that perform actions. Some of the character-agents are more "intelligent" than others. Matsu's family members act more intelligently than the fish. There are other intelligent "non-human guided" character-agents in the piece — we included more than user-controlled characters in the space. Intelligent character-agents occupy our world as well. For example, Matsu's family members have preset animations and timelines, "knowing" they have to drown unless they can be saved. The number of participants and the kinds of interactions these users foster will thus change the story. Thus, we have more than just user-controlled buttons in our space; character-agents assume a new level of responsibility in the piece. What are the implications of creating a religious story that can change? Does virtual performance in this case become one of many folk interpretations of cultural history, or does it become a form of cultural imperialism, dismantling long-held beliefs with new technology?

Interactive, on-line performance can define itself as a unique genre at sites where it will be able to serve as an integration of several approaches, combining them with scientific ways of expression to generate a unique experience. As Robert Smythe says of creating good puppet theater, "The true magic lies within those who create so much from so little, and in those who are willing to believe us when we do."

Works Cited

Chinnock, C. "Technology Information: Virtual Reality Goes to Work." *Byte,* 21:3 (1996), 26(2).

Currell, D. *The Complete Book of Puppet Theatre.* London: A & C Black, 1974.

Damer, B. *Avatars!* Indianapolis: New Riders, 1997.

Dinkla, S. "From Participation to Interaction: Toward the Origins of Interactive Art." *Clicking In: Hot Links to a Digital Culture,* Ed. Hershman Leeson, 279–290, 1996.

Flanagan, Mary. *Matsu: Goddess.* On-line project. www.maryflanagan.com/matsu/default. htm. 1999.

McKenzie, J. "Virtual Reality: Performance, Immersion, and the Thaw," *TDR* Cambridge, Mass. 38 (4), (1994, Winter), 83.

Mclean's. "Stepping into the Future of Dance." (Dancers Pierre-Paul Savoie and Jeff Hall Integrate Live Performance and Virtual Reality in 'Poles'), (1996, October), 71.

Rotzer, F. "From Image to Environment." *UNESCO Courier,* 36 (2) (1996, December).

SmartLab Centre. *Flutterfugue.* July 2002 performance. www.smartlabcentre.com. 2002.

Smythe, R. "Are Puppets Alive?" *Sagecraft Puppetry Homepage.* www.sagecraft.com/pup petry/philosophy/alive.html.

Stalberg, R. H. *China's Puppets.* San Francisco: China Books, 1984.

Taipei Economic and Cultural Office in Houston (TECO). "Puppetry: The Taiwan Tradition." www.houstoncul.org/culdir/pupp/pupp.htm. 1996.

"VRML Humanoid Animation Working Group." http://ece.uwaterloo.ca/~h-anim/. 1997.

Appendix A: Selected Additional Puppetry Collections

Steve Abrams

Collections of Over Five Hundred Puppets

These collections are in addition to the collections described in preceding essays (American Museum of Natural History, Ballard Institute, Bread & Puppet Theater Museum, Center for Puppetry Arts, Detroit Institute of Arts, Harvard Theatre Collection, and the UCLA Fowler Museum of Cultural History).

The Detroit Children's Museum. 6134 Second Avenue, Detroit, MI 48202. The Children's Museum has six hundred and nine puppets in its collection and four hundred puppets in the Lending Department. The collection, much of it donated by Helen Reisdorf, includes a number of toy puppets by Pelham, Steiff and Hazelle. Also puppets by Phil Molby, Ray Moore, Harry Burnett, Martin Stevens, Paul McPharlin, Gisela Lohmann, and Roberto Lago. Traditional puppets include Indonesian shadowpuppets, Punch and Judy sets, Sicilian marionettes, and puppets from Germany, the Czech Republic and Mexico. In addition, there are many prints, books, posters and other materials related to puppetry.

Gary Busk Collection. Carrollton, TX. poaavlib@dhc.net. A private collection of over one thousand puppets. Large collection of puppets by Mabel Beaton and Sky Highchief. Other artists include Bil Baird, Frank Paris, Pady Blackwood, Martin and Olga Stevens, Poppinjay Puppets, Phillip Huber, Tony Urbano, Ray

Moore, Bob Baker, Tatterman, Rene, Jimmy Rowlands, Marjorie Batchelder, Paul McPharlin, Tony Sarg, Cole Marionettes, Sue Hastings, Ron Herrick, Sid and Marty Krofft, George Latshaw, Lou Bunin, Ed Johnson, Kathy Piper, Joe Owens, Herbert Scheffel, Alfred Wallace, Lea Wallace, Arlyn Coad, Ronnie Burkett, Dolores Hadley, and Jim Gamble.

COPA (Conservatory of Puppet Arts). 965 Fair Oaks Ave., Pasadena, CA 91103. Project of Community Partners located at the Armory Center Northwest. **The Alan Cook Collection.** 626-296-1536. www.COPA-puppets.org; mail@ copa-puppets.org. More than three thousand puppets from China, Taiwan, Sri Lanka, Java, Bali, Burma, Turkey, and Greece. Also Punch and Judy sets, Guignol, Caspar and Sicilian marionettes. A large collection of vaudeville marionettes used by Len Ayers (The Mantell Manikins). Other artists include Tatterman, Frank Paris, Turnabout Theatre, Donald Cordry, Martin and Olga Stevens, Art Clokey, Roberto Lago, Walton and O'Rourke, Gilberto Ramirez, Tony Sarg, Blanding Sloan, Bil Baird, Bob Brown, Poppinjay, Jewell Manikins and many others.

Museum of International Folk Art. P.O. Box 2087, 706 Camino Lejo, Santa Fe, NM 87505. 505-476-1200. www.moifa.org. Approximately one thousand eight hundred puppets. Includes hand, shadow, rod, and finger puppets from North America, South America, Asia, and Europe.

Pittsburgh Children's Museum. 10 Children's Way, Pittsburgh, PA 15212. 412-322-5058. www.pittsburghkids.org. Collection of several hundred puppets includes puppets by Margo Lovelace, Tony Sarg, Turnabout, WPA, one *bunraku*, Jim Henson, and Johnny Faust.

Collections in Natural History, Archeology, Anthropology, and Ethnography: Cultures Around the World

Bishop Museum. 1525 Bernice St., Honolulu, HI 96817. 808-847-3511. www.bishopmuseum.org. Three rare Hawaiian puppets.

Burke Museum of Natural History and Culture. University of Washington, 17th Ave. and N.E. 45 St., Seattle, WA 98195. www.washington.edu/burke museum. Fifty puppets. Indonesian shadow and rod puppets; four string puppets from Burma, six huge shadow puppets from Thailand, three Vietnamese water puppets, four from North America, including one from Alaska. The Tlingit and Kwakwaka'wakw are hand puppets, and the Tsimshian is a string puppet.

Chinese Temple. 1500 Broderick St., Oroville, CA 95965. Oroville Parks Dept., 530-538-24115. www.cityoforoville.org/Parks/ChineseTemple.html. Hand puppets from Oroville Chinese Opera Theatre and shadow puppets.

The Field Museum. 1400 South Lake Shore Drive at Roosevelt Road (Grant Park), Chicago, IL 60605. 312-922-9410. www.fieldmuseum.org. One hundred sixty-three puppets, including ninety-five from Taiwan, thirty-six from China, fifteen from Indonesia, twelve from Iran, and one each from New Hebrides, Thailand, Canada, Alaska, and Arizona.

Phoebe A. Hearst Museum of Anthropology. Kroeber Hall, Bancroft Way and College Ave., University of California at Berkeley, Berkeley, CA. 510-643-7648. www.hearstmuseum.berkeley.edu. An unknown number of puppets including ones from African-Ibibio and Java.

Mingei International Museum. Balboa Park, 1439 El Prado, San Diego, CA 92101. 619-239-0003. www.mingei.org. Over one hundred puppets, mostly from Asia; also some from Italy and USA.

National Museum of African Art. Smithsonian Institution, 950 Independence Ave SW, Washington, DC 20506. www.nmafa.si.edu. 202-357-4600. Twelve puppets: five from Ibibio-Nigeria, two from Bozo-Burkina Faso, and five from Bamana-Mali.

National Museum of the American Indian. George Gustav Heye Center, Smithsonian Institution, 1 Bowling Green, Battery Park, NY 10004. 212-514-3700. www.conexus.si.edu and www.nmai.si.edu. Extensive Native American collection, including masks and some rare puppets. Fewer than ten marionettes from the Northwest Coast (Kwakiutl, Nisga'a, Gitksan; Tsimshian), a few tourist-style marionettes from Mexico, and one ceramic articulated figure catalogued as "Aztec." A new museum will open on the Mall in Washington, DC, in 2004.

National Museum of Natural History. Smithsonian Institution, Constitution Ave & 10th St. NW, Washington, DC 20560. 202-237-2700. www.mnh.si.edu. Two hundred thirty-five items from the following areas: Thirteen marionettes from Burma, one Native American puppet (Haida), five from Ceylon, one from China, about one hundred seventy rod and shadow puppets from Java, seven from Bali, twenty from Korea, seven from New Hebrides, one from African-Bambara, two from Mexico, six from Hawaii, and two from Zambia.

Spooner Museum of Anthropology (or KUMA). 48 University of Kansas, 1340 Jayhawk Blvd., Lawrence, KS 66045. 785-864-4245. www.anthro.ku.edu. Approximately one hundred thirty puppets donated by Hazelle Rollins.

University of Pennsylvania Museum of Archaeology and Anthropology. 33rd & Spruce St., Philadelphia, PA 19104. 215-898-4025 (Museum Education

Department). www.museum.upenn.edu. Approximately two hundred fifty puppets: forty goleks, two hundred and eight Java shadow puppets, some from China, all in storage.

Collections from Art Museums with Collections from Traditional Cultures

Cleveland Museum of Art. 11150 East Blvd., Cleveland, OH 44106. 216-421-7340. www.clevelandart.org. Eighteen Indonesian puppets in the education collection.

Fine Arts Museum of San Francisco. M. H. De Young Memorial Art Museum, 75 Tea Garden Drive, Golden Gate Park near 10th and Fulton, San Francisco, CA 94118. Museum closed since 2001, new museum to open in 2005. Temes nevinbur puppet, New Hebrides. (From *Traditional Puppets of the World*, Michael Malkin.)

Metropolitan Museum of Art. 1000 Fifth Ave at 82nd St., NY, NY 10028. www.metmuseum.org. Michael Rockefeller Collection. Arts of Oceania, Africa and the Americas. A few African puppets, also perhaps puppets from Sumatra.

Peabody Essex Museum. 150 Essex St., Salem, MA 01970. 978-745-1876. www.pem.org. Ten puppets from Java and two from Japan, perhaps others.

Seattle Asian Art Museum. 1400 E. Prospect St. (Volunteer Park), Seattle, WA 98112. 206-654-3100. www.seattleartmuseum.org. Three hundred sixty Chinese shadow puppets (exhibited in 1999 for the Seattle Festival). The puppets can be seen on-line.

Collections Associated with Theaters

Bob Baker Marionette Theater. 1345 West First St., Los Angeles, CA 09926. 213-250-9995. www.bobbakermarionettes.com. In addition to his own puppets, works by film pioneer George Pal, Turnabout, Tatterman, Frank Paris and others.

Meredith Bixby Marionette Exhibit. P.O. Box 198, 141 E. Michigan Ave., Saline, MI 48176. 734-429-4494. www.salinechamber.com. Permanent exhibition of the work of Meredith Bixby (1910–2002).

Chinese Theatre Works. 37–45 84th St., #31, Jackson Heights, NY 11372. Kuang-Yu Fong and Stephen Kaplin (skactw@tiac.net). The Pauline Benton collection of Chinese shadow puppets.

Cleveland Playhouse. 8500 Euclid Ave., Cleveland, OH 44106. 216-795-7000. www.clevelandplayhouse.com. Three puppets from the 1916 production of *The Death of Tintageles*. Puppets from the 1922 production of *Aladdin's Lamp*, and the entire cast of Shakespeare's *A Midsummer Night's Dream* (1925), directed and designed by Julie McCune Flory.

In the Heart of the Beast Theatre. 1500 E. Lake St, Minneapolis, MN 55407. 612-721-2535. www.hbot.org. Puppets exhibited at Frederick R. Weisman Art Museum.

Magic and Movie Hall of Fame. O'Shea's Hilton Casino, 3555 Las Vegas Blvd., Las Vegas, NV 89109. 702-737-1343. www.nvohwy.com/m/magmvhal/htm. Valentine Vox collection includes ventriloquist figures. "I Can See Your Lips Moving," 1985.

Northwest Puppet Center. 9123 15th Ave. NE, Seattle, WA 98115. 206-523-2579. Chris and Stephen Carter. www.nwpuppet.org and nwpuppet@earth link.net. Active puppet theater, opened in 1993. Rarest puppets are 21 hand puppets of the Bergamo (c. 1890). Also high-quality Sicilian and Chinese puppets, contemporary make, traditional style; African and Indonesian puppets; and hundreds of puppets by the Carters. Early editions of the first puppet histories and publications.

Puppet House Theater. 128 Thimble Island Rd., Stony Creek, CT 06405. 203-488-5752. Tim Gable and James Weil. www.puppethouse.org. Formerly the "Macri-Weil Sicilian Puppet Theater," opened in 1963. Fifty-two large Catania Sicilian marionettes and sixty Palermo-style marionettes.

Puppet Showplace Theatre. 32 Station St., Brookline, MA 02445. 617-731-6400. www.puppetshowplace.org. Puppets of Mary Churchill and Paul Vincent-Davis.

Puppet Works. 338 6th Avenue at 4th St., Brooklyn, NY 11215. 718-965-3391. www.puppetworks.org and puppetwork@aol.com. Finely crafted marionettes adorn the walls of Nicholas Coppola's theater.

Aurora Valentinetti Puppet Museum. 249 Fourth Street, Bremerton, WA 98337. 360-373-2992. Curator Stanley W. Hess (s.w.hess@worldnet.att.net). The museum is a division of the Evergreen Children's Theatre. Founded with the collection of Aurora Valentinetti, of the University of Washington faculty (1943–1992), and Marshall Campbell. Over three hundred international puppets, as well as puppets associated with the University of Washington School of Drama.

Other Collections

American Museum of the Moving Image. 35th Ave. and 36th St., Astoria, NY 11106. 718-784-4520. www.ammi.org. Thirty-five puppets from the Morey Bunin (1910–1997) Collection, including Foodini. Also Yoda from *The Empire Strikes Back.*

Brooklyn Historical Society. 128 Pierrepont St., Brooklyn, NY 11201. 718-222-4111. www.brooklynhistory.org. A vent figure of John Cooper, the ventriloquist who taught Shari Lewis.

Canadian Museum of Civilization. 100 Laurier St, Hull PQ JBX 4H2. 819-776-7000. www.civilization.ca. Curator Constance Nebel. 819-776-8235. 400-puppet collection that includes traditional puppets of various cultures and 20th century Canadian puppets. *Canadian Puppets*, Ken McKay (1980).

Circus World Museum. 426 Water St., Baraboo, WI 53913. 608-356-8341. www.circusworldmuseum.com. "Punch and Judy at the Circus" exhibit has puppets used by Ray Turner (puppets by Pinxy).

Cooper-Hewitt National Design Museum. Smithsonian Institution, 2 E. 91st St. at Fifth Ave., NY, NY 10028. 212-849-8400. www.si.edu/ndm. The original collection includes French shadow puppets from the Theatre Seraphin (1776–1870), a Guignol booth, and nine eighteenth-century puppets, all in the 1949 exhibit "Small Wonders." In 1976 Frank Haines (1891–1988) and Elizabeth Haines (1903–1977) donated four hundred and eight items, including marionettes, advertising puppets, stage props and accessories, scripts, and paper files. Puppets are hand-carved wood and dressed with exquisite costumes. Productions represented include *Nightingale, Connecticut Yankee in King Arthur's Court, Christmas Carol, The Owl & the Pussy Cat.* Advertising figures include Reddy Kilowatt and Elsie, the Borden Cow.

Denver Museum of Nature and Science. 2001 Colorado Blvd., Denver, CO 80205. 303-370-6383. www.dmns.org. Six puppets: one Native American Kwakiutl puppet and one marionette made by an Indian student at Haskell Institute, c. 1935. Also three rod puppets and one shadow puppet from Java.

George Mason University. Fenwick Library Special Collections and Archives, 4400 University Drive, Fairfax, VA 22030. www.gmu.edu. Institute of the Federal Theatre Project, Dr Lorraine Brown. Audiotape oral histories and transcripts of WPA puppeteers include Bil Baird, Bob Bromley, Ralph Chessé, Max Leavitt, Molka Reich, Len Suib, and Grace Wilder.

Hirshhorn Museum and Sculpture Garden. Smithsonian Institution, Independence Ave & 8th St. NW, Washington, DC 20506. www.hirshhorn.org. Seven marionettes by Alexandra Exter (1882–1949), a Russian set designer living in Paris in the 1920s. Cubist puppets made in 1926 include two Harlequins, Columbine, Pierrot, Lady in Red, American Policeman, Judy.

Historical Society of Western Pennsylvania. Senator John Heinz Pittsburgh Regional History Center, 1212 Smallman St., Pittsburgh, PA 15222. 412-454-6000. www.pghhistory.org. Ninety-one items, including marionettes, heads, stages, and props. Two hand puppets from the mid-twentieth century designed by Ida Mae Stilley Maher. Czech puppets collected and used by Milan Getting (1878–1951). See William Keyes, *Pennsylvania Heritage Magazine* (1994) and *Czechoslovak-American Puppetry*, Ed. Vit Horejs (1994).

Institute for Advanced Study, Princeton. East Asian Library, 33 First Campus Center, Room 310, Princeton, NJ 08540. Approximately two thousand five hundred Chinese shadow puppets in the Gest Oriental Library, including all set pieces, heads, etc.

McGill University Library. Rosalynde Stearn Collection, Rare Books Dept., 3459 McTavish St., Montreal, Que H3A 1Y1. 414-398-6555. www.library.mcgill. ca. 100 well catalogued puppets and extensive printed material.

Mercer Museum. Bucks County Historical Society, 84 S. Pine St. at Ashland St., Doylestown, PA 18901. 215-345-0210. www.mercermuseum.org. Fourteen Sicilian marionettes, Punch & Judy sets and tobacconist figure of Punch, the symbol of the museum. Some puppets labeled as Chinese, but are actually from Java.

Michigan State University Museum. E. Grand Ave., East Lansing, MI 48824. 517-355-2300. www.museum.cl.msu.edu. Eighteen Lano marionettes and hand puppets, including a skeleton, a dog, clowns, black natives, and an Arab. Original typed manuscript of puppeteer David Lano's book *A Wandering Showman, I* includes unpublished material. Photos of Lano and other related paper memorabilia, including information about Lano's puppet shows and presentations for the WPA in the 1930s.

Museum of Broadcasting and Communications. Chicago Cultural Center, 78 E. Washington St., Chicago, IL 60202. 312-629-6000. www.museum.tv. Clippings and tapes of radio and TV shows featuring Edgar Bergen's Charlie McCarthy Theater. Exhibit opened April 2001 named Puppets, Pies and Prizes: Children's TV Chicago Style. Includes work of Roy Brown (1933–2001), "Garfield Goose," which aired in 1953.

Museum of the City of New York. 1220 Fifth Ave. and 103rd St., NY, NY 10029. 212-534-1672. www.mcny.org. Excellent collection of material about the New York theater and an unknown quantity of puppets. Some puppets by Rolain Rochelle and print material on the Yiddish Puppet Theatre, Bil Baird, and Herb Scheffel.

Museum of Jewish Heritage. One Battery Park Plaza, NY, NY 10004. 212-968-1800. www.mjhnyc.org. Puppets by Simcha Schwarz (1900–1974), designed by Marc Chagall.

Museum of Science & Industry. 5700 S. Lake Shore Drive (Jackson Park), Chicago, IL 60630. 773-684-1414. www.msichicago.org. One hundred sixty puppets from Kungsholm Theatre, opera with puppets. Puppets on exhibit.

Nantucket Historical Association. P.O. Box 1016, Nantucket, MA 02554. 508-228-1894. www.nha.org. Tony Sarg material, including books, photos, and four puppets. Also six puppets not made by Sarg.

Newark Museum. 49 Washington St., P.O. Box 540, Newark, NJ 07101. 973-596-6550. www.newarkmuseum.org. Twenty-seven puppets including twenty-two from Asia, two from Africa, and three from the United States.

Oakland Museum. 1000 Oak St., Oakland, CA 94607. 510-238-2200. www.museumca.org. Four puppets by Ralph Chessé.

Harry Ransom Humanities Research Center. University of Texas, Austin, P.O. Box 7219, 21st and Speedway, Austin, TX 78713. 512-471-8944. www.hrc.utexas.edu. Sixty-two Sicilian marionettes and ten Rajasthani marionettes.

Santa Barbara Museum of Art. 1130 State St., Santa Barbara, CA 93161. www.sbmuseart.org. Doll gallery, Schott collection of eighteenth-century French and Italian puppets, German hand puppets, one small Sicilian puppet, Java rod and shadow puppets.

Santa Fe Museum of Fine Arts. 107 W Palace Ave., P.O. Box 2087, Santa Fe, NM 87503. 505-476-5061. www.museumofnewmexico.org. Eighty puppets of Gustave Bauman (1881–1971), documented in a special catalog by Ellen Zeiselman.

C. V. Starr East Asian Library. 300 Kent Hall, Mail Code 3901, Columbia University, 1140 Amsterdam Ave., New York, NY 10027. starr@libraries.cul.columbia.edu. More than twenty thousand *bunraku* photographs, programs in English and Japanese, texts of the plays performed, and audio and video recordings, donated by Barbara Adachi. The collection includes two or three puppets (not *bunraku*) and two or three heads.

Vent Haven Museum. 33 W. Maple Ave., Fort Mitchell, KY 41011. 606-341-0461. www.venthaven.org/wsberger.htm. Exhibit by Cincinnati Museum. Approximately five hundred ventriloquist figures. Collection of W. S. Berger (1878–1972). A major collection, opened in 1973, mostly exhibited.

Whitman College. 345 Boyer, Walla Walla, WA 99362. 509-527-5111. www.whitman.edu. Sixteen *bunraku* heads. These can be seen on-line at www.whitman.edu/offices_departments/sheehan/DollTheater/11.html.

Whitney Museum of American Art. 945 Madison Ave. at 75th St., NY, NY 10021. 212-570-3676. www.whitney.org. The Calder Circus may be considered a collection of puppets.

The Jane Voorhes Zimmerli Art Museum. Rutgers University, 71 Hamilton St., New Brunswick, NJ 08901. 732-932-7237. www.zimmerlimuseum.rutgers. edu. Eight zinc shadow puppets from the French *Le Chat Noir* cabaret and nine French hand puppets.

Collections of Puppetry Videotapes

Library of Congress. 101 Independence Ave. SE, Washington, DC 20540. 202-707-5000. www.loc.gov. The Library preserved many films, including early Edison films using puppets.

Museum of Television and Radio. 25 W. 52nd St., NY, NY 10019. 212-621-6800. www.mtr.org. Collection of rare TV shows with puppets, including extensive work by Jim Henson and Burr Tillstrom.

New York Public Library for the Performing Arts. Dorothy & Lewis Cullman Center, 40 Lincoln Center Plaza, NY, NY 10023. 212-870-1641. www.nypl. org. The Theatre and Film Archive includes a collection of videotapes from all Henson Festival performances.

The Puppeteers of America Audiovisual Library. 3827 Westminster, Carrollton, TX 75007. www.puppeteers.org; poaavlib@dhc.net.

Appendix B: Films and Videos on Puppetry at the Donnell Media Center of the New York Public Library

JOSEPH YRANSKI

All of these films and videos may be viewed on site in the Study Center. This service is provided to the general public by appointment made at least two working days in advance for viewing. To gain access to the New York Public Library catalogue, log on to www.nypl.org, then click on to Leoline. All of the materials within the library are listed by title, name or subject.

Film: Act Without Words, 10 min.
Films Inc/Jacques Forgeot, 1964
Puppet animation is used to express the tenor of Samuel Beckett's existential universe.

Film: The Adventures of Elmo in Grouchland, 73 min.
Swank Motion Picture, 1999
When "Sesame Street's" Elmo dives into a garbage can to save his beloved blanket, the Muppet characters all come forward to help him out.

Film: Alice, 84 min.
First Run/Icarus, 1988

Jan Svankmejer pays tribute to Lewis Carroll's wonderland tales in this feature-length film that is populated with sinister puppets.

Film: Blue Like an Orange, 26 min.
UNESCO/McGraw-Hill, 1968
French puppeteers of the Alexandre Expedition for the Mutual Appreciation of Eastern & Western Culture pursue a survey of little-known puppet troupes and well-known puppeteers, emphasizing their similarities rather than their cultural and ethnic differences.

Video: Brother Bread, Sister Puppet, 60 min.
Cinema Guild, 1992
Documents the Bread & Puppet Theater's 1988 *Domestic Resurrection Circus*, located at the company's home in Northern Vermont. Founding puppeteer Peter Schumann and the company discuss politics, puppets, music and performance.

Film: Chinese Shadow Play, 10 min.
Chinese Film Enterprises of America, 1947
Traditional rod puppets made out of donkey skin parchment and accompanied by traditional Chinese music are presented behind a translucent screen. The classic legend of the White Snake Lady.

Film: Cinderella, 40 min.
Thames Television/Media International, 1983
Mark Hall's puppet animation of the classic fairy tale is done without the use of narration.

Film: Corduroy, 16 min.
Weston Woods Studio, 1984
Based upon the book by Don Freeman, a teddy bear waits patiently for someone to buy him. When a mother refuses to buy him because he is missing a button on his overalls, the bear embarks on a storewide search for it.

Film: Crane's Feather, 10 min.
Soyuzmult Film, 1978
Irina Garina's puppet-animation version of a Japanese tale of an old woman who rescues a crane in the snow.

Video: Curious George, 14 min.
Churchill Films, 1984
Puppetry-animated version of H. A. Rey children's book of a curious monkey who is taken from the jungle and brought to a big city.

Video: Curious George Goes to the Hospital, 15 min.
Churchill Films, 1983
Further adventures of H. A. Rey's curious monkey, George.

Film: Dick Whittington and His Cat, 15 min.
Israel Berman/Sterling Educational Films, 1965
    An animated puppet film of the classic English legend.

Video: Early Russian Cinema Volume #3: Starevitch's Fantasies, 58 min.
Milestone Film & Video, 1992
    Ladislas Starevitch's early puppet animation from the Khanzhonkov Studios includes *The Dragonfly and the Ant* (1913), *Christmas Eve* (1913), *The Lily of Belgium* (1915).

Film: The Epic of Gilgamesh, 11 min.
First Run/Icarus, 1981
    The Brothers Quay produce a swift and savage animated tale about a tricycle-riding monster who lures a winged creature to its lair.

Film: Frog and Toad Are Friends, 18 min.
Churchill Films, 1985
    John Matthews's animated puppet film of Arnold Lobel's book.

Film: Frog and Toad: Behind the Scenes, 10 min.
Churchill Films, 1985
    John Matthews shows how he made the puppets, what they are made of, and how he brings them to life.

Film: The Hand, 19 min.
McGraw-Hill, 1965
    Jiri Trinka's puppet animation is an allegory about a man whose only pleasure is the flower to which he devotes his love.

Film: Hiawatha, 19 min.
Israel Berman/Sterling Educational Films, 1967
    Puppetry version of Henry Wadsworth Longfellow's classic poem.

Film: The Hungry Walrus, 6 min.
Beacon Films, 1982
    Puppet-animated version of an Inuit tale about Orfix the carver, who carves a snow statue of a walrus.

Film: Interlude by Candlelight, 13 min.
M. van der Linden, 1963
    A photographic interpretation of the puppets and strange driftwood forms collected by the Dutch artist Henry van Tussenbroek.

Film: It's One Family: Knock on Wood, 24 min.
Tony De Nonno, 1982

Documentary on Mike and Ida Mantero, who remain bound to the sixteenth-century Sicilian marionette tradition. In their Brooklyn theater they continue to perform the saga of Orlando Furioso from the court of Charlemagne.

Film: Kid Stuff, 6 min.
National Film Board of Canada, 1990
   Pierre M. Trudeau uses puppets and drawings to convey the effects of family discord upon a small child.

Film: Kumak, The Sleep Hunter, 13 min.
Dunclaren Productions, 1953
   Puppet version of an Inuit tale of a hunter who is given magical powers that allow him to become a great hunter.

Film: The Legend of the Cruel Giant, 11 min.
Soyuzmultfilm Studio/Carousel Films, 1970
   Puppet animation about a fisherman who releases a genie/giant and then is rewarded with gold and jewels.

Film: The Little Giraffe, 8 min.
Puppet Film Studios/McGraw-Hill, 1962
   Inflated puppets tell the story about the adventures of a giraffe who falls off a Ferris wheel in this Polish film.

Film: The Little Match Girl, 17 min.
Gakken Productions/Coronet, 1978
   An animated puppet version of the Hans Christian Andersen story.

Film: The Little Players, 27 min.
Robin Lehman, 1982
   Frank Peschka and Bill Murdock use their own creative drive in adapting action to their puppets. The five puppets who make up the "little players" perform material from Shakespeare, Nöel Coward and Oscar Wilde.

Film: The Lover's Exile, 87 min.
Films Inc., 1980
   Bunraku puppeteers and master puppeteer Tamao Yoshida breathe life into Monzaemon Chikamatsu's classic drama of a messenger boy and a prostitute.

Film: Magic Gifts, 18 min.
Fleetwood Films, 1959
   Animated puppet film of the traditional folktale in which a poor man is given three magic gifts, only to have them stolen by a wicked innkeeper.

Film: The Man Who Wanted to Fly, 11 min.
Gakken Company, Ltd./Coronet 1969

A Japanese tale adapted in puppet animation about a clever man who manages to fly with the ducks.

Film: The Meadow's Green, 28 min.
George Griffin & Dee Dee Halleck, 1975
Documents the Bread & Puppet Theater's *Domestic Resurrection Circus*, performed in July 1975. The political stories enacted by the puppets are as basic as the bread that is baked and passed out to all those who attend.

Film: A Muppet Christmas Carol, 89 min.
Swank Motion Pictures, 1992
Brian Henson continues the excellent work of his father in this re-telling of the Charles Dickens story.

Film: The Muppet Movie, 98 min.
Swank Motion Pictures, 1979
Jim Henson introduces his popular Muppets in their feature film debut.

Film: Muppet Treasure Island, 99 min.
Swank Motion Pictures, 1996
The Muppets under the direction of Brian Henson create their usual havoc in this version of Robert Louis Stevenson's classic tale.

Film: Muppets in Space, 88 min.
Swank Motion Pictures, 1999
The Muppets help Gonzo find his place in the universe, with a little bit of help from a spaceship.

Film: The Muppets Take Manhattan, 93 min.
Films Inc., 1984
Jim Henson's popular Muppets come to New York City after their graduation in order to fulfill their dreams.

Film: Nightangel, 15 min.
National Film Board of Canada, 1986
Jacques Drouin and Brestislav Pojar use puppets and pinpoint animation to illustrate the fantasy life of a man temporarily blinded in an accident.

Film: Pirro, 11 min.
Pat Patterson/Macmillan, 1980
Puppeteer Pat Patterson sets up situations, both verbally and in sign language, with the aid of her clown marionette, Pirro.

Film: The Princess and the Dragon, 9 min.
Film Polski/Sterling Films, 1947
Animated puppets tell the tale of a cobbler who saves the kingdom from a fire-breathing dragon.

Film: Puppet Animation, 16 min.
Educational Media International, 1983

David Johnson's notorious Australian puppet film star, "Dennis the Dragon," is interviewed on a television talk show about the techniques used in puppet animation.

Video: Puppetry: World of Imagination, 43 min.
Cinema Guild, 2001

The best of contemporary puppetry includes works by Ralph Lee, Basil Twist, Michael Curry, Janie Geiser, Leslee Asch and Cheryl Henson of the Biennial Henson Puppetry Festival and footage of the Greenwich Village Halloween Parade.

Film: Puppets, 15 min.
Stelios Roccos, 1966

Stelios Roccos presents a variety of methods for making puppets, beginning with stick puppets and advancing to more sophisticated types.

Film: Puppets: How They Happen, 18 min.
FilmFair Communications, 1986

A puppeteer introduces an unruly group of children, ages six to ten, to the art of puppets. Using "found" materials, the children develop characters and voices for their puppets and perform *The Bremen Town Musicians.*

Film: Revenge of the Kinematograph Cameraman, 9 min.
Festival Films, 1912

Ladislas Starevitch's puppet-animation fable of an insect couple's marital infidelity.

Film: The Rolling Rice Ball, 11 min.
Gakken Company, Ltd./Coronet, 1967

A puppet film adaptation of a Japanese fairy tale of a poor woodcutter who is rewarded for helping the Land of the Mice.

Film: Sesame Street Presents: Follow That Bird, 88 min.
Swank Motion Pictures, 1985

Jim Henson's Big Bird is taken away from his "Sesame Street" neighbors by busybody social workers. This causes one of the greatest bird hunts in the history of film.

Film: The Seventh Master of the House, 13 min.
Caprino Films/Modern Learning Aids, 1969

Norwegian puppet-animated tale of P. C. Asbjornsen and Jorgen E. Moe's story. A lone traveler asks for shelter in a farmhouse set deep in the woods, only to discover that the owners are incapable of making any decisions.

Film: Shadow Puppet Theatre of Java, 22 min.
Baylis Glascock Films, 1970
   Oemartopo presents an all-night Indonesian *wayang kulit,* including the flower battle. Puppets are shown being made, and the meaning of different puppet shapes and details is discussed.

Film: The Shoemaker and the Elves, 15 min.
Institut fur Film und Bild/Films Inc., 1971
   Puppet-animated version of the classic story by the Brothers Grimm.

Film: The Snow Girl, 9 min.
Featurette Film Studio/McGraw-Hill, 1972
   Lucjan Dembinski's animated puppet version of the Russian tale of the snow girl who comes to life and lives with an old childless couple.

Film: Some Secrets Should Be Told, 12 min.
MTI Teleprograms, 1982
   Susan Linn and her two hand puppets discuss sexual abuse of children.

Film: The Song of Roland, 40 min.
Richard Tomkins Productions, 1975
   The film records performances and backstage activities that reveal the origins of Sicilian puppetry folk art.

Film: Sticks and Stones, 14 min.
BBC-TV/Vedo, 1973
   Puppeteer Rick Jones creates and animates "Fingermouse," who collects a variety of objects that he brings back to the puppeteer in order to tell one of Aesop's fables.

Film: Street of Crocodiles, 21 min.
B.F.I./First Run/Icarus, 1986
   The Brothers Quay use three-dimensional puppet animation to tell the story of a caretaker at a museum who mistakenly turns on a kinetoscope.

Film: Tanya the Puppeteer, 25 min.
Sunrise Films Ltd./Coronet, 1981
   Noted Russian puppeteer Sergei Obratsov's beginning puppet class is seen through the eyes of a twelve-year-old student.

Film: The Teddy Bears, 15 min.
Edison Company, 1907
   Edwin S. Porter's retelling of the Goldilocks legend features a puppet-animation sequence viewed through a knothole.

Video: Turnabout: The Story of the Yale Puppeteers, 58 min.
Filmakers Library, 1993

Documents puppeteer Harry Burnett, composer Forman Brown, and the rest of the Turnabout Theatre Company. Their unique mixture of topical marionette parodies, coupled with live cabaret, made them a Hollywood landmark for over thirty-five years.

Video: Where the Wild Things Are, 40 min.
BBC-TV/Films Inc., 1985

Fantasy opera by Christopher Swann based upon the book by Maurice Sendak, in which a boy who creates havoc in his home is sent to bed without his supper.

Selected Bibliography

Aaseng, Nathan. *Jim Henson: Muppet Master*. Minneapolis: Lerner Publications, 1988.

Allen, Arthur Bruce. *Puppetry and Puppet Plays for Infants, Juniors and Seniors*. London: Allman, 1937.

Anderson, Dee. *Amazingly Easy Puppet Plays: 42 New Scripts for One-Person Puppetry*. Chicago: American Library Association, 1997.

Aquino, J. L, et al. *Statistical Analysis of Subsidised Dance, Drama, and Puppetry Companies, 1974–78 Activity and Financial Statistics for Twenty-Eight Performing Arts Companies Receiving General Grants From the Theatre Board of the Australia Council*. Australian Theatre 1. North Sydney N.S.W.: The Arts Information Program of the Australia Council, 1980.

Astell-Burt, Caroline. *I Am the Story: The Art of Puppetry in Education and Therapy*. London: Souvenir Notes, 2001.

Bany-Winters, Lisa. *Onstage Theater Games and Activities for Kids*. 1st ed. Chicago: Chicago Review Press, 1997.

Batchelder, Marjorie Hope, and Vivian Michael. *Hand-and-Rod Puppets: A New Adventure in the Art of Puppetry*. Columbus, 1947.

Bell, John. *Puppets, Masks, and Performing Objects*. Cambridge, MA: MIT Press, 2001.

Ben-Shalom, David, and Rotem Petrakovsky. *Madrikh Le-Bubatron*. Israel: h. mo. l, 1986.

Bibliothèque Nationale de France, and Département des Arts du Spectacle. *Bibliothèque Nationale, Département des Arts du Spectacle*. Alexandria, VA: Chadwyck-Healey France, 1991–1993.

Binyon, Helen. *Puppetry Today: Designing and Making Marionettes, Glove Puppets, Rod Puppets, and Shadow Puppets*. London: Studio Vista, 1966.

Bittleston, Gisela. *The Healing Art of Glove Puppetry*. Edinburgh: Floris Books, 1978.

Bufano, Remo, and Arthur Richmond. *Book of Puppetry*. New York: Macmillan, 1950.

Bunraku Kashira no Meisaku Kankokai, and Seijiro Saito. *Masterpieces of Japanese Puppetry Sculptured Heads of the Bunraku Theater.* 1st ed. Rutland, VT: C. E. Tuttle, 1958.

Center for Puppetry Arts. *Puppetry of China: A Rare Exhibition of Figures Which Illustrate the Four Styles of Chinese Puppet Theater.* Atlanta, GA: Center for Puppetry Arts, 1984.

_____. *Puppetry of India: An Exhibition of Figures Celebrating India's Culture.* Atlanta, GA: Center for Puppetry Arts, 1986.

_____. *Futurism Conference: Futurism Conference Report, July 12–15, 1990.* Atlanta, GA: Center for Puppetry Arts, 1990.

Chen, Yimin, Junxiang Liu, and Zhiyun Fang. *Zhongguo quyi, za ji, mu ou xi, pi ying xi: Chinese quyi, acrobatics, puppetry and shadow theater.* Beijing di 1 ban ed. Chinese Culture and Art Series: Zhongguo Wen Hua Yi Shu Cong Shu (Beijing, China) 10. Beijing: Culture and Art, 1999.

Chevalier, Alain, et al. *Bibliographie des Arts du Spectacle.* Bruxelles, New York: P.I.E.-Peter Lang, 2000.

Coca-Cola Company Collection (Library of Congress). *One-Minute Bible Stories — New Testament .* United States: RCA/Columbia Pictures Home Video, 1985.

_____. *One-Minute Bible Stories — Old Testament.* United States: RCA/Columbia Pictures Home Video, 1985.

Condon, Camy, et al. *Global Family Puppets.* St. Louis, MO: Institute for Peace and Justice, 1984.

_____. *Puppets for Peace.* St. Louis, MO: Institute for Peace and Justice, 1984.

Creegan, George, and Dorothy Stephenson. *Sir George's Book of Hand Puppetry.* Chicago: Follett, 1966.

Crothers, J. Frances. *The Puppeteer's Library Guide: The Bibliographic Index to the Literature of the World Puppet Theatre.* Metuchen, NJ: Scarecrow Press, 1971–1983.

Currell, David. *The Complete Book of Puppetry.* London: Pitman, 1974. (1st American ed. Boston: Plays, 1975.)

_____. *The Complete Book of Puppet Theatre.* Totowa, NJ: Barnes & Noble Books, 1987.

Douglas, Helen M. *The ABC of Puppetry.* New York: Binney & Smith, 1944.

Efimova, Nina Iakovlevna Simonovich. *Adventures of a Russian Puppet Theatre.* Birmingham, MI: Puppetry Imprints, 1935.

Fraser, Peter. *Introducing Puppetry.* London: Batsord, 1968.

_____. *Puppets and Puppetry.* New York: Stein and Day, 1982.

Geertz, Armin W., and Michael Lomatuway'ma. *Children of Cottonwood: Piety and Ceremonialism in Hopi Indian Puppetry.* American Tribal Religions v. 12. Lincoln: University of Nebraska Press, 1987.

Glut, Donald F. *The Frankenstein Catalog.* Jefferson, NC: McFarland, 1984.

Hainaux, René. *Recherches et formation théâtrales en Wallonie (Organization). Les*

Arts Du Spectacle Bibliographie : Ouvrages En Langue Française Concernant Théâtre, Musique, Danse, Mime, Marionnettes, Variétés, Cirque, Radio, Télévision, Cinéma, Publiés Dans Le Monde Entre 1900 Et 1985 (Books in French About Theatre, Music, Dance, Mime, Puppetry, Light Entertainment, Circus, Radio, Television, Cinema Published Between 1900 and 1985). Brussels: Editions Labor, 1989.

Hamilton, Jake. *Special Effects in Film and Television.* 1st American ed. New York: DK Publishing, 1998.

Hanford, Robert Ten Eyck, and Ted Enik. *The Complete Book of Puppets & Puppeteering.* New York: Sterling Publishing, 1981.

Hansen, Carol, Peggy Mueller, and Marilyn Turkovich. *Shilpa Folk Dances, Music Crafts, and Puppetry of India.* New Delhi, India: Educational Resources Center, University of the State of New York, State Education Dept., 1980.

_____. *Shilpa.* 1990 rev. ed. Wellesley, MA: World Eagle, 1990.

Harp, Grace. *Handbook of Christian Puppetry.* Denver: Accent Books, 1984.

Harrison, Shirley C. *Puppets and Puppetry.* Eunice, LA: Ledoux Library, 1981.

Horejs, Vit. *Czechoslovak-American Puppetry.* New York: GOH Productions, 1995.

Indian Ministry of Education and Culture. *Puppet Theatre in India: Our Cultural Fabric.* New Delhi: Ministry of Education and Culture, 1982.

Jurkowski, Henryk, and Penny Francis. *A History of European Puppetry.* Lewiston: Edwin Mellen Press, 1996–1998.

Kamath, Bhaskar Kogga. *Story of Kogga Kamath's Marionettes.* Udupi, India: Regional Resources Centre, 1995.

Kawajiri, Taiji. *Nihon Ningyogeki Hattatsushi Ko.* Tokyo: Bansei Shobo, 1986.

Kohen, Gabriela, and José Ramón. *The Theater.* Torrance, CA: Laredo Publishing, 1992.

Krishnaiah, S. A. *Karnataka Puppetry.* Udupi, Karnataka, India: Regional Resources Centre for Folk Performing Arts, 1988.

Kumar, Sunil, S. M. Mushtaq Ahmad, and Hemanta Kanitakara. *Puppetry: A Tool of Mass Communication.* Varanasi, India: National Council of Development Communication, 1989.

Lago, Roberto, and Lola V Cueto. *Mexican Folk Puppets, Traditional and Modern.* Birmingham, MI: Puppetry Imprints, 1941.

Latda Nilamani. *Hun Læ Lakhåon Samrap Dek.* Phim khrang thi l ed. Bangkok: Witthayalai Khru Suan Dusit. Chamnai thi 'Ongkan Kha khåong Khurusapha, Suksaphanphanit, 2520.

Latshaw, George. *Puppetry: The Ultimate Disguise.* 1st ed. New York: Richards Rosen Press, 1978.

_____. *The Complete Book of Puppetry.* Mineola, NY: Dover Publications, 2000.

Lê, Bá Sinh. *Marionnettes Sur Eau (Water Puppetry).* Hô Chí Minh City: Doàn rôi nu oc dân tãoc, 1993.

Leeper, Vera. *Indian Legends Live in Puppetry: A Creative Manual.* Healdsburg, CA: Naturegraph, 1973.

Leleu-Rouvray, Geneviève, et al. *Bibliographie Internationale De La Marionnette.* Charleville-Mézières: Institut international de la marionnette, 1997.

Los Angeles County Museum. *History of Puppetry* [an Exhibition] Sponsored by Los Angeles County Museum and Los Angeles County Guild of Puppetry: Los Angeles, 1959.

MacNamara, Desmond. *Puppetry.* London: Arco Publications, 1965. (1st American ed., New York: Horizon Press, 1966.)

Malík, Jan. *Puppetry in Czechoslovakia.* 1st ed. Prague: Orbis, 1948.

March, Benjamin, and Paul McPharlin. *Chinese Shadow Figure Plays and Their Making.* Detroit: Puppetry Imprints, Handbook XI, 1938.

Marcus, Joan. *Disney Presents The Lion King with Photographs from the Broadway Musical.* New York: Disney Press, 1998.

McKay, Kenneth B., and Andrew Oxenham. *Puppetry in Canada: An Art to Enchant.* Willowdale, ON: Ontario Puppetry Association Publishing, 1980.

McPharlin, Paul. *Puppetry: A Yearbook of Puppets & Marionettes.* Detroit, 1919.

_____. *Puppet Heads and Their Making: A Theorem, with Woodcuts.* Detroit: The Inland Press, c1931.

_____. *Marionette Control.* Highland Park, MI: Puppetry Handbook VII, 1934.

_____. *Animal Marionettes.* Birmingham, MI: Puppetry Imprints, Handbook X, 1936.

_____. *Puppets in America, 1739 to Today with an Account of the First American Puppetry Conference.* Birmingham, MI: Puppetry Imprints, 1936.

_____. *A Repertory of Marionette Plays.* Mellen Studies in Puppetry, v. 2. rpt. Lewiston, NY: Edwin Mellen Press, 1997.

Milligan, David Fredrick. *Fist Puppetry.* New York: A.S. Barnes, 1938. (2nd ed., South Brunswick, NJ: A. S. Barnes, 1976.)

Mitra, Sanat Kumar. *Pa Scimabangera Putulanaca.* Lokasamskrti Gabeshana Granthamala 2. Kalikata: Lokasamskrti Gabeshana Parishada. Paribeshaka Pustaka Bipani, 1989.

Mulholland, John. *Practical Puppetry.* New York: Arco, 1968.

Nelson, Nicholas, and James Juvenal Hayes. *Trick Marionettes.* Birmingham, MI: Puppetry Imprints, 1935.

Miller, Jr., George B., et al. *Puppetry Library: An Annotated Bibliography Based on the Batchelder-McPharlin Collection at the University of New Mexico.* Westport, CT: Greenwood Press, 1981.

Nguyên, Huy Hông. *Nghãe Thuãat Múa r Ôi Viãet Nam.* Hà-nãoi: Van hóa, 1974.

_____. *Water Puppetry of Vietnam.* Hanoi: Foreign Languages Publishing House, 1986.

_____, and Trung Chinh Tran. *Vietnamese Traditional Water Puppetry.* Hanoi: The Gioi, 1992.

Nikolais, Alwin. *Index to Puppetry: A Classified List of Magazine Articles Published Between 1910 and 1938.* Hartford, 1938.

Oatman, Kae, and D. Jeff Essery. *Breaking Through the Barrier Puppet Play with the Profoundly Handicapped.* Willowdale, ON: Ontario Puppetry Association Publishing, 1981.

Painter, William M. *Musical Story Hours: Using Music with Storytelling and Puppetry.* Hamden, CT: Library Professional Publications, 1989.

Paritta Chalmphao Kåo`anantakun. *KhwamplianplµNg Læ Khwamtåon Ang Nai Sinlapa KansadµNg Nangtalung.* `Ekkasan Wichakan mailek 33. Krung Thep: Sathaban Thaikhadisuksa, Mahawitthayalai Thammasat, 1982.

Payant, Felix, Adolphe Appia, and Geoffrey Archbold. *A Book of Puppetry.* Columbus, OH: Design Publishing Company, 1936.

Pearson, Mary Rose. *Perky Puppets with a Purpose: A Complete Guide to Puppetry & Ventriloquism in Christian Ministry.* Springfield, MO: Gospel Publishing House, 1992.

Philpott, A. R. *Modern Puppetry.* Blishen Books. London: Joseph, 1966. (1st American ed. Boston: Plays, 1967.)

_____. *Dictionary of Puppetry.* 1st American ed. Boston: Plays, 1969.

_____. *Puppets and Therapy.* London: Educational Puppetry Association, 1975.

Plowright, Poh Sim. *Mediums, Puppets, and the Human Actor in the Theatres of the East.* Mellen Studies in Puppetry v. 4. Lewiston, NY: Edwin Mellen Press, 2002.

ProQuest Information and Learning Company. *International Index to the Performing Arts IIPA.* Ann Arbor: ProQuest Information and Learning, 2001–.

Puppeteers of America. *Handbook and Directory.* Macedonia, OH: Puppeteers of America, n.d.

Puppetry Handbooks. Detroit: 1931–.

The Puppetry Journal. Macedonia, OH : Puppeteers of America, 1949–.

The Puppetry Yearbook. Lewiston, NY: Edwin Mellen Press, 1995–.

Quan, Elizabeth. *The Immortal Poet of the Milo: The Story Behind Boat Festival and Other Chinese Puppet Plays, The Dragon.* Toronto: Sounds Canadian, 2001.

Ransome, Grace Greenleaf. *Puppets and Shadows: A Selective Bibliography to 1930.* Mellen Studies in Puppetry v. 1. Lewiston: Edwin Mellen Press, 1997.

Raya, Mohita. *Nadiyara Putulanaca.* Kalikata: Karuna Praka sani, 1995.

Renfro, Nancy. *Puppetry and the Art of Story Creation.* Puppetry in Education Series. Austin, TX: N. Renfro Studios, 1979.

_____. *Puppetry, Language, and the Special Child Discovering Alternate Languages.* Puppetry in Education Series. Austin, TX: N. Renfro Studios, 1984.

Robinson, Stuart, and Patricia Robinson. *Exploring Puppetry.* London: Mills & Boon, 1967.

Roser, Albrecht. *Gustaf Und Sein Ensemble Beschreibungen Eines Puppenspielers.* 1. Aufl ed. Gerlingen: Bleicher Verlag, 1979.

Sedana, I Nyoman. *Festival Wayang Kulit Cupak 1995 Siasat Seniman Dalang Dalam Pembinaan Seni Pewayangan: Laporan Hasil Penelitian (The 1995*

Contest of Wayang Cupak Shadow Theatre: Puppeteer's Strategy in Improving the Arts of Puppetry). Denpasar: Proyek Pengkajian dan Penelitian Ilmu Pengetahuan Terapan, 1996.

Shah, Anupama, and Uma Joshi. *Puppetry and Folk Dramas, for Non-Formal Education.* New Delhi: Sterling Publishers, 1992.

Sherzer, Dina, and Joel Sherzer, eds. *Humor and Comedy in Puppetry: Celebration in Popular Culture.* Bowling Green, OH: Bowling Green State University Popular Press, 1987.

Stockwell, Alan. *Puppetry with Line Drawings and Photographs.* Collins Nutshell Books. London: Collins, 1966.

Szilágyi, Dezso. Union internationale des marionnettes, and Publikationskommission. *Die Welt Des Puppenspielers.* 1. Aufl ed. Berlin: Henschelverlag, 1989.

Tilakasiri, J. *Puppetry in Ceylon.* Arts of Ceylon 1. Colombo: Dept. of Cultural Affairs, 1961.

_____. *Puppetry in Sri Lanka.* The Culture of Sri Lanka 4. Colombo: Dept. of Cultural Affairs, 1976.

_____. *The Asian Shadow Play.* 1st ed. Ratmalana: Sarvodaya Vishva Lekha, 1999.

Tillis, Steve. *Toward an Aesthetics of the Puppet: Puppetry as a Theatrical Art.* Contributions in Drama and Theatre Studies no. 47. New York: Greenwood Press, 1992.

Tilroe, Robert. *Puppetry and Television.* Willowdale, ON: Ontario Puppetry Association Publishing, 1981.

Tô Sanh. *Nghāe Thuāat Múa r Ói Nu Oc.* Hà-nāoi: Van Hóa, 1976.

Tribble, Keith. *Marionette Theater of the Symbolist Era.* Mellen Studies in Puppetry v. 3. Lewiston, NY: Edwin Mellen Press, 2003.

UNIMA-USA, Inc. *À propos (American Center of Unima): À propos.* Laguna Beach, CA: American Center of UNIMA, 1971.

Vaneck, Florence Marion. *The Art and Technique of Puppetry.* St. Louis, MO: Hart Publishing, 1934.

Venu, Ji. *Puppetry and Lesser Known Dance Traditions of Kerala.* 1st ed. Natana Kairali Folklore Series no. 1. Irinjalakuda, Trichur District, Kerala, India: Natana Kairali Research and Performing Centre for Traditional Arts, 1990.

Wall, Leonard Vernon, and Educational Puppetry Association. *The Puppet Book: A Book on Educational Puppetry.* London: Faber and Faber, 1950.

Wanthani Muangbun, and Sathaban Natduriyangkhasin (Thailand). *Laksana Pratimanawitthaya Khøong Hun R Ang Rammakian Khøong Krom Phraratchawang Bøowøonwichaichan.* Krung Thep: Sathaban Natduriyangkhasin, Krom Sinlapakøon, 2539.

Warshawsky, Gale Solotar. *Creative Puppetry for Jewish Kids.* Denver: Alternatives in Religious Education, 1985.

Whanslaw, H. W. *Animal Puppetry.* London: W. Gardner, 1939.

_____. *A Bench Book of Puppetry Containing Useful References in Alphabetical Order*. Redhill, Surrey: Wells Gardner, Darton, 1957.

_____. *A Second Bench Book of Puppetry Containing Useful References in Alphabetical Order*. Redhill, Surrey: Wells Gardner, Darton, 1957.

Works Progress Administration. *Puppetry Manual Recreation Training & Demonstration Program*. New York, 1940.

About the Contributors

Steve Abrams writes frequently about puppetry. He is the associate editor of *Puppetry Journal* and past president of Puppeteers of America. Based in Philadelphia, he has worked as a professional puppeteer for over twenty-five years.

Vincent Anthony founded the Center for Puppetry Arts in Atlanta in 1978 to focus on the global aspects of puppetry; he continues to serve as its executive director. He has served as general secretary of UNIMA-USA, the U.S. division of Union Internationale de la Marionette, the international puppetry organization, and is currently vice president of UNIMA International.

Leslee Asch was associated with The Jim Henson Company for over twenty years. As director of exhibitions, she was responsible for nationally and internationally acclaimed touring exhibitions. Asch also served as executive director of The Jim Henson Foundation and was producing director of the Henson International Festival of Puppet Theater for ten years. She is the editorial advisor for *Puppetry International.*

John Bell is Assistant Professor of Performing Arts at Emerson College, where he teaches theater history and puppet theater. He is also a member of Great Small Works, a theater collective with whom he has conceived and directed *A Mammal's Notebook: The Erik Satie Cabaret.* He is a contributing editor to *The Drama Review* and *Puppetry International.*

Dwight Blocker Bowers is a cultural historian at the Smithsonian Institution's National Museum of American History. His expertise in documenting performing arts history has resulted in exhibitions, publications, a research- and collection-based museum performance series and over fifty archival recordings, which have produced three Grammy Award nominations.

Phyllis T. Dircks is Professor of English at Long Island University, where she teaches contemporary American drama. A specialist in popular entertainment, she is the author of *David Garrick* (1985), *Two Burlettas of Kane O'Hara* (1987), and *The Eighteenth-Century English Burletta*, as well as numerous essays in national and international scholarly journals.

Annette Fern was research and reference librarian at the Harvard Theatre Collection at the time her chapter was written.

Mary Flanagan investigates the intersection of art, technology and gender study through critical writing, art work, and activism. Her essays have appeared in *Art Journal, Wide Angle, Convergence,* and *Culture Machine*; she has co-edited *Reload: Rethinking Women + Cyberculture* (2002). She is associate professor at the University of Oregon.

Kathy Foley is Professor of Theatre Arts at the University of California, Santa Cruz. She is the Southeast Asia editor of *Asian Theatre Journal* and has written extensively on Southeast Asian performance for *TDR, Cambridge Guide to Asian Theatre, Puppetry International* and other publications. She also performs Punch and Judy, making her a real professor of puppetry.

Mina Gregory is the associate conservator at the Museum of New Mexico in Santa Fe, working on the collections, outloans, exhibits and pest management programs of the Museum of Fine Arts, the Palace of the Governors, the Museum of Indian Arts and Cultures, and the Museum of International Folk Art. She has recently completed a set of storage and handling guidelines for the Gustave Baumann Marionette collection at the Museum of Fine Arts.

Roy W. Hamilton is curator of Asian and Pacific collections at the UCLA Fowler Museum of Cultural History. He is the editor and principal author of *Gift of the Cotton Maiden: Textiles of Flores and the Solor Islands* (1994) and *From the Rainbow's Varied Hue: Textiles of the Southern Philippines* (1998). He has organized numerous exhibitions, including The Art of Rice: Spirit and Sustenance in Asia, a major project that will tour North America in 2003–2005.

Ellen Roney Hughes is a cultural historian in the Smithsonian Institution's National Museum of American History, specializing in American sport and leisure history, popular culture, and material culture. Dr. Hughes is the director of the Smithsonian's American Sport Oral History Project and is currently preparing two new exhibitions: America Plays: Sports Entertainment and Music and Sports: Breaking Records, Breaking Barriers.

Richard Leet, an educator and award-winning artist, was the founding director of the Charles H. MacNider Museum, Mason City, Iowa, 1965–2000. He received the Lifetime Distinguished Service Award of the Midwest Museums Conference of the American Association of Museums in 1995 and was named to the Hall of Fame of the Iowa Museum Association in 2001.

Bernard F. Reilly is past director of research and access at the Chicago Historical Society.

Maureen Russell is the associate conservator of objects and sculpture at the Los Angeles County Museum of Art, having previously served at the Museum of

Fine Arts, Boston, and the National Gallery of Art in Washington, DC. She is a former fellow in objects and sculpture conservation at Harvard University.

Elka Schumann is currently the Bread & Puppet Museum Director and publisher and editor of the Bread & Puppet Press. Since the Bread & Puppet Theater was founded in 1963 by her husband, Peter Schumann, Ms. Schumann has held a variety of positions in the company, including treasurer, secretary, archivist, and occasional performer and musician. In addition, she founded and directed the Dancing Bear and Hardscrabble Puppet Theater for children.

Nancy Lohman Staub is a *membre d'honneur,* a member-at-large and former president of the Council of UNIMA, Union Internationale de la Marionnette, where she is a member of both the Research and Publication Commissions. She serves as the North America editor for the *World Encyclopedia of Puppetry Arts.* She has contributed numerous articles on puppetry to several publications.

Lowell Swortzell is Professor of Educational Theatre at New York University, where he teaches American theater, theater for young audiences and play development. He has written eighteen published plays and edited four play anthologies, for which he has received several awards, including *The New York Times* "Notable Book of the Year," designation, as well as *Choice* Magazine and American Alliance for Theatre and Education awards.

Cara Varnell is currently a textile conservator in private practice. Her clients include corporate and private collectors, as well as many museums and archives. She specializes in, though is not limited to, the conservation and exhibition of historic costumes. She was formerly the associate textile conservator at the Los Angeles County Museum of Art.

Fredric Woodbridge Wilson is the curator of the Harvard Theatre Collection. Previously, he was a curator at the Pierpont Morgan Library in New York. He is a musicologist, a conductor, and a music editor, and he has organized more than twenty exhibitions. He has written and lectured widely on Victorian theater and the operas of Gilbert and Sullivan. He was awarded a Guggenheim fellowship in 1996 for research in theatrical publishing.

Alan Woods grew up in Massachusetts, put on puppet shows in high school, and spent a year in Southeast Asia after college. Otherwise his experience differs from that of Julie Taymor. He has directed the Jerome Lawrence and Robert E. Lee Theatre Research Institute at Ohio State University since 1979, and explores popular culture in essays, lectures, and classes.

Anne Wright-Parsons is director of the Anthropology Museum at Northern Illinois University; previously she was assistant to the curator of the Asian Collection at the American Museum of Natural History in New York. Her interest in puppetry was cultivated during her many years of residence in Indonesia and Thailand.

Joseph Yranski is Senior Film and Video Historian for the Donnell Media Center of the New York Public Library. In addition to his extensive film programming experience around the country, he has contributed to numerous video documentaries and film books and has co-curated several exhibitions.

Roberta Zonghi is the keeper of rare books and manuscripts at the Boston Public Library, a post she has held since 1998. She has been interested in William Addison Dwiggins, his typographical work, his book design and illustrations and his marionettes throughout her career at Boston Public Library, which dates from 1970.

Index

Numbers in *italics* indicate illustrations.

315